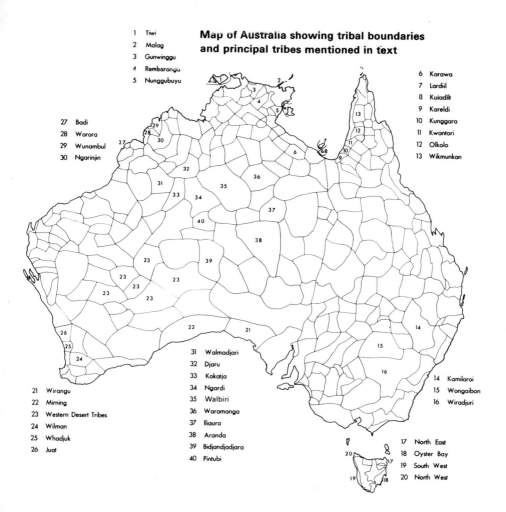

Map of Australia showing tribal boundaries and principal tribes mentioned in text

1 Tiwi
2 Malag
3 Gunwinggu
4 Rembarunga
5 Nunggubuyu

6 Karawa
7 Lardiil
8 Kaiadilt
9 Kareldi
10 Kunggara
11 Kwantari
12 Olkolo
13 Wikmunkan

27 Badi
28 Worora
29 Wunambul
30 Ngarinjin

31 Walmadjari
32 Djaru
33 Kokatja
34 Ngardi
35 Walbiri
36 Waramanga
37 Iliaura
38 Aranda
39 Bidjandjadjara
40 Pintubi

21 Wirangu
22 Mirning
23 Western Desert Tribes
24 Wilman
25 Whadjuk
26 Juat

14 Kamilaroi
15 Wongaibon
16 Wiradjuri

17 North East
18 Oyster Bay
19 South West
20 North West

RESEARCH MONOGRAPHS ON HUMAN POPULATION BIOLOGY

General Editor: G. AINSWORTH HARRISON

ABORIGINAL MAN ADAPTING

The human biology of Australian Aborigines

R. L. KIRK

CLARENDON PRESS

1981

Oxford University Press, Walton Street, Oxford OX2 6DP

OXFORD LONDON GLASGOW
NEW YORK TORONTO MELBOURNE WELLINGTON
KUALA LUMPUR SINGAPORE HONG KONG TOKYO
DELHI BOMBAY CALCUTTA MADRAS KARACHI
NAIROBI DAR ES SALAAM CAPE TOWN

Published in the United States by
Oxford University Press, New York

British Library Cataloguing in Publication Data

Kirk, R L
    Aboriginal man adapting. — (Research monographs
on human population biology).
    1. Human ecology — Australia
    2. Australian aborigines
    I. Title   II. Series
    994'.0049915   GF801   80-41152
    ISBN 0-19-857532-7

Typeset by Anne Joshua Associates, Oxford
Printed in Great Britain at the University Press, Oxford
by Eric Buckley, Printer to the University

PREFACE

For the greater part of the two million years or so during which man has been evolving he has exploited the environment by using the technology of the hunter–gatherer. This phase lasted in most parts of the world until a little less than 10 000 years ago. Then, in centres in south-east Asia and the Middle East, the domestication of animals and the deliberate scattering of seed introduced the agricultural revolution. Agriculture spread from these centres throughout most of Asia, across Europe, and into Africa.

There were, however, areas of the world where the impact of the agricultural revolution was not felt until relatively recently. When Europeans settled the Australian continent a mere two centuries ago the Aboriginal populations there were exclusively hunter–gatherers. Hunter–gatherer communities still existed also in many parts of America, Africa, Asia, and Oceania when Europeans first made forays into these regions.

The effect of European contact following the voyages of exploration was to alter, in nearly every case, the indigenous economic system, grossly disturbing the relationship between man and his environment which had been built over a period of many thousands of years. Today there are left in the Americas only a few hunter-gatherers in the remoter jungle areas of the south and in the extreme arctic areas of the north. Much has been learnt from written records made during the early years of contact and we know that human societies in the Americas had a rich and varied structure and that many of these maintained their integrity well into the last century. Although we may learn something of their social organization and biological relationships from those remaining now, they certainly do not represent the full range of such societies which were in existence before Europeans arrived.

In Australia there is no evidence of any significant disturbance of the basic economic pattern until European settlement occurred two hundred years ago. Contacts between Aborigines along the north coast and Macassans fishing for trepang had taken place for several centuries before Europeans arrived. But although the Macassans introduced some changes into Aboriginal culture they did not modify the life-style of the Aborigines in any significant way. More important is that although the European invasion obliterated Aboriginal society in the richer agricultural regions large areas of the continent remained relatively unaffected until well into this century. For this reason Australia provides an important opportunity for understanding not only the manner in which hunter–gatherer economy was adapted to different ecological situations but also the way in which human biological adaptation occurs when a dominant culture attempts to displace a culture whose technology is at a simple level of development.

In many parts of Australia the interaction between the two cultures is still in progress. The present book seeks to explore the biological consequences of this interaction as well as to help us understand the range of adaptation which had occurred already in Australia during the previous 40 000 years. Much of our knowledge of this adaptation is incomplete, and I hope that many more people will fill in the gaps in the future. Aborigines in Australia still offer to the rest of the world a unique chance to understand, in detail, the place of man in the natural world.

During the last twenty years I have been indebted to many friends and colleagues, both in Aboriginal and white communities, who have shared their knowledge with me and who have made possible my own studies across Australia. Although it is invidious to single out a few names from so many, both Gerard Vos, during the earlier, and Max Blake, during the latter phases of these studies made significant contributions: to them I express my sincere gratitude. Where I have drawn on the work of others I hope their views have been presented fairly and that they will recognize the blemishes remaining as due solely to my own inadequacies. Various chapters of this book have been read critically by experts in particular areas and their comments have helped very much to improve the argument. Among those to whom I express my special thanks are Nicolas Peterson, Alan Thorne, Betty Meehan, Rhys Jones, Ronald Berndt, Victor Macfarlane, Tasman Brown, Michael Gracey, and H. C. Coombs. In addition, Mildred Kirk has assisted me in many ways to present my views with greater clarity.

The task of preparing the manuscript in its various drafts has been carried out with great facility by Robina Williams and Suzan Ellis. Finally, I express my appreciation to Geoffrey Harrison for his guidance in the development of the theme for the present volume and to the editorial staff of the OUP for steering the volume through the critical transition from the typed manuscript to the printed book.

Canberra   RLK
December 1979

ACKNOWLEDGEMENTS

I am indebted to the following persons and publishers for permission to use original photographs or material which has appeared elsewhere:

Professor Tasman Brown for Fig. 9.3(a); Mr Ted Deveson for the original sketch of Fig. 8.1; Professor W. W. Howells for Figs. 5.8 and 5.9; Dr Bronya Keats for Fig. 7.2; Mr F. D. McCarthy and the Trustees of the Australian Museum, Sydney, for Fig. 4.7; Dr Betty Meehan for Figs. 4.2 and 4.3; Professor C. D. Rowley for a quotation which appears on p. 197 from *The destruction of Aboriginal society*; Dr Alan Thorne for Figs. 2.3 and 2.5; Professor Stephen Wurm for Fig. 6.4. The Australian Bureau of Statistics for Figs. 1.2 and 1.3 and the Australian National University Press for Figs. 1.4, 9.1, 9.2 and Table 9.5. The Australian Institute of Aboriginal Studies, Acton, Canberra, for Figs. 1.5, 4.10, 5.4, 5.5, 5.7, 5.9, 7.3, 7.4 and Tables 8.1, 8.2, and 8.3. The University of California Press for Figs. 3.2, 3.5 and Table 3.3. The University of Chicago Press for Figs. 3.3 and 3.4 which appeared in an article by J. B. Birdsell in *The American Naturalist* vol. 87, 1953. The Editor and the University of Sydney for Fig. 4.9 which appeared in an article by R. Gould in *Oceania* Vol. 39, 1969. For Figs. 3.1 and 3.5 copyright © 1968 by the Wenner-Gren Foundation for Anthropological Research Inc. Reprinted with permission from *Man the hunter* edited by Richard B. Lee and Irven de Vore (New York: Aldine Publishing Company). The *Journal of Applied Physiology* for Fig. 8.2. Figures 2.6, 2.8, 2.9, and 4.4 from *Sunda and sahul* and Figs. 4.1 and 5.2 from the *Journal of Human Evolution* Vol. 6, 1977 are copyright by Academic Press Inc. (London) Ltd.

CONTENTS

1

THE LAST CONTINENT

Australia assumed its present shape and area when the rising level of the sea at the end of the last ice age drowned the land between New Guinea and the tip of Cape York in the north, and between Tasmania and the Australian mainland in the south. Some 15 000 years ago the seas began to rise steadily, until finally these two land-bridges disappeared some time between 10 000 and 8000 years before the present (BP); and for the last 6000 years Australia's geography and climate have varied little from what they are now.[1]

It was to this setting that the Aborigines had become adapted when European settlers, just 200 years ago, began what was to be a drastic change in the social economy and ecology of the continent. The effect which this change has had on the distribution, health, and population numbers of the Aborigines will be discussed later. At this stage, however, we will outline the main ecological factors which were operating at the time of contact with the Europeans and which had prevailed during the previous few thousand years, and also examine the climatic fluctuations and consequent changes in the flora and fauna which occurred during the latter part of the Pleistocene, the period when man first arrived in the Australian region.

The geographic outline

The present area of Australia is 7 500 000 km^2 (2 900 000 square miles), almost the same as that of the United States of America or of Europe. Nearly 40 per cent of its land-area lies within the tropics, but only a small part of the continent has the type of ecology usually associated with the wet tropics: the most characteristic climatic feature of most of the continent is its aridity.

Geologically, Australia is an old and mainly stable area and there is now none of the volcanic activity and uplifting which still characterizes New Guinea and the other islands to the north. As a result the country has been subject to a long period of weathering and erosion which has produced a surface of generally low elevation with relatively few striking topographic features. Only near the coasts and in a few scattered localities elsewhere has there been geologically recent mountain-building or other land-form changes: those in the east have been particularly important in producing the mountain chain of the Eastern Uplands which runs from Cape York down to Tasmania.

Fig. 1.1. Major land-form areas in Australia.

The Eastern Uplands were an important influence on the distribution of Aboriginal populations. They are lower in the north, and set further back from the coast than in the southern half of their length. In the north the crests are rarely more than 600 metres above sea level, the abrupt scarp being cut through by rivers flowing rapidly eastward across the fertile coastal plain. In the central area of the Eastern Uplands, they broaden out into wide tablelands which, because of their elevation, create a more temperate climate even in that part of their area which lies within the tropics. Further south the broad tablelands are significantly colder than the adjacent coastal plains, a factor which was also important in determining human settlement patterns. The highest areas of the Uplands occur at their southern end, with a maximum elevation of 2000 metres. It was in this relatively small area in the Snowy Mountains and Southern Alps on the mainland that glaciation occurred during the Pleistocene. Tasmania, in broad terms, is an extension of the Eastern Uplands, and during the Pleistocene its mountains were also glaciated and dissected in the higher parts, giving rise to what is in the present island a complex of hills and valleys with a relatively restricted area of flat land.

In the interior of Australia the geography is dominated by desert land-forms with extensive areas of sand-dunes, large weathered outcrops, intermittent stream beds, and interior drainage basins leading to lakes with fluctuating levels and salinity. In the west the uplifted edge of the Western Shield, which occupies about 60 per cent of the continent, has been cut through in places in the Darling Scarp, to form gorges running down to the coastal sedimentary plain; in the Kimberley area of north-western Australia, the Shield has been raised into ranges, which are also cut through towards the coast by deep gorges. On the southern edge of the Shield is a treeless limestone plain which, because of the scarcity of surface-water, has always been an area difficult for human habitation.

Between the Western Shield and the Eastern Uplands are the Central Plains, composed of relatively young sediments which have a high fertility when water is available. Only two major rivers, however, flow across the southern portion of the central plains. The Darling and the Murray both rise in the Eastern Uplands, flowing westwards and south, until, joining together, they finally enter the sea near the present city of Adelaide. Despite their length, which, together with their other major tributaries the Murrumbidgee and the Lachlan, totals more than 4000 miles, the volume of water is not great and is also subject to marked fluctuations. Even the Murray has been known to dry across, and the Darling, which in flood can cover vast areas of country, is reduced during times of drought to a series of lagoons. Despite this, the Murray–Darling basin has been an important determinant of human habitation throughout the whole period that man has been in Australia, and some of the densest populations of Aborigines were living along the lower stretches of the river at the time of first European contact.

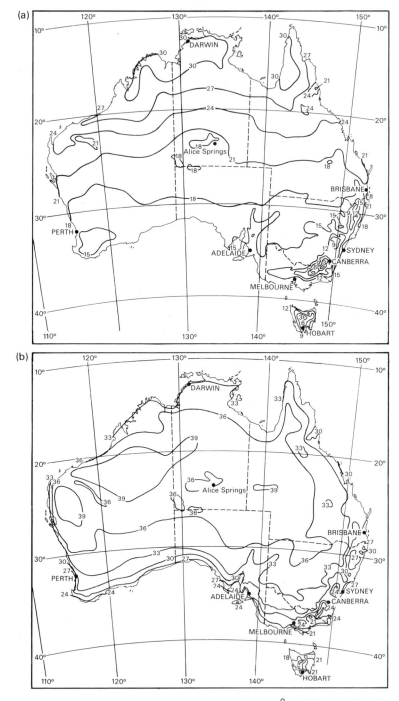

Fig. 1.2. Average daily maximum temperature in °C: (a) winter (July);
(b) summer (January).

Macroclimatic patterns

Plant life and its dependent animal — including human — life, is adapted to and influenced by climatic factors: solar radiation, temperature, and water. It is important to examine these factors in their Australian setting.

Because of its size and geographical position Australia has a wide range of climates, though, owing to its latitude and its unusual topography, their distribution is different from that found in the other continents; and this in turn markedly influences the distribution of Australia's vegetation zones.

The dominating influences on the climate are, first, the seasonal northward and southward movements of the pressure systems which travel from west to east across the continent; and, secondly, the position of the Eastern Uplands, which deflect much of the moisture in the onshore winds from the Pacific Ocean on to the narrow coastal plain along the east coast, casting a rain-shadow on the westward side of the ranges.

The southward movement of the pressure systems during the summer produces monsoonal conditions for four or five months along the north coast, which penetrate with diminishing effect several hundred kilometres to the south. During the monsoon period rainfall is heavy, rising to a maximum of 45–56 cm in the wettest month. In winter conditions in the north are reversed, with dry, warm weather prevailing. The land which was flooded during the monsoon dries out and rivers are reduced in volume and may stop flowing. By contrast the coastal areas south of the tropic receive their maximum rainfall during the winter months.

South of the monsoonal belt rainfall is sparse and irregular, showing wide fluctuations in annual totals. Thus for Alice Springs, with a mean annual rainfall of 9.0 cm, the range is from less than 2 cm to over 100 cm. Periods of drought may persist for many years, a factor of great importance in the human exploitation of these vast areas of country. Much of the interior of the continent is arid and, as the isothermal maps indicate, the summer temperatures can be extreme. Of importance also is the great diurnal range of temperature in the centre: lack of cloud-cover leads to high temperatures during the day, but equally to a rapid fall at night. Minimum night temperatures are frequently less than 10 °C and can drop to freezing or below — conditions which demand cultural and/or physiological adaptation for human survival and comfort.

A third major climatic zone is the eastern coastal plain. Moist onshore winds ensure a regular rainfall, which is distributed more

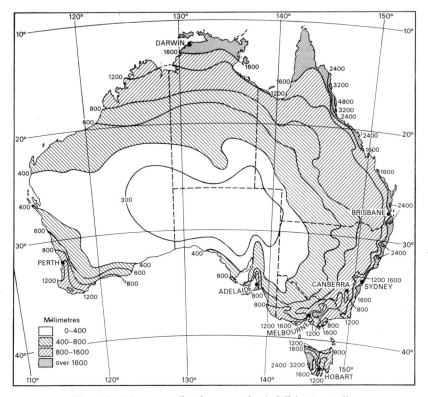

Fig. 1.3. 90 percentiles for annual rainfall in Australia.

evenly throughout the year, and which, in the north, reaches 225 cm or more per year. This, combined with the higher temperatures prevailing in the tropics, has led to the development on the eastern slopes of the Eastern Uplands of areas of tropical rain forest — formerly more extensive than at present.

In the south-west of the continent and also along parts of the southern coast near the mouth of the Murray River the climate approximates to that of the Mediterranean, with mild, wet winters and hot dry summers. Tasmania, lying furthest from the equator, has a more temperate climate, with cold winters and mild, wet summers. The topography of the island produces major regional differences, precipitation being heavy along the west coast. The mountainous interior considerably reduces the rainfall eastwards.

Plant-growth determinants

Radiation, temperature, and rainfall, and their variation from season to season, all contribute to determining the type of plants which will grow and the density which they will attain on a given area of land. Each species has its own characteristic requirements for growth and achieves a balance between these climatic factors and other environmental determinants, such as soil fertility.

In Australia attention has been given recently to the growth characteristics and yield for various plant species of economic importance to the pastoralist industry. Using information on the amount of dry matter produced for varying intensities of solar radiation it is possible to calculate a light index (LI). Similarly for dry-matter production in relation to temperature a thermal index (TI) can be derived, and for dry-matter production in relation to a function of rainfall and evaporation a third index, a moisture index (MI), can be calculated. All three indices can be combined to give a composite growth index, defined as:

$$GI = LI \times TI \times MI$$

E. A. Fitzpatrick and H. A. Nix[2] of the Commonwealth Scientific Industrial Research Organization (CSIRO) have charted the distribution of GI values across the continent for various plant species. Figure 1.4 (a) and (b) shows these values for tropical and temperate grasses respectively. Combining these data, it is clear that maximum yields of plant material occur in relatively restricted zones across the north, down the east coast, and in the south-west corner of Australia. In the past animal species, including man, which needed to utilize the plant resources for their own growth, must also have had a distribution density related to the GI values for adapted species in the native flora. A more detailed study of these relationships, however, still needs to be developed.

Plant growth, of course, is influenced by other factors in addition to those just discussed. Of these, topographic features which influence the availability of water will be outlined more fully in the next section. One other important factor is that of soil type and soil fertility.

Since Australia is geologically an old continent, it is eroded over large areas and its soils are thin and leached. There are relatively few modern soils: only about 20 per cent of the land has both fertile and well watered soils, and of this area about a half is deficient in various trace elements. Some of the trace-element deficiencies are potential causes of serious disease in both animals and man, and widespread

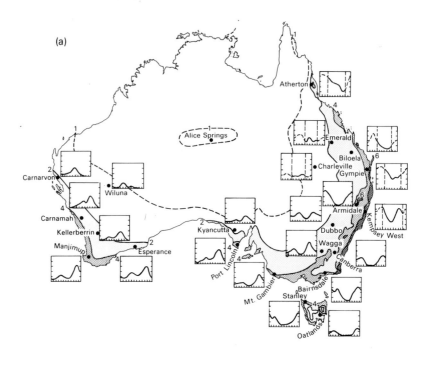

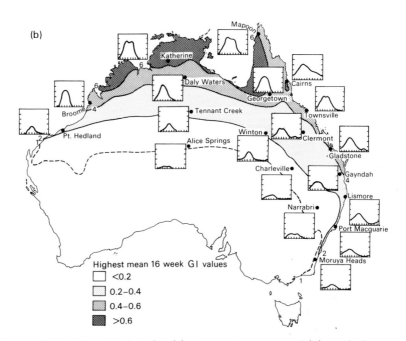

Fig. 1.4. Growth index values for (a) temperate grasses and (b) tropical grasses.

zinc deficiency in Australian soils will be discussed more fully later in relation to retarded growth of Aboriginal children.

Drainage basins and culture areas

The climatic patterns of radiation, temperature, and rainfall have also to be considered in relation to the very high rates of evaporation which prevail over most of the continent, and the generally low relief (only 7 per cent of the total land-area is above 600 m). One important consequence of this is that there are no reserves of snow to equalize river flows between wet and dry seasons: many of the rivers are subject to severe flooding after heavy rain or are reduced during summer to dry stream-beds, with small water-holes at intervals along their length. This combination of factors emphasizes the need for utilizing the scarce water supplies efficiently, especially in inland areas. For this reason attention has been focused on drainage basins as important determinants of human associations.

Nicolas Peterson, of the Australian National University, argues that watersheds between drainage basins will be areas with the lowest water resources; which, in turn, means that they will be areas with the lowest plant and animal food-resources which can be utilized by hunter–gatherers.[3] He has found good agreement between the boundaries of drainage divisions, and in many cases drainage basins, and Aboriginal tribal, linguistic, and cultural boundaries.

On the basis of cultural traits Peterson has subdivided some of the 12 major drainage divisions given in the *Atlas of Australian resources*,[4] and has designated the 17 culture areas shown in Fig. 1.5. Many of these culture areas correspond well with the broad geographic zones into which the continent has been divided. This is true of the Riverina area, which coincides with the Murray–Darling drainage basin. It is true also for areas like the South-Western, characterized by short streams rising on the western edge of the Shield and running across the narrow coastal plain to the Indian Ocean; and it applies also for Tasmania.

By contrast the monsoonal north covers several culture areas, not all of them related to drainage basins. In the Timor drainage region, for example, Peterson has introduced three culture areas, Kimberley, Fitzmaurice, and Wagait, together with another culture area in the north-east corner of Arnhem Land. And as a final example, in the Pacific Slope drainage basin, characterized by a large number of short streams rising in the Eastern Uplands and flowing across the narrow coastal plain into the Pacific Ocean, Peterson recognizes four culture areas, with a small rain-forest enclave

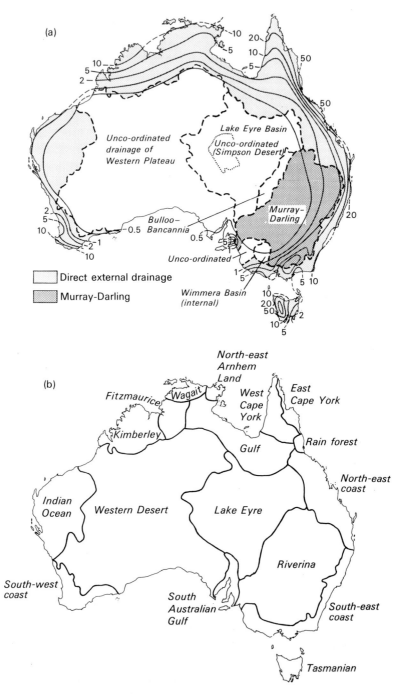

Fig. 1.5. (a) Natural drainage divisions in Australia;
(b) Aboriginal culture areas as proposed by Peterson.[3]

separating the East Cape York area from the North-East Coast and South-East Coast areas.

The importance of Peterson's attempt to relate cultural patterns to environmental variables is very great and Australia offers a unique opportunity for working out this relationship in detail.

Indigenous plants and animals[5]

Australia's isolation over a long period of geological time has given rise to a unique flora and fauna which is adapted to the prevailing climate and soil conditions and, in many areas, to the aridity which characterizes the greater part of the country. It must be remembered when vegetation zones are described in broad outline that within any given area there may be considerable heterogeneity. This will be referred to again when discussing population size and distribution in Chapter 3.

The areas of closed forest, with a continuous canopy, are located along the east coast and down into Tasmania; and there are also small areas in the south-west. Parts of this closed forest are rain forest, often with more than one layer of canopy, creepers and epiphytes, and a thick litter with mosses and liverworts. In the north the rain forest is composed mainly of Malaysian species and is similar to the rain forest of New Guinea. Smaller areas of rain forest occur further south, and there are patches of rain forest along the wet west coast of Tasmania.

Elsewhere the closed forest is composed of eucalypt species, often of great height reaching 100 metres or more, both in the south-east and south-west of the continent. There is, in many areas of closed forest, a second tree layer and also tree ferns and a well developed shrub layer. In drier areas the ferns and tree ferns disappear and different eucalypt species predominate. Moving further inland there is a broad area of more open forest or woodland, composed also of eucalypt species, which sweeps across the north and down parallel to the east coast and diagonally in the south-west from the Bight to the Indian Ocean south of Shark Bay. The woodland area is variable, depending on soils and topography, with patches of grass and other plants between the trees.

The open forest passes into wide areas of grassland, particularly in the east, mixed with areas of scrubland with low trees of acacia, or mulga, or of stunted eucalypts, known as mallee, adapted to dry conditions. The grasses are of various kinds, but large areas are of hummock grass composed of spinnifex (*Triodia* spp) or tussock grasses (*Astrebla, Stipa,* etc.). Finally, in the centre of the continent

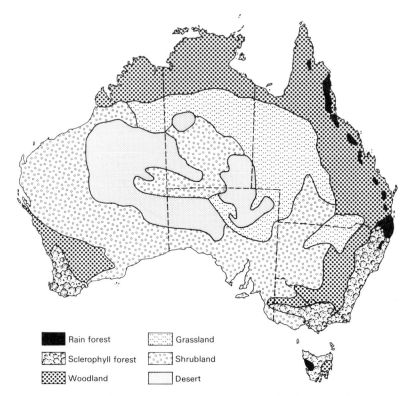

Fig. 1.6. Simplified map of natural vegetation in Australia.

there are large areas of desert complex, sparsely vegetated with xerophytic grasses and with a scattering of salt bush, patches of spinnifex, and occasional trees, generally along watercourses. The desert is discontinuous, with areas of fixed or moving dunes in the Tanami, Sandy, Gibson, Victoria, and Simpson Deserts, and with areas of spinnifex grassland or shrubland between. These central areas are the least productive and have supported either very low densities of human population or none at all.

Also of importance to a hunting–gathering people is the type and abundance of the animal species available. For populations living along the coasts, or in lake or river environments, fish or other aquatic species like turtles are a major source of food. But even coastal peoples sometimes supplement their diet with terrestrial animals. For populations living away from water, terrestrial forms, of course, are the only ones on which they can rely.

Australian faunal associations are dominated by the marsupial mammals: there are approximately 120 living species, and some additional species, which are now extinct, were present when man first arrived. The marsupials, a large proportion of which are herbivores, have radiated to fill a wide variety of ecological niches: there are tree-climbing and gliding forms (phalangers and possums and the koala), the large macropods (kangaroos and wallabies), burrowing forms or nest builders (wombats, rat kangaroos), and carnivorous forms (marsupial 'mice' and 'moles', native 'cats', 'devils', the Tasmanian 'wolf' and ant-eaters or numbats) and a group of omnivores, the bandicoots. There is a small number of true placental mammals, apart from those introduced since the first European settlement. These include bats, rats, and mice, having affinities with similar species to the north. Another mammalian species, the dog (*Canis familiaris*), entered the continent after the end of the Pleistocene, probably in association with man. The Australian form of the dog, known as the dingo, is now feral and widely distributed. According to Macintosh the dingo is morphologically distinct from the Pacific-Islands dog reported from some archaeological sites in New Guinea.

Of the non-mammalian fauna, the most numerous are the birds, including the large flightless emu, and the now extinct *Genyornis*. Other forms, which were important food sources for the Aborigines, include a varied reptilian fauna, among them turtles, more than 200 species of lizard, a large number of snakes, and two species of crocodile restricted to rivers in the monsoonal north. There are numerous insect and spider species, and a limited number of amphibians, many in the drier areas, with specialized burrowing adaptations. Freshwater crustacea and fish occur in many inland waters and were important sources of food in some areas. Marine fishes, crustacea, and molluscs are abundant in many coastal areas and were also exploited extensively.

Changes in climate during the late Pleistocene

During the last glaciation (Wisconsin or Wurm), which marked the end of the Pleistocene epoch, several periods of cold alternated with periods of warmer temperatures. When temperatures were low, vast quantities of water in the world's seas were immobilized in sheets of ice, and sea-levels fell. As temperatures rose and the ice melted, sea-levels rose again and covered large areas of land, particularly in regions where there are wide continental shelves.

The lowest sea-level in the Australian region occurred 15 000 to 17 000 years ago and was approximately 150 m lower than at present. There was another low level about 28 000 years ago, when the coastline was closer to the existing one; another very low level

at 53 000 years BP; and a further three low levels back to the beginning of the Upper Pleistocene, just over 100 000 years ago.[6] For
the greater part of this period Australia and New Guinea were
joined by a broad isthmus of low land, and the sea gap between
this single land-mass (Sahul Land) and the islands and South-East-
Asian land-mass (Sunda Land) to the north-west was also greatly
reduced. At the maxima of lowered sea-levels accidental or deliberate
crossing by man from the Indonesian Islands into Australia – New
Guinea would have been facilitated. At such times the distance
between Timor and the Australian coast was approximately 100 km,
and crossings of this gap, even using rudimentary water-craft, could

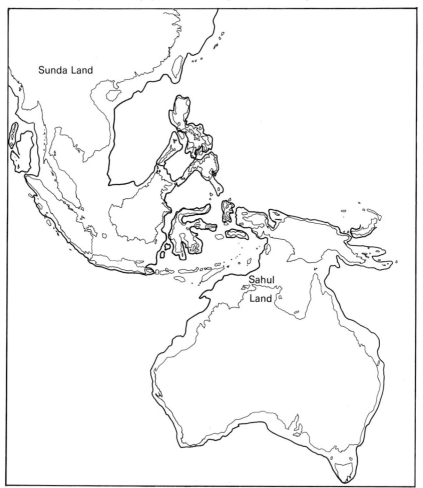

Fig. 1.7. The Sunda and Sahul land-masses at the end of the Pleistocene.

have happened on more than one occasion. But other migration routes are almost as probable, such as from Sulawesi through Sula Island and Ceram to New Guinea. (Here the shortest sea-crossing might have been no more than 50 km.)

We know that by about 40 000 years ago people had penetrated to the south-east corner of Australia. How long before that they made their first landfall remains to be established by further research. However such research may be difficult since if the early arrivals were people adapted to a coastal environment the evidence of their activities would now lie under more than 100 m of water. Only as the rising seas pushed them further back, and as population numbers grew, would it have been necessary to migrate into new areas and to adapt their technologies to exploit unfamiliar environments.

Rising sea-levels would have had important consequences for the human occupants of Sahul Land, the name we can use for the single, enlarged, Australia–New-Guinea land-mass during the late Pleistocene. One of these, noted above, is the contraction of the total land-area, but this by itself would have been counteracted by an increase in the total length of coastline available for exploitation by a littoral population. Although the total length of coastline when the sea was at its lowest levels is difficult to estimate, mainly because of lack of knowledge of the shape and extent of estuaries, it is clear from the map in Fig. 1.7 that the length of coast around Sahul Land 17 000 years ago was substantially less than the combined lengths of the coasts of Australia and New Guinea today. A further element of uncertainty about the impact of climatic changes on the human population at the end of the Pleistocene lies in our lack of knowledge about the effect of altered sea temperatures and currents on the near-shore fishes and other animals being used as food-sources during these earlier periods of colonization.

Although we do not know exactly what the coastline was like and how best it could have been utilized during the periods of lowered sea-levels, estimates have been made of the broad climatic changes which affected the continent as a whole. These would have been of great significance not only for man, but also for the plant and animal associations on which he depended. One such estimate is that at the height of the glacial maxima the sub-tropical high pressure systems which control much of the present Australian climate moved closer to the equator, and the surface-temperature of the sea was lower. In the north of Australia this would have meant a climate somewhat drier than it is now, with temperatures, on average, about 4 °C lower than at present.

The postulated fall in mean temperature and lowered rainfall in the northern parts of the country would have had a corresponding impact on the vegetation zones. In Sahul Land, Nix and Kalma[7] have suggested that some 20 000 years ago the dense closed tropical forest on the southern slopes of the New Guinea mountain chain was about the same as at present, but there was a considerable expansion of the more temperate woodland areas, which spread across most of the land now covered by the Arafura Sea. Because of its relatively low slope this area would also have had numerous swamps. In addition, the flatness of the terrain very close to mean sea-level may have made access to good supplies of fresh water difficult, a factor which in its turn could have limited the use of some of the shorelines along the north-western edge of Sahul Land, and may have forced some groups to exploit the higher ground inland, in what is now Arnhem Land.

In the south the late Pleistocene climate had more complex effects. The colder conditions resulted in some permanent glaciation. Though this was restricted to a relatively small area in the southern part of the Eastern Uplands and in Tasmania, the neighbouring periglacial areas in the Eastern Uplands would have been too cold to support a human population. Further away from the mountains, climatic factors seem to have been more favourable to man than at present. Many lakes in south-eastern Australia, now dry, were full during the Pleistocene, and archaeological evidence, which will be discussed in detail in the next chapter, indicates an active human economy going back to at least 40 000 BP. Some experts believe this indicates an increased rainfall during this period. An alternative explanation, however, is that the lower mean temperature resulted in a striking reduction in evaporation, allowing the balance between run-off and evaporation to change in favour of increased water flows, which also resulted in full lakes.

The changing climate which altered the distribution of the vegetation zones during the latter part of the Pleistocene was the end of a longer-term alteration in climate which had been taking place since the end of the Tertiary some one million years ago. At that time Australia was wetter and warmer than it is now, and tropical species of plants were more widespread, as also were the areas of forest. This was the era of the giant marsupials, large animals, some of which were adapted to browsing from trees and taller shrubs. As temperatures dropped and the climate became drier, woodlands contracted and the large browsing kangaroos became less successful in competition with the smaller grazing species. Eventually the large browsing forms became extinct, as also did some of the large flightless birds and the flamingoes, many species of which once added variety to the Australian avian fauna.

Some of the now extinct species overlapped with the arrival of man in Australia. Rhys Jones,[8] among others, argues that man altered the environment by his hunting activities, particularly by the practice of deliberately lighting fires to burn the bush. Jones believes that what he calls 'firestick farming' was used deliberately by the Aborigines to increase yield, and in this way their activities led to the extinction of the species with whom they were in competition. John Calaby[9] of the CSIRO Wildlife Division, however, sees the extinction of the large marsupials as the end result of a long-term change in the total ecology of the continent. Man, he believes, may have hastened the extinction of some of the species, but his continued absence from the continent would not have halted the change to the new balance which was being established before he arrived. The archaeological record, although revealing the presence of extinct forms at a few sites, still provides only scanty evidence that they were being hunted by the Aborigines of 15 000–20 000 years ago. The remains associated with hearths at that time suggest that mammals of any kind, particularly kangaroos, provided a relatively small part of the diet. But at one site near Lake Bolace in south-eastern Australia Peter Coutts[10] of the Victorian Archaeological Survey has recently found remains of butchered bones from a giant kangaroo. The site is claimed to be at least 15 000 years old and the burnt, possibly cut, bones were found in association with charcoal and stone tools. Further research in this area may well settle the argument about the importance of human activity in altering the faunal balance in Pleistocene Australia.

2

EARLY SEAFARERS

The first colonists to arrive in Sahul Land, the single land-mass consisting of an enlarged Australia and New Guinea, must be credited with being the earliest seafarers. Colonization of the Americas, which occurred almost certainly at a later period, was probably achieved by foot across the Bering land-bridge. Movement of people into Sahul Land, however, involved a sea voyage of at least 50–100 kilometres.[1] From what point the voyage started, by what means of transport it was effected, and where the landfall was made are unknown. All that is certain is that 35 000–40 000 years ago stone tools were being used in south-east Australia, and abundant evidence now testifies to the presence of man at places ranging from the New Guinea Highlands to the extreme tip of Western Australia up to 20 000 years ago.

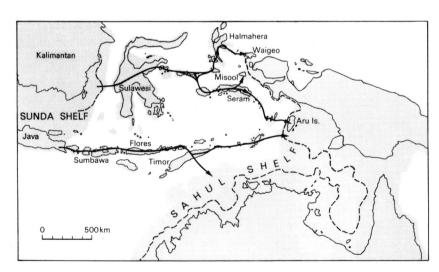

Fig. 2.1. Birdsell's postulated routes for Pleistocene entry to Sahul Land.

Firm evidence for the earliest human occupation comes from excavations at the site of Lake Mungo in south-east Australia. As the Pleistocene period reached the peak of its last glaciation the climate of this part of the country was cooler than at present, and the now relatively dry area between the Darling and the Lachlan and Murray Rivers was filled by a series of shallow lakes abounding in fresh-water fish and crustacea and surrounded by country with a wide range of marsupials including the now extinct giant kangaroo, *Procoptodon*. Remains of more than forty human skeletons have been recovered from this area, which is called the Willandra Lakes system, and the skeletons have been dated within a period from 10 000 to 28 000 years ago. The remains of hearths and of stone artefacts push the evidence for human activity here back to approximately 35 000 BP, possibly even earlier.

One of the most dramatic finds was made in 1974 at Lake Mungo,

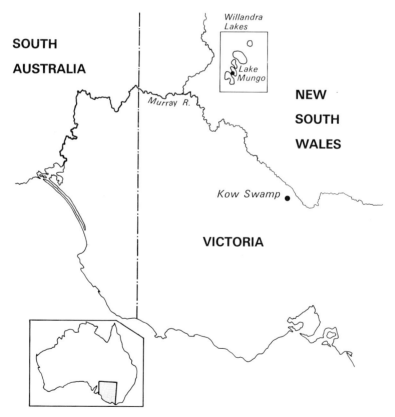

Fig. 2.2. The Willandra Lakes system in South-East Australia.

the location of which is shown in Fig. 2.2. Dr J. M. Bowler, of the Australian National University, was studying the stratigraphy of the surface material deposited some 25 000 to 40 000 years ago during the period of high lake level when he noticed the exposed left side of a carbonate-encrusted human skull protruding above the sandy surface. Two days later Bowler was joined by other workers from the National University, and the team was able to excavate the complete skeleton of an adult male.[2] This was not the first set of human remains uncovered at Lake Mungo, but they were the most complete. Careful stratigraphic studies suggest that this skeleton, Mungo III, was laid in its shallow grave 28 000 to 30 000 years ago: pink staining of the soil around the skeleton indicates also that red ochre had been sprinkled over the body and this provides us with the earliest example in Australia of ritualistic practice associated with burial.

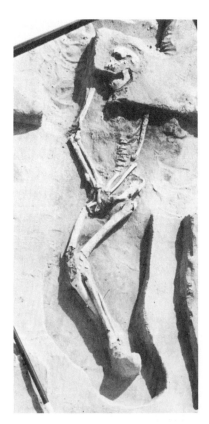

Fig. 2.3. The Mungo III skeleton during excavation.

Mungo III, in common with the earlier discovered cremated remains of Mungo I, has delicately structured bones, giving it a 'gracile' appearance and placing it morphologically within the range of modern Aboriginal skeletal material. This contrasts with the more 'robust' structure of the skeletons from the site excavated by Dr Alan Thorne at Kow Swamp, 300 km to the south-east of Lake Mungo. The Kow Swamp site has revealed more than 40 crania and mandibles, with a smaller number of post-cranial remains. Dating by carbon-14 analysis shows the burials to be much more recent than at Lake Mungo, the earliest being less than 14 000 years BP, and the most recent 9000 years BP.[3]

As a group the Kow Swamp crania are larger and heavier than either the Lake Mungo or modern Aboriginal crania. The brow ridges are relatively well-developed, the post-orbital constriction is conspicuous, and the frontal bones are flattened and broader anteriorly. In many of the specimens the cranial bones are also thicker than in modern skulls. Thorne,[4] in reviewing the Kow Swamp material,

Fig. 2.4. Archaeological sites in Australia.

concludes that there are certain groups of features of these crania
that support earlier suggestions that some Aboriginal crania show
relationships with Solo and Pithecanthropine forms in Java. Especially, the overall form of the frontal bones of some of the Kow
Swamp crania are similar to those of Pleistocene human remains in
Indonesia.

It is important to emphasize at this stage the dichotomy between
the 'gracile' but older Lake Mungo skeletons and the 'robust' more
recent remains from Kow Swamp. This dichotomy is reflected in the
remains from other sites. Of these the Keilor skull, discovered in
1940 in a terrace of the Maribyrnong River near Melbourne, and

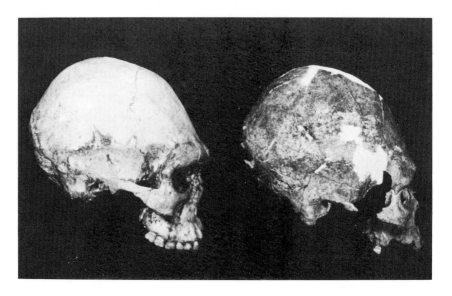

Fig. 2.5. The Cohuna (*left*) and Kow Swamp V (*right*) crania.

dated at 13 000 BP, falls into the 'gracile' group, whereas Cohuna
(not dated, but very probably 10 000–15 000 BP), Mossgiel (>4600
BP), and Lake Nitchie (6000 BP) fall into the 'robust' group. Thorne,
who has examined all the older skeletal material and compared it
with measurements made on museum collections of Aboriginal
material from more recent burials, as shown in Fig. 2.6, has illustrated the relationship between the fossil material from south-east
Australia and that representing more modern populations, showing
the ranges of variation where more than one representative was available for measurement.

Recently Freedman and Lofgren[5] have given a detailed description of skeletal remains found in 1972 at Cossack on the central West Australian coast. It has not been possible to date the skeleton itself, but the geomorphology of the site in which it was found suggests it was buried not more than 6500 years ago. Measurements and other features of the Cossack skull show that it is very different from recent West Australian Aboriginal skulls and is more similar to the Kow Swamp skulls, thus providing the first evidence for the widespread occurrence of these robust forms of man across the continent.

One possible explanation of the dichotomy between the gracile and robust skulls is that they represent extremes of the range for skull types in Aborigines, these extreme forms having been selected in the localities where they were found by dietary or other environmental factors. It seems unlikely, however, that such extreme morphological differences could arise in this way. A more probable hypothesis is that Kow Swamp and Lake Mungo skeletons are representatives of two separate waves of immigrants into Australia.

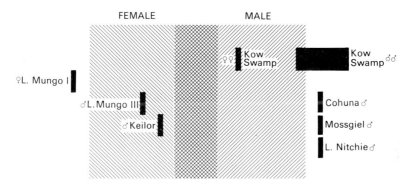

Fig. 2.6 Ranges for skull features in Aboriginal fossil (solid bars) and recent crania (hatched area) (from Thorne).[4]

Both these types maintained their identities for a long period of time, with the distinction between them gradually breaking down to give rise to the characteristics of Aborigines today. As more skeletal material is discovered in other parts of the continent, particularly for the period of 40 000 to 10 000 BP, it may be possible to resolve further the reason for the striking difference between these gracile and robust ancestral forms of Aboriginal man.

Another case for a multiple origin of the Aboriginal population has been argued by Loring Brace using evidence from the size of teeth. Brace finds that tooth size in Aborigines, as determined from museum specimens, varies over a wide range. The smallest teeth,

Table 2.1. Some radio-carbon dates for Pleistocene sites in Australia (localities are shown in Fig. 2.3)

Locality	Source of dated material	Years BP
Lake Mungo	Occupation	32 750
Keilor	Occupation	32 000
Lake Mungo	Burial	30 000
Lake Yantara	Hearth	26 200
Lake Mungo	Cremation	25 500
Malangangerr	Ground axes	24 800
Devil's Lair	Occupation	24 600
Koonalda Cave	Rock art	23 700
Lake Arumpo	Shell midden	22 600
Kenniff Cave	Occupation	18 800
Miriwun	Occupation	18 000
Clogg's Cave	Occupation	17 720
Seton, Kangaroo Is.	Bone tools	16 150
Puntutjarpa	Rock shelter	10 170
Kow Swamp	Burial	10 000

on average, are found in the north and the largest in the south along the Murray River. The difference is larger than that for any other set of modern populations in an area of comparable size. Brace believes that tooth size in the Murray Basin series represents the result of selective forces which maintained a robust dentition and a well-developed post-cranial skeleton from the Middle Pleistocene right on up to the beginning of the Holocene, and this robustness is reflected in the physiques of the modern inhabitants of this area. But he concludes also that the cline in tooth size, increasing from Cape York southwards, is due to the introduction of people with smaller teeth into the Cape York Peninsula and a gradual penetration of the genes for smaller tooth size into populations further removed. He envisages this introduction and penetration as a continuous process rather than discrete waves of migration or invasion. We shall see later (Chapter 5) that this cline in tooth size is paralleled by a similar gradation in other skull features, and the case for the penetration of outside genes into northern populations is strengthened by the evidence in Chapter 6 based on blood genetic markers.

Not all experts accept the simple model proposed by Brace to account for the striking difference in tooth size across Australia. Tooth size is only partly under genetic control and there is also considerable variation in tooth size within a single population. Further,

since skull features, including tooth size, are influenced by diet, it
is likely that dietary differences between the tropical and semi-
tropical north, the desert areas of the centre and the more temperate
regions in the south, account for some of the observed variability in
tooth size.

The stone-tool traditions

Most of the evidence for the antiquity of human occupation in Australia and New Guinea comes not from the skeletal material but from
the careful dating of deposits in which stone tools or other evidence
of human activity have been found. Rhys Jones[6] and also John
Mulvaney[7] have recently summarized this evidence in a way which
makes it possible to distinguish the broad sweep of cultural development through time.

The oldest dates are in southern Australia. Both at Lake Mungo
and in the river terraces at Keilor, stone tools go back probably to
40 000 years BP, possibly even much earlier. At Burrill Lake in New
South Wales, Clogg's Cave in Victoria, and Devil's Lair in Western
Australia dates range from 17 000 to 24 000 BP. Dates in this latter
range have come from Cave Bay Cave, on Hunter Island off the north
coast of Tasmania, and from Kangaroo Island, South Australia. In
the tropical north, rock shelters at the base of the Arnhem Land
escarpment, Miriwun in the Kimberley and the Early Man site, and
probably Laura in Queensland have dates from 18 000 to 24 000 BP,
whilst in the Highlands of New Guinea evidence of human occupation goes back to 26 000 BP.

Jones argues that the stone tools from these Pleistocene sites, even
though widely separated geographically, bear strong resemblances to
one another, although regional differences can be vaguely discerned.
The tool-kits all have large dome-shaped, horse-hoof core scrapers
and several kinds of steep-edged, notched, and nosed scrapers often
with step-flaked edges: sometimes different edges have been worked
on to the same blank. The wide dispersal of types is demonstrated
by the presence on Kangaroo Island of large 'waisted blades' worked
on both sides, which are similar to some of the stone tools found in
the Highlands of New Guinea from Pleistocene down to recent times.

It is believed that 'waisted blades' were fastened to wooden shafts,
and such hafted tools were common in New Guinea. In New Guinea
another development was the careful grinding of the edges of the
adze which, in its most developed state, produces a highly polished
implement. In Australia, too, examples of bifacially flaked adzes
have been found on which the cutting edge has been ground to a

bevel, and some of these tools have grooves which could have been used for hafting.[8] These edge-ground adzes were discovered in rock shelters near Oenpelli in Arnhem Land, and have been dated to 18 000 to 20 000 years BP. Further excavations in the same area and at Laura in Cape York have confirmed the presence of edge-ground tools up to at least 10 000 years ago.

If the stone-tool assemblages in Australia are examined from a chronological point of view it appears that a dramatic change began to take place about 6000 years ago. At sites in many parts of the country which are more recent than this, there are new additions to the stone tools present, particularly points and backed blades. In contrast to the heavy core and scraper implements characteristic of the tools dated back as far as 40 000 BP, these small points and blades were often finely shaped by percussion and pressure flaking techniques; thus the period starting 6000 years ago gave rise to what has been called 'the Australian small-tool tradition'.

The widespread distribution of these small tools and their appearance in a relatively short period of time has suggested that the new technology was brought in by the arrival of a wave of immigrants soon after the end of the Pleistocene. This hypothesis is made more attractive by the arrival, at some time after this, of the native dog or dingo. Dingo bones have been dated reliably at less than 4000 years BP, but of course it is possible that older examples may be found in the future (see p. 13 and ref. 5). Dingos did not reach Tasmania, so it is reasonable to argue that they entered Australia after the rising sea-level had separated Tasmania from the mainland. For the same reason the Australian small-tool tradition did not reach Tasmania. Here, the Pleistocene large-core-and-scraper tradition continued unaltered until the time of discovery by Europeans.

Small blades, points, and hafted adzes however did not completely replace the older tool traditions. Over a span of 20 000 to 30 000 years there was a tendency for reduction in the size of the larger cores and scrapers. As noted above, some of these had been edge-ground, and some had waists or grooves to enable them to be fastened to handles. In addition, small flakes were present at many of the older sites, and some show signs of working to produce indentations around the edge, whilst at Devil's Lair in South-West Australia, Dortch and Merrilees[9] found evidence of plant-gum adhering to flakes as old as 25 000 BP. Such gum is still used to attach adzes to the handles of spear-throwers.

Other tool traditions

Stone survives in the archaeological record for a very long time. Not so, however, other materials which can be, and frequently are, used for making tools. Only under certain conditions is bone preserved well enough for its use to be inferred: wooden or fibre implements fare even worse, and are rarely recovered from archaeological sites.

At the time of contact by Europeans, wood was being used extensively for tool production, being fashioned as spears, either with or without stone points and as spear-throwers, digging-sticks, clubs, and carrying utensils. Both returning and non-returning boomerangs were also in use in many parts of the country, but not in Tasmania. Though it may be inferred that wooden implements have been in use over a long period of time, only recently has evidence become available to lend support to this possibility. Luebbers,[10] excavating a peat bog at Wyrie in South Australia, has uncovered not only digging-sticks and a barbed spear-head, but also boomerangs. These finds have been dated to about 10 000 B P.

Bone tools, on the other hand, have been reported from a number of sites. Some of the earliest examples are nearly 20 000 B P from Devil's Lair in south-west Australia, from Cave Bay Cave in Tasmania, and possibly an even older bone artefact, pointed at both ends, from Lake Mungo. The Seton site on Kangaroo Island has yielded bone tools dated at 16 000 B P and Clogg's Cave in Victoria at 12 000 B P. In Tasmania bone tools have been recovered from the basal levels at Rocky Cape at 8000 B P. More recent bone points have come from sites in Arnhem Land, down to immediate pre-contact specimens, pointed either at one or both ends, from rock shelters and coastal middens in Victoria.

Contemporary observations in the last century in Victoria indicated that pointed bones of various sizes were used in the manufacture of skin cloaks, and that bone spatulae were employed to smooth the seams where skins were sewn together. The polished form of some of the bone points from the older levels in places such as Devil's Lair suggests that they could have been used for making skin cloaks. Small pointed bones were used also as tips to fish-prongs, as barbs on spears, or as part of fish-gorges.

The use of bone in fishing is paralleled in the utilization of shell to make fish-hooks. Coastal sites at many places have produced shell fish-hooks of many different types, in addition to stone files used in cutting the shell to the appropriate hooked shape.

Terminal Pleistocene economies

Economic activity of the hunter–gratherer type must have been the
predominant form throughout the whole range of the archaeological
record in Australia, contrasting in this respect with New Guinea
where evidence for the beginning of horticulture goes back to at least
10 000 BP. Though there is contemporary evidence for the careful
tending of solanaceous plants in parts of northern Australia it is not
known for how long this had persisted. There is good evidence also
that grasslands were fired deliberately, a practice which results in
increased production of seed during the next season. Indeed, this
practice has been termed firestick farming. But apart from this
suggestion of the tending of plants and the firing of grasslands,
no tools or arrangement of dwellings have been found in the archaeological record to suggest anything other than the exploitation of the
natural flora and fauna in the local region, with the first stages in the
development of agriculture being manifest in some places.

Most sites have been discovered, of course, where local conditions
favoured the congregation of people. Caves and rock shelters rank
high in this regard, not only because they provided shelter for the
human inhabitants, but also because the debris left behind was
similarly protected from disruptive agencies. Thus at sites such as
Devil's Lair in south Western Australia human occupation may have
extended back 40 000 years, with good evidence of use by man for
longer than 22 500 years. Some shelters in the Alligator River area
of Arnhem Land have been associated with human occupation from
25 000 BP to the present day. In this area numerous examples of
grindstones have been found, at least three of which have been dated
to 18 000 BP. A grindstone of the same age has come from Miriwun
in the Kimberley area of Western Australia. From similar levels,
in Arnhem Land, as noted earlier, there are also examples of edge-
ground axes, making this area the oldest known in the world for the
use of a grinding technology.

Recent studies of present-day populations reveal that in many
localities there is a seasonal movement influenced by fluctuations in
the abundance of the food-source. In the tropical north this is controlled by the monsoonal climate which makes it difficult to live on
the low-lying flood plains near the coast during summer months.
At this time the population moves inland to higher ground. Carmel
White, investigating one such site, found evidence that it was used
for the manufacture of stone tools during the wet season.[8] She
believes these tools were the ones used at lower sites during the dry
season for the manufacture of artefacts made from plant materials.

At Clogg's Cave in south-eastern Australia Josephine Flood has carefully documented the evidence for human occupation from 18 000 to 8000 BP.[11] After that date Aborigines may have visited the cave sporadically but they do not seem to have used it as a habitation. This limestone cave is 37 km from the present coastline and only 76 m above sea-level, and the surrounding countryside at the time of European contact was a mixture of grassland, open woodland, and dry sclerophyll forest; it has a mild climate ranging from means of about 9 °C in winter to 20 °C in summer. Analysis of vegetation remains at Clogg's Cave and nearby sites suggests that climatic changes in the area were gradual, from an earlier wetter and colder phase about 32 000 BP to one very similar to the present by 21 000 to 25 000 BP. If there was any increase in mean temperature or decrease in rainfall in the area during the last 20 000 years it was not sufficient to alter significantly the local plant associations.

Of equal interest is the evidence of the faunal remains. Below the levels where human artefacts were found there were bones of now extinct marsupials, including the giant kangaroo *Macropus titon* and the now locally extinct Tasmanian Devil. Another species, still found in Tasmania, was the rodent *Pseudomys higginsi* which was present in the lower levels of the cave but disappeared later, being replaced by other species of *Pseudomys*.

The stone-tool types in the cave deposits representing the 10 000-year span from the time of the earliest occupation to its abandonment 8000 years ago were remarkably uniform. Pebbles which had been brought into the cave were burnished in a manner which suggested that they had been used for making skins pliable: some pebbles were pitted, probably as a result of their being used for making other stone tools. The majority of these other tools were scrapers of various types. Close comparison of these with scrapers from other places reveals a striking similarity between the Clogg's Cave tools and those from the lower levels at Rocky Cape in north-western Tasmania, even though the materials used to make the tools in the two localities were different. This similarity supports the view, documented by Davidson 40 years ago, that the Tasmanian culture was derived from that on the mainland during the late Pleistocene, when the Bass Strait land-bridge was still in existence. Flood points out that there were local variations in the tool traditions: for example, at Rocky Cape there were notched and round-edged scrapers in the lower levels, a type not found in the Clogg's Cave deposits.

The 10 000-year range of dates for the use of Clogg's Cave as a habitation-site raises questions in relation to the changes in the human exploitation of the local environment. Why was the cave not

visited before 18 000 BP and why was it abandoned after 8000 BP?
Recently Sandra Bowdler[12] has put forward a hypothesis which goes
a long way toward answering these and similar questions for other
parts of Australia.

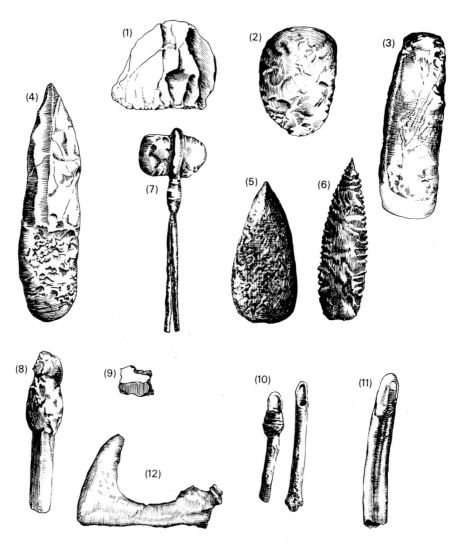

Fig. 2.7. Examples of Australian stone and bone implements: (1) horsehoof
core; (2) uniface pebble implement; (3) edge-ground adze; (4) leilara blade;
(5) pecked axe; (6) Kimberley point; (7) edge-ground axe with hafted vine-stem
handle; (8) gum-hafted quartzite flaked knife; (9) microlithic burin; (10) bone
awls; (11) dugong-tooth chisel; (12) kangaroo-shoulder-blade yam-slicer.

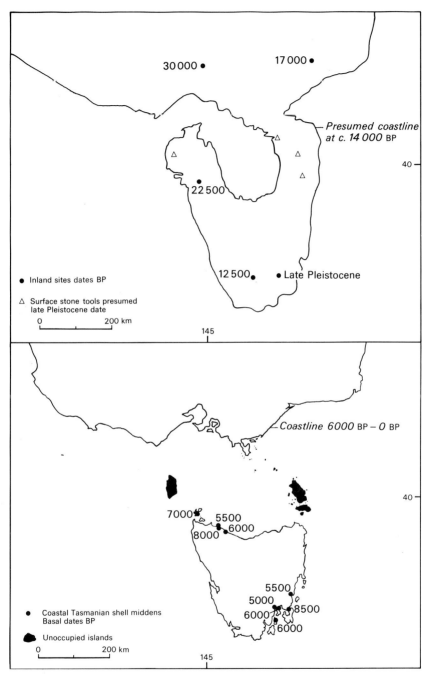

Fig. 2.8. Main archaeological sites and dates in Tasmania and Bass Strait showing shore-line at *c*. 14 000 BP and at 6000 BP to the present.

The earliest arrivals in Australia, she argues, were successful ex-
ploiters of a marine environment. Indeed, it was because of this
type of activity in their original homeland that they crossed the
50–100 km of sea to the northern edges of Sahul Land. It would
be expected that they would have continued to exploit the marine
environment; and their migrations as the population grew would be
along the coast rather than uniformly in all directions across the
continent — a land of unfamiliar plants and animals in unfamiliar
environments. This coastal expansion may have been quite rapid
and, in turn, would have led to the exploitation, first of estuarine
and then of riverine environments.

Having reached the south coast of Australia one of the best
riverine environments undoubtedly would have been the lower
reaches of the Murray River. From here expansion inland would have
followed the Murray and its tributaries, and some 40 000 years ago
these early settlers would have been exploiting the fish, molluscs,
and crustacia of the Willandra Lakes system, which at that time
was part of the Murray–Darling Basin. It is significant that the
Mungo I site, dated at 26 000 BP, had abundant remains of freshwater fish and mussels, and a number of small land-mammals, the
largest being the hare wallaby, in addition to some lizards and birds
and fragments of emu shells. The older site, Mungo II, however, with
a date of nearly 33 000 BP yielded remains of only mussels together
with stone artefacts. It was not until the lakes had started to dry up,
at about 15 000 BP, that sites have been found in the Willandra Lakes
area with remains of larger land-mammals, kangaroos and wallabies.
It is at this period also that grindstones first occur at these sites,
suggestive evidence for a change in the economy, supplementing the
now diminishing supply of freshwater food not only with larger land
animals, but also with plant foods.

Another consequence of the hypothesis put forward by Bowdler
is that at the height of the last glaciation, about 18 000 BP, when sea-
levels were at their lowest, the evidence of coastline settlements
would have been destroyed by the subsequent rising sea, until it
reached to near present levels by 8000 years BP. The consequences
of these late Pleistocene changes were not the same in all parts of
the continent. The glacial maximum meant not only a lower mean
temperature, but was associated in many areas with increased aridity.
Up to 18 000 BP increasing aridity in the north was severe enough
to force the exploitation of better watered but non-marine environments on the Arnhem Land escarpment, at that time a considerable
distance from the coast. Bowdler believes that the dating of grindstones in the Alligator River area to 18 000 BP is an indication that

the greater aridity in the north was forcing changes which led toward the exploitation of plant resources, in a way similar to that occurring slightly later in the south as the Willandra Lakes began to dry. Interestingly, evidence for expansion into the arid interior indicates the earliest date for this at Puntutjarpa in the Western Desert was relatively recent, at approximately 10 000 BP. Here kangaroo bones were common, and grindstones were already part of the artefact assemblage.

The implication of Bowdler's hypothesis for the interpretation of sites like Clogg's Cave is clear. Its earliest use by man at 18 000 BP coincided with the last glacial maximum, and the Cave would have provided welcome shelter on the edge of the glaciated areas of the Eastern Uplands. The sparsity of artefacts in the Cave suggests however that its use was never intensive, except for a brief time at about 8000 BP. At the earlier date there was a sparsity of sites in the whole area of present coastal south-east Australia, for indeed the traces of those people who were exploiting the marine environment of that time are buried beneath the sea. It is not until the end of the Pleistocene that we find records of sites along the present coast and in the adjacent Blue Mountains, and by 6000 BP there is abundant evidence for sites along the coast. These coastal people were exploiting not only the marine environment, but also, probably on a seasonal basis, an area of the hinterland. From this time on there is also evidence of the addition to the tool-kit of the smaller, more finely worked microliths. This new technology would have had an important impact on the hunting of land-mammals and on the manufacture of fish-hooks, with undoubted feedback on the production of better artefacts in wood and other plant materials. It is from the end of the Pleistocene, therefore, that the expansion of the human population led finally to the exploitation of virtually the whole continent. Only areas of extreme aridity, and some of the highland areas of the south-east and of Tasmania, remained unoccupied up to the time of European contact.

A Tasmanian interlude

The relationship between climatic factors and economic activity in a hunter–gatherer society has been brilliantly explored by recent studies of the now extinct Tasmanians. Mainland Australia became separated from Tasmania at the end of the Pleistocene, and sea-levels were close to their present position by 6000–7000 years ago. At the height of the last glaciation a broad area of land formed a bridge between Tasmania and the mainland and the similarity of the stone tools found in Tasmania with those from sites such as Clogg's Cave makes it clear that Tasmanian culture was derived from mainland sources. What is clear also is that the severance of the land connection prevented further exchange, and for the last 10 000 years at least the Tasmanians retained many of the older traits of the Pleistocene period and were isolated from the newer microlith technology of the mainland and from gaining the companionship of the dingo dog. However, despite their isolation the Tasmanians did develop some traits of their own and were evolving a tool-kit which differed from that of the mainland.

Shell middens on the present Tasmanian coast yield dates for the earliest occupation of any intensity from about 8000 BP. A date of 12 600 BP for the aptly named Beginner's Luck Cave in the southwest of Tasmania is associated with indications that the cave was used only sporadically, and implies that the main focus of the population was elsewhere. Bowdler[12] has interpreted her excavation of Cave Bay Cave, on Hunter Island off the north-west tip of Tasmania, as indicating also only sporadic use of the cave during much of the period when it was visited by man.

At the lowest level in Cave Bay Cave there are hearths established 20 000 to 22 750 BP. For the next 2000 years it appears to have been used only occasionally. There was one isolated hearth about 15 400 BP and then a long interval to 7000 BP with little evidence for human use. At this date there are two layers of midden material indicating a marine economy, followed by a return to sporadic use up to the time of contact by Europeans.

Bowdler has employed the same argument to explain the varied strata in Cave Bay Cave as she used for the distribution and use of sites on the mainland. The Tasmanians were a people exploiting the sea as the main base for their economy, supplementing this by catching game in the hinterland. The earliest level at Cave Bay Cave coincided with a time of raised sea-levels during the last interstadial. At 22 000 BP the coast would not have been far from Cave Bay Cave, and it could have been visited by people making expeditions into the coastal hinterland to hunt species such as the brush wallaby, bandicoots, and native cats (Dasyurus). At the peak of the last glaciation at 18 000 BP, however, the coast would have moved further away from the site of the cave, and the human population followed the coast and abandoned even sporadic visits to it. Only when the rising level of the sea brought the coast back to near the cave, do we find evidence of more intense occupation by people exploiting the marine environment. It was at this time that other sites around the present coastline were beginning to be used. There is a basal date of 8700 BP for Carlton Midden, 5000–6000 BP for middens on the east bank of the Derwent River, and 4700 BP for Little Swanport. Rhys Jones[13] interprets these dates as a good indication that people were pushed back up the short, steep slope by rising sea-levels in the south-east as well.

The Tasmanians continued to be primarily dependent on a littoral economy, making only seasonal use of the hinterland. On the western and southern coastlines they developed the use of bark canoes to increase the exploitation of marine resources of nearby islands. Rhys Jones has analysed the ethnographic and archaeological evidence, as well as experimental evidence using reconstructed canoes, to postulate the factors controlling the extent of such exploitation. Larger islands with areas greater than 90 km^2 and with minimum water crossings of 4 km could support a resident band of approximately 50 people. These bands periodically visited the mainland and adjacent islands, and received reciprocal visits from mainlanders. Smaller islands, less than 70 km^2 and with minimum crossings ranging from 1–8 km, received seasonal visits but did not support a resident population. Islands in this category at the upper distance limit were visited only by parties of experienced adults. Islands involving a water crossing greater than about 13–15 km, no matter what their size, were never visited.

Although small offshore islands add a substantial amount to the marine resources which can be utilized by a coastal people, clearly the benefits have to be balanced by the dangers involved in making sea crossings in primitive craft. Jones has used the same argument to explain the absence, at the time of European contact, of a human population on islands in the middle of Bass Strait and also on Kangaroo Island, off the coast of South Australia. The Bass Strait islands were once part of the land-bridge connecting the main continent with Tasmania, and the few stone tools which have been found on them were most probably left behind during visits from people living on the neighbouring shore-line. No shell middens have been found on these islands, nor any other evidence which dates to post-Pleistocene times. Whilst the islands were used before they became surrounded by sea at times when movement by land was possible, after the sea-level rose and access to them necessitated long sea crossings, their size and economic resources were not adequate to maintain a minimal human population, and their distance from other areas of permanent settlement was too great to enable them to be used seasonally.

Another valuable example is provided by Kangaroo Island, now 14.5 km from the nearest point of the South Australian coast. In this case, as sea-levels rose and the gap between mainland and island became greater, visits between the two areas became less frequent until, finally, they ceased altogether. Once again, the size and economic resources of the island alone were not sufficient to maintain a human population.

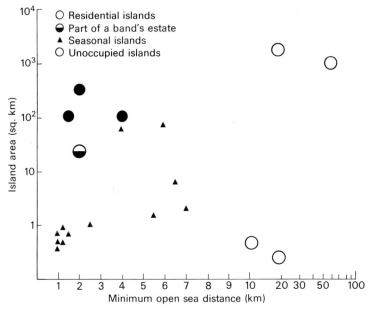

Fig. 2.9. Relationship between area, minimum sea distance, and occupation for islands around Tasmania (after Jones).[13]

The beginnings of non-material culture

Man is distinguished from other animals by his capacity for symbolic thought and his ability to communicate this symbolism in langauge and in a variety of other behavioural activities. The earliest development of this capacity during human evolution is difficult to establish. It is not until the archaeological record reveals human endeavour not immediately related to satisfying simple biological needs that we can infer that non-material aspects of culture had achieved some significance. In Europe the simple notching or scratching of bone and stone, together with the appearance of ochre pigment and pierced teeth used as personal ornaments can be dated to perhaps 30 000–40 000 years ago. By 20 000 BP painting and engraving on rocks and the beginning of sculpture in the form of 'venuses' was established, and from then on the evidence indicates a rapid growth in the complexity and extent of non-material culture.

In Australia evidence for comparable development of non-material culture has a similar time-scale to that of Europe.[14] By 30 000 BP ritual was established in connection with death. The Mungo I remains had been cremated, and the Mungo III burial was associated with a deposit of ochre, possibly smeared on the body at the time of burial. Fragments of ochre have been found at many sites dated between 15 000 and 20 000 BP and the pigment could have been used not only for body decoration, but also for painting on rock in a manner similar to that practised in many parts of the continent in more recent times. Unfortunately, the dating of paintings in caves is difficult, though there is suggestive evidence for cave painting at Laura in north Queensland as early as 13 000 BP. But although painting on rock is difficult to date because of deterioration, except in very special situations, the engraving of rock is more likely to be recovered and dated.

In Koonalda Cave on the Nullarbor Plain, simple linear markings in the soft limestone have been dated to more than 20 000 BP, and at Ingaladdi water-hole in the Northern Territory linear engravings on rock, similar to those associated with rainmaking ceremonies by living Aborigines, has an age of 5000–7000 years. By inference, the tradition of rock engravings of stylized circles and bird tracks found at Mount Cameron West in Tasmania must have considerable antiquity. The oldest of the extant engravings may be no older than 1000 years, but they bear a strong stylistic resemblance to similar engravings in central Australia: the isolation of Tasmania from mainland influences over a period of 10 000 years implies the persistence of an art tradition for at least this length of time.

One of the most unusual associations in Australia was the discovery of a male burial at Lake Nitchie, in south-east Australia, with a necklace of pierced Tasmanian Devil (Sarcophilus) teeth. No other example of pierced-teeth necklaces has been found in Australia, but the Lake Nitchie burial took place more than 5000 years ago.[15]

All these pieces of evidence indicate that concern with ritual has a long history in Australia, as it has in other parts of the world. It emphasizes also that in interpreting the signs of material culture allowance must be made for possible effects of the non-material aspects of culture on human economic activity. Thus the abandonment of a particular site may have been due to the enforcement of a taboo rather than a change in climate. Perhaps the most striking example of a taboo on economic activity is Jones's interpretation of the cessation of fish-eating in Tasmania, as evidenced by the absence

of fish bones in middens from 3000 BP up to the time of European
contact.[13] Other marine foods were still represented in the middens,
and fish bones were abundant prior to 3000 BP. Jones believes the
archaeological record in Tasmania indicates the beginning of a food
prohibition which remained operative in all Tasmanian tribes for
more than 100 generations.

3

PEOPLE IN BALANCE

Australia offers a unique opportunity to study the relationships
of man to land at a simple level of economic activity. At the time of
European contact the whole continent was occupied: the archaeological evidence indicates that it had been so for many thousands of
years without any dramatic interference through the movement of
people or ideas from other areas into the country and without the
opportunity, if population increased, for people to move out. A
pattern of life had developed, therefore, which enabled the population to remain in balance with its environment.

No census of the entire country was, or could have been, taken
at the time of contact. But as exploration and settlement by Europeans expanded notes were made on the distribution and number of
Aborigines encountered.

Using such sources, supplemented later by more anthropologically
oriented studies, the Polish sociologist Ludwik Krzywicki listed the
size of a large number of Australian tribes in *Primitive society and its
vital statistics.*[1] Krzywicki's figures have been used selectively by
some later writers, but he did not give estimates of the total population by State at the time of first European contact. This was done by
A. R. Radcliffe-Brown, Professor of Anthropology at Sydney University, who made some of the earliest studies of Aboriginal social
structure. His estimates were published in the *Year book of the
Commonwealth of Australia* for 1930.[2]

Radcliffe-Brown's minimum population for the entire continent
was 251 000. He stated, however, that 'it could have been quite
possibly, or even probably, over 300 000'. His minimum figure
represents a density of 1 person per 31 km^2 (12 square miles). If
allowance is made for uninhabitable desert areas, the average density
becomes 1 person per 18 km^2 (7 square miles).

Radcliffe-Brown recognized that the population was not distributed

Table 3.1. Radcliffe-Brown's estimate of the Aboriginal population[2]

	Population in 1000s	Density: No. of persons per km^2
Western Australia	52	49
South Australia	10	98
Victoria	11.5	21
Queensland	100	18
New South Wales	40	21
Northern Territory	35	39
Tasmania	2.5	28
Total	251	31

evenly across the continent, and his estimates range from 1 person per 18 km^2 in Queensland to 1 person per 98 km^2 in South Australia. More recent estimates indicate almost a hundredfold difference in density between the most favoured environments and the harshest extremes. Coastal areas, particularly some of those in the north and around Sydney, were able to sustain relatively high densities of population. The east coast of Cape York, for example, has yielded one estimate of 22 persons per km of coastline. This is 4.6 persons per km^2 when related to the area claimed by the same people as their territory, although a more realistic figure for the same locality is 1 person per km^2. A lower density occurred on the west coast of Cape York, approximating 1 person per 5 km^2. Even early estimates made before the end of the eighteenth century indicated that the coastline around the present city of Sydney supported a population of 2.5 persons per km of coast, or 2 persons for each km^2.

Riverine environments were also very favourable in some situations. The explorers Eyre and Sturt, in the last century, both reported large groups of Aborigines at various points along the Murray River, and Eyre's observations over an extended period of time showed that groups utilizing river resources were relatively stable communities. A reasonable estimate based on Eyre's records is 2.5 persons per km of river. Near the mouth of the Murray River, Tindale has shown that localized populations exploiting the tidal estuarine environment achieved densities of nearly 1 person per km^2.

In contrast to the relatively abundant resources of the coast and larger rivers, the vast arid areas of the interior could support only a sparse population. But even in these situations there were significant local variations in the carrying capacity of the land, in addition to longer-term cycles in any one locality because of periods of drought or plenty, which sometimes extended over several years, M. J. Meggitt[3] has estimated that one of the largest tribes, the Walbiri in central Australia, had a pre-contact population of only 1 person per 90 km^2 of the 100 000 km^2 area of undulating sandhill desert territory they inhabit. Their neighbours, the Aranda, occupied a relatively more productive territory of 65 000 km^2: with a total population of 2000 the Aranda would have required little more than 30 km^2 to support one person. Even within these vast territories the population density was not uniform. Meggitt recognized four major divisions within the Walbiri; the smallest of these, the Lander country, had an area of 20 000 km^2 and supported the densest population, whilst the Walmala country, in the west of the Walbiri territory, with more limited plant and animal resources, was the least densely populated.

For other parts of the continent, recent estimates of population suggest similar differences in density. In the Kimberley region of Western Australia the average density may have approximated 1 person per 17 km^2; on the more fertile Daly River in the Northern Territory one small group lived at a density of 1 person per 13 to 18 km^2, whilst in north-eastern Arnhem Land the average density was somewhat less with one person per 20–23 km^2. In Tasmania, Rhys Jones has estimated the pre-contact population to have been between 3000 and 4000 persons, or a density for the whole island of one person per 12 to 20 km^2. However, Jones points out that since one-third of the land-area was never inhabited the more realistic density would have been 1 person per 10 to 15 km^2 of occupied land.[4]

Social structure

To understand more fully the factors which operated to control the density and distribution of population it is necessary to examine, in outline, the main features of traditional Aboriginal social organization. Close study reveals differences between different areas, but some generalizations about the ways in which people structured their relationships with other people apply over the whole of Australia.[5]

The family group. The basic social unit is the family, consisting of a man with his wife or wives, and dependent children. Older relatives might be attached to the family group in some cases. The family group is sometimes referred to as the 'hearth group'.

Bands. The unit of economic activity is the local group, or band, which is what Radcliffe-Brown referred to as a 'horde'. The band consists of families who join together to take part in hunting or food-gathering and to provide daily social contact. But the membership of a band is not static. The number of families in the band depends on the terrain and season, and at certain times it might be enlarged by visitors from other groups. In a good coastal or riverine environment a local group might consist of 25 to 50 or more persons. By contrast, where resources are poor, as in desert areas, families disperse and frequently spend considerable periods on their own, congregating to form larger local groups again when conditions improve.

Jeremy Long made several journeys into remote parts of central Australia during 1957-64.[6] He observed groups ranging in size from 2 to 25 persons consisting generally of one or two families and he concluded that in these arid areas there were loose associations of families which foraged independently but often within a day's walking distance of each other.

At times the foraging family units come together at a single camp. When conditions are particularly favourable, for example after rain when food becomes abundant, members of several of these loose associations of families gather together to take part in ceremonies. Such gatherings represent mainly people belonging to the same tribe and may number from 100 or so up to 400–500 persons.

Local descent groups. The local groups discussed above must be distinguished from the land-owning groups, which are the core of Aboriginal social structure. The composition of these land-owning groups is made up of persons bound to the same locality by ties of descent and kinship as well as of religion. Most important to an Aboriginal is his or her membership of a group which 'owns' a particular area of land, identified by certain natural features such as water-holes, hills, caves, and lakes, which were created by or associated with the activities of mythical beings. Membership of this land-owning group depends on the group to which the individual's father belongs, although sometimes additional factors may operate, such as the locality in which the child was reported to have been conceived, either physically or 'spiritually'. These patrilineal land-owning groups are also exogamous.

Local descent group territory in each case is defined mainly on the basis of the sites in it which have religious significance, and ownership of these is inalienable. This does not mean that members of other local descent groups cannot enter into the area, and they may and do hunt game and collect food over the estates of other local descent groups. What is more important is that, although the economic unit, the local group of hunters and food-gatherers, comprises members of the local descent group, it is more frequently made up of members from a number of local descent groups. This appears to be based on the need for co-operation in exploiting the food-resources available, which influences not only the number of families that camp together in the same vicinity at a particular time but also how far they move from their own estates into neighbouring areas when foods are seasonally more abundant there.

Tribes. The term 'tribe' is somewhat controversial. In traditional Aboriginal Australia there was no formal political organization which held members of various local groups together, nothing indeed which can be used conveniently to define a tribe, a supertribe, or a nation, even though groupings of several thousand persons loosely affiliated to each other did exist in some parts of the continent. It has been suggested that because of the meaning which the term 'tribe' has in other parts of the world it should be replaced in Australia by the term 'local group clusters'. However, since the term 'tribe' is firmly entrenched in Australian use it will be retained here.

'Tribe' in the Australian Aboriginal context can be used to refer to a group of people who occupy a recognized area of country over which they claim both religious and hunting and food-gathering rights. Members of a tribe speak the same language or dialect as recognized by themselves and by their neighbours. In addition, members of a tribe consider they have more in common with one another than with members of other tribes; and a tribe is, up to a point, a relatively self-contained entity with its own kind of social structure. As part of this perspective, marriage rules emphasize preference for unions within that range. Members of a tribe may have a name for themselves, or their neighbours may have a name for them, though sometimes there is no overall name for the whole tribe. As we will note later, boundaries between these larger constellations in some cases may easily be defined by distinctive natural features, such as a river or a line of hills. But in other cases the boundary is less precise, and members of one tribe may have hunting rights over country held by another.

Social categories. As well as what could be called more broadly 'tribal' membership, including membership of a local descent group, with its own sacred sites associated with its 'estate', each individual belongs to one social category or another. The names of these social categories and their complexity varies in different parts of the country, and in some places has been undergoing change during the last fifty years at least, indicating an ability to adapt the pattern of social regulation to pressures from outside.

Catherine and Ronald Berndt have recently given an excellent outline of Aboriginal social categories in *Pioneers and settlers: the
Aboriginal Australians.*[7] What follows is a brief note on some points
in their discussion.

At the simplest level of classification alternative generations are
grouped into separate categories. Everyone in your own generation
belongs to the same category as yourself, and so does everyone in
your grandparent's and grandchildren's generations. Everyone in
your parent's and your children's generations belong to the other
category. This simple, two-category social system is endogamous:
marriages take place between persons in the same generation. This
type of alternating generation system is found especially in the
Western Desert.

Another simple two-category system operated in many parts of
the continent. In this system society is divided into two named
moieties, which are exogamous: that is husband and wife must
belong to different moieties, since marriages between members of
the same moiety are not acceptable. In north-east Arnhem Land,
membership of a moiety is determined by patrilineal descent; in
other words, the children are assigned to the same moiety as their
father and father's father. In western Arnhem Land, on the other
hand, membership of the two traditionally recognized moieties is
determined by matrilineal descent; children belong to the named
moiety of their mother and mother's mother. During recent years the
named patrilineal moieties of eastern Arnhem Land have spread into
western Arnhem Land, possibly because they accord better with the
patrilineal ownership of land in the local descent groups which are
part of the overall system there. In a few areas, including western
Arnhem Land, each moiety is divided into two parts, which can be
called semi-moieties, and membership of these rests on similar rules.

A somewhat similar four-category system but with partly different
rules operates in other parts of the continent. For simplicity we can
call the four categories, sections A, B, C, and D. If a man in section A
marries a woman in B, as he should do, their children will be in
section D. A man in section C should marry a woman in section D
and their children will be in section B. If an A woman marries a
B man the children will be assigned to C, but if a C woman marries
a D man the children will be assigned to A.

In this four-section system, which is still important in, for instance,
the centre and north-west of the continent, no distinction in terms is
made to indicate sex. That differentiation is included in an eight-
category system, in which each of the four sections is subdivided
into A_1 and A_2, B_1 and B_2, etc. One form of the sub-section term in

each of the divisions indicates males, the other females. Reference should be made to the Berndts' book for fuller details of the way in which the eight-category system operates. What is worth noting here is that both the four- and the eight-category system have been spreading during the last fifty years into areas in the Northern Territory, South Australia, and Western Australia where they had not been operating before, and the eight-category system has been spreading more widely.

Kinship. Finally, social relations are regulated by classifications of relationships related also to biological factors, although set within a social framework. In different places, not only the terms used to define these kinship relationships may differ, but the types and the strengths of the bonds implied by the terms also differ.

All persons within a community, or tribe, acknowledge a kin relationship with everyone else in that community, either consanguineal or more distant. Kin terms in Aboriginal society categorize relationships in different ways from the patterns recognized in Australian–European society. Thus Aboriginal children call not only their biological father, but all his brothers by the same 'father' term. Similarly all their mother's sisters are 'mothers' to them. But their father's sisters and their mother's brothers are addressed and referred to by different terms. The children of all 'fathers' and all 'mothers' are also all brothers and sisters, but the children of father's sisters and the children of mother's brothers are put in a different category, corresponding to what are termed cousins in Australian–European society, with an added distinction made between cousins on the father's side and cousins on the mother's side.

All of this kinship classification is important in regulating marriage choices. Not only must the two marriage partners belong to the appropriate moieties, sections, or sub-sections, they must also stand in the right kin relationship. And, when all these conditions are satisfied, other factors also enter into the final arrangement, factors which are important to particular families in terms of prestige and social security.

Biologically, the moiety, section, and subsection systems maintain the practice of exogamy, and also maintain marriages no closer than the first-cousin level in the four-section system and no closer than second-cousins in the eight-section system.

Though moieties and semi-moieties, or sections and subsections, have different names in various parts of the continent, the essential ordering of social relations is everywhere carried out according to the principles outlined above. But there are exceptions, and the

Aboriginal social system is flexible enough to accommodate them. For instance, a person from outside the tribe is assigned to an appropriate section of his host tribe on the basis of his or her social classification in the previous tribe.

More importantly, recent studies indicate that there may have been a significant proportion of marriages which were not contracted according to the category rules. One such study by Ralph Piddington[8] reports that among the Karadjeri in Western Australia there existed both 'alternate' and 'wrong' marriages; and he points out that Phyllis Kaberry[9] studying Kimberley tribes recorded 7 to 38 per cent 'alternate' marriages and 4 to 25 per cent 'wrong' marriages. Piddington's results have been criticized because they were obtained from groups already subject to severe modification through contact with European culture, and Piddington himself believes it is now too late to determine the incidence of irregular marriages in pre-contact times.

Perhaps in the past social anthropologists have placed too much emphasis upon the 'construct' system regulating social relationships, including marriage, in Aboriginal society. The literature has been filled with examples of tribes with 'mixed' systems and those where there are exceptions to the strict application of the rules. Some time ago F. G. G. Rose[10] argued forcibly that it was necessary to determine not whether individuals in any particular locality behave according to the 'construct' rules but to record their own perception of how their behaviour is regulated. He draws attention to Turner's study of the people on Groote Eylandt in the Gulf of Carpentaria. This work is relevant to an understanding of the relationship between a person's membership of his or her local group or clan and the division of society into moieties or sections with a complicated structure of kinship categories regulating social behaviour. Rose argued that kinship terms for an Aboriginal in traditional society were more important in expressing economic relationships and the rights and obligations between groups rather than in indicating blood relationships; and that the details of what he calls a *kinship–local-group-generation* system have to be established in each Aboriginal population.

In a recent study Neville White[11] has found, among two intermarrying dialect groups, Ridarngu and Wagilag, in north-central Arnhem Land, that the size of the local group varied during the four years of his study from 31 to 60 persons (in 5 to 8 households). Approximately 75 per cent of the marriages were between members of these two dialect groups. White argues that this represents a transition stage between the tribal structure characteristic of western

Arnhem Land, represented by the endogamous Rembarranga, which is a single linguistic unit, and the other extreme in north-eastern Arnhem Land, where dialect units are exogamous.

There has been much speculation about the significance and the origin of the moiety and section systems and of the role of kinship in the economic life of the community. Their origin, of course, is impossible to elicit; but it is clear that they have certain functions, not only in making exogamy mandatory, but in prohibiting marriage with many of the women in the appropriate social group. This may lead to a greater social stability, but the exogamous categories may have a more important consequence for a hunter–gatherer community. Exogamy provides a set of interlocking social relationships which extends the ranges of land to which the group may have access in times of shortage. This will be significant in a four-section system, but will provide an even wider set of ranges in an eight-section system. Perhaps it is because of its economic importance that this latter system was adopted widely in the more arid areas of the continent. Kinship also ensures that people are linked together in wider co-operative units.

The ecological significance of section and sub-section systems in an arid environment has been discussed by Aram Yengoyan,[12] who points out that section terms extend beyond tribal boundaries. They allow ready classification of persons belonging to another tribe and this overlapping network of related individuals and groups makes possible relocation of camps into neighbouring areas for the exploitation of resources during periods of economic stress. Yengoyan continues 'In central and western Australia the almost limitless extension of social ties through section categories and groupings provided each local group with the ability to expand and contract their movements into adjacent areas during times of hardship. Not only did local groups continuously readjust to minute environmental pressures, but the composition of local groups also varied as individuals re-aligned themselves with adjacent bands through the extension of kinship and section terms' (p. 125).

Not everyone agrees with Yengoyan's idea, particularly his claim that the section system meant an almost limitless expansion of social ties. It did mean some expansion, but the focus was always on the group's own sites in its own country, which imposed a severe limit on the expansion which could take place. What is of interest also is that in the area with which Yengoyan is concerned the section and sub-section system came into operation relatively recently: the traditional system in the Western Desert was that of alternating generations.

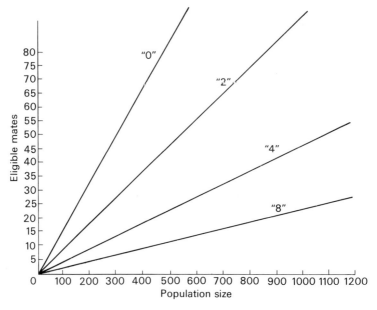

Fig. 3.1. Population size and number of eligible mates in relation to different sets of marriage restrictions: '0' = local group exogamy; '2' = moiety restrictions; '4' = section restrictions; '8' = sub-section restrictions (from Yengoyan).[12]

   Neville White has also recently provided evidence for the importance of the ecological determinants of marriage patterns for populations in northern Australia, particularly for those in north-eastern Arnhem Land. Here the evidence indicates that marriage distances are greater when the ecological situation is poorer or unreliable. He points out that this may be simply an inverse relationship because of the lack of availability of spouses when population density decreases. But he suggests that it may also be an adaptive strategy to maximize resources. When conditions are poorer it will be advantageous to use marriage as a means of extending one's range of movement into different areas. If this involves moving into a superior environment, as for instance when an 'inland' man marries a 'coastal' woman, there is an insurance against times when the inland resources are depleted. White finds that the shortest marriage distances are found among coastal populations in Arnhem Land, where tribal size and area is smallest and population density greatest. As tribal size decreases he finds the proportion of intertribal marriage increases, the linear regression between the two being significant. White points out that under these conditions, where there are small population units with high densities and short marriage distances, one might expect to find genetic diversity due to microevolutionary processes such as genetic drift. That is, in the most favourable areas will be found genetically distinguishable clusters of neighbouring tribes with greater genetic diversity per unit area than is found in less favourable areas with great marriage distances.

Demography of traditionally oriented communities

Vital statistics for poulations in pre-contact times do not exist. With a few exceptions, it is only during the present century that records have been made for people whose life-style is still traditionally oriented. Where such records refer to ages, in general they are only to broad age categories. Only in cases where birth dates have been recorded can an accurate age assessment be made. Further, when dealing with local groups whose total population may not exceed 50 persons, chance factors will result in large variations from group to group.

Norman Tindale[13] has collected much detailed information on the composition of local groups. Figure 3.2 illustrates and age and sex composition of three such local groups in the Western Desert area. In the Rawlinson Ranges 62 per cent were estimated to be aged 20 and under, compared with 40 per cent at Tomkinson Ranges and 54 per cent at Bellock Range. The ratio of males to females at the same three localities was 0.91, 0.76, and 1.2. Similar data were collected by W. W. Denham[14] during 1970–2 among the Alyawara-speaking people of Central Australia. The groups combined totalled 264 persons of whom 51 per cent were under 20 and the ratio of males to females was 2.03. Among these Alyawara, however, 32 per cent were under 10 years of age, a figure which probably indicates the impact on their population structure of the modern medical services to which these people had access at the time.

In the north comparable figures are available for several populations, and one example will indicate the situation during the 1930s. Lauriston Sharp[15] made a careful census among several groups living on the western side of Cape York. A church mission had been established in the region since 1905 and a segment of the population, about 30 per cent, was more or less permanently domiciled there when Sharp made his studies. A further 30 per cent were still living what Sharp considered to be a traditionally oriented life and the remaining 40 per cent were at an intermediate stage of the 'acculturation' process. The total population in 1933 was 376 persons and only 24 per cent were recorded as pre-pubertal, whilst 53 per cent were recorded as being over 25 years of age.

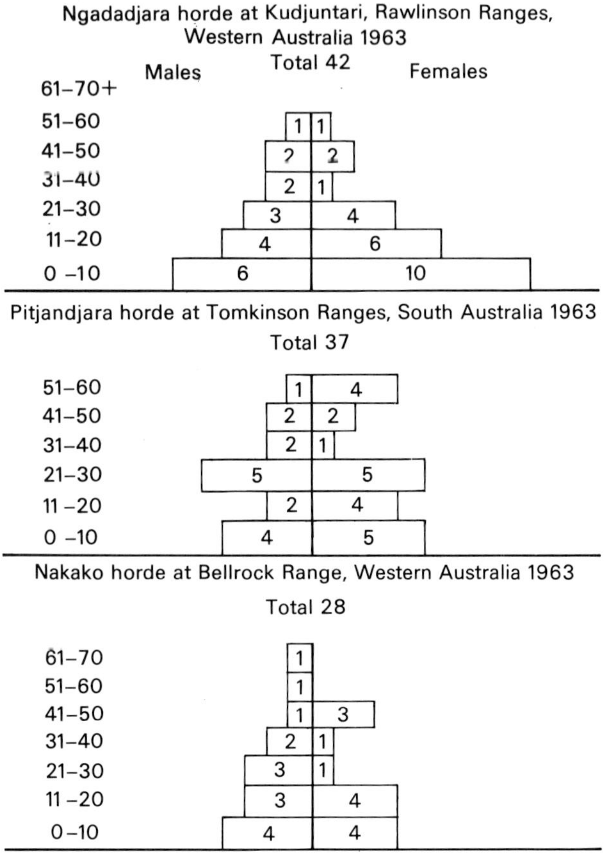

Ngadadjara horde at Kudjuntari, Rawlinson Ranges,
Western Australia 1963

Total 42

Age	Males	Females
61–70+		
51–60	1	1
41–50	?	2
31–40	2	1
21–30	3	4
11–20	4	6
0 –10	6	10

Pitjandjara horde at Tomkinson Ranges, South Australia 1963

Total 37

Age	Males	Females
51–60	1	4
41–50	2	2
31–40	2	1
21–30	5	5
11 –20	2	4
0 –10	4	5

Nakako horde at Bellrock Range, Western Australia 1963

Total 28

Age	Males	Females
61–70	1	
51–60	1	
41–50	1	3
31–40	2	1
21–30	3	1
11 –20	3	4
0 –10	4	4

Fig. 3.2. Age-structure of three hordes in the Western Desert (from Tindale).[13]

Sharp's attempt to define the composition of the traditionally-oriented group was of little value: his figures indicate clearly that the mission had been active in attracting young people away from the bush, and this applied particularly to the young girls. It is known also that the mission was not the only contact experience for this population. The Dutch visited the area in 1623, and at least some Aborigines were killed: much later, in 1864, over thirty men from one tribe were killed by the Jardine expedition, and diseases spreading from white communities in Cape York during the nineteenth century caused great morbidity, and presumably mortality, in the area. All these factors must have altered the population structure, both in its age and sex composition, from that which prevailed in the pre-contact period.

One other significant demographic parameter can be extracted from the records. With the exception of Tasmania, all traditional Aboriginal societies were polygynous, though not all men had more than one wife. Sometimes a girl was betrothed at birth, and the common pattern was for women to be married to much older men. This marriage pattern changed considerably after contact, but was still present when some of the more recent local censuses were taken. For example, among the Walbiri of central Australia in the early 1960s, Meggitt reported that 34 per cent of husbands were polygynous, the distribution of the number of wives per married man being given in Table 3.2.[3]

Table 3.2. Number of wives per married man among the Walbiri
         (from Meggitt)[3]

No. of wives	1	2	3	4	5 and over
Per cent of married men (Total No. 175)	66	24	5	3	2

Varying proportions of polygynous unions have been reported for other parts of the continent. Phyllis Kaberry reports 13 per cent in the Kimberley, Sharp gives 19 per cent among the traditionally-oriented group in Cape York, and Ronald and Catherine Berndt state that the number of wives per married man in the desert regions may be as many as six, with two or three being more usual. Larger numbers occur in Arnhem Land in a small proportion of cases: Hart and Pilling[16] in their study of the Tiwi on Bathurst and Melville Islands noted a few men had as many as twenty to thirty wives assigned to them. Polygynous unions are important, of course, not only in terms of sexual relations, but also economically and from the point of view of prestige. The Berndts have outlined the functions of obtaining wives in these terms, particularly for the Arnhem Land region, where reshuffling of wives can occur as new alliances are formed.

Men under the age of 25 rarely had wives betrothed to them, and since betrothal for the girl may have been at birth, there was inevitably a large gap between the age of husband and wife. When the wife reached the age of puberty, the husband could be 40 years of age. In a polygynous household, the gap in age would become even greater as the man accumulated more wives. During recent times, not only the proportion of polygynous unions but also the difference in age between husband and wife has been decreasing. For the Alyawara in central Australia Denham found the mean age difference between spouses to be 14 years. The mean age difference for men in the 65 and over age group, however, was 28 years suggesting that these older men had acquired a 'new generation' of younger wives.

Denham found that the age-gap was different if looked at from the point of view of the women. Women under 39 years of age were 17 years younger than their husbands, women in the 40–49 age group were ten years younger than their husbands, whilst women over 49 were an average of only five years younger than their husbands, and a few women in fact were older than their husbands.

The decreasing gap in age between spouses as women become older is due to the death of older men with relatively young wives. These widows may remarry, frequently with men who have not yet had a young wife assigned to them. Among the Tiwi on Bathurst and Melville Islands, all such widows were expected to remarry and they became part of the exchange system. Not all such widows remarry, however, and Denham records that among the Alyawara at the time of his survey 12 per cent of the women who had been married were widowed, compared with 5 per cent of widowers among men who had been married. There was, on the other hand, a much larger proportion of males than females in the community who were not married at that time. This reflects the age difference between the sexes in the age of marriage: the youngest female with a spouse was 14 years old, but the youngest male with a spouse was 26 years old.

Does the institution of polygyny have any consequence on the fertility of individuals in the group? Lauriston Sharp's records for the 1933–4 period on the western side of Cape York suggest that there is no difference: 20 women who were living in polygynous households had an average of 2.4 children, whilst 60 women living in monogynous households had 2.3 children each. The data for the Alyawara in central Australia suggest also that women in polygynous households are still fertile: the mean difference of 2.4 years between the age of adjacent siblings under 5 years old indicates that Alyawara women do not remain sexually inactive or infertile for any appreciable period after the birth of a previous child. One advantage in the polygynous household is the possibility that since women are most likely to have co-wives during the years of their highest fertility they are most likely to benefit from additional assistance in caring for the children.

Ecological factors controlling population density

The density of population in a demographically stable hunter–gatherer community obviously must be related in some way to environmental factors which control the energy flow and essential nutrient resources of the land on which the community is dependent, even though such factors need not be completely deterministic. The number of these controlling factors are many and their inter-actions complex. In Chapter 1 the studies by Fitzpatrick and Nix were used to illustrate how physical variables like moisture, light, and temperature can be combined into a growth index related to dry-matter production for particular plant species. In any one locality, however, the actual productivity will depend on such factors as soil type, trace-element level, contours affecting water run-off, and, for coastal areas, ocean currents, closeness to estuaries, and the nature of the beach and its accessibility.

In addition to these physical determinants there are cultural factors, of which the most important is the level of technological development directly concerned with obtaining food: a bow and arrow for instance, is more efficient for some types of hunting than a spear; a fish-trap more effective in most situations than a line with a shell hook. As well as direct cultural effects on the extractive technology, there are many other cultural factors which will exert an effect. For example we noted in the last chapter the suggestion that a food prohibition prevented the utilization of fish as a food in Tasmania during the last 3000 years, a prohibition which may have altered significantly the energy balance in Tasmanian populations.

Few attempts have been made to quantify such variables as they operate in communities at the simplest levels of economic activity. In Australia one important exception is the work of J. B. Birdsell. In his first discussion of this topic Birdsell[17] used the mean annual rainfall as a simple measure of one of the more significant variables in the environment, and, since there were few records of the actual population size of Aboriginal tribes he substituted tribal area as the dependent variable. He argued that if 'in a statistical sense' the size of a tribal population was a constant then area would be a direct function of population density. Tribal areas were estimated from the 1940 tribal map published by Norman Tindale,[18] and correlation coefficients were calculated for the relationship beween the estimated mean annual rainfall and area for each tribe. For a total series of 409 tribes Birdsell obtained a coefficient of curvilinear correlation of 0.59. He recognized, however, that there might be factors other than mean annual rainfall affecting population densi-ties and that cultural factors might result in deviations from the assumed constant tribal size of 500 persons.

To remove the effect of other ecological factors Birdsell eliminated all tribes except those whose resources are primarily terrestrial in origin, and whose territories are essentially watered by rainfall which falls within their territories. Thus, tribes whose domain included islands, coastal tribes, and tribes which depended on resources from rivers whose water came largely from sources outside the tribal territory were not included. Cultural factors were taken into account by excluding tribes whose populations were known to depart significantly from the assumed constant size of 500. After the eliminations were made Birdsell was left with a series of 123 tribes which he considered to be ecologically and culturally constant in the characteristics relevant for his analysis. These tribes were distributed in three blocs; the largest, constituting two-thirds of the total, centred in Queensland; the other two blocs, of about 20 tribes each, occupied a portion of the central desert area and a region in the south-east of the continent inland from the coast and extending from the southern portion of the Dividing Range to near the mouth of the Murray River.

Figure 3.3 reproduces the scattergram of the relationship between mean annual rainfall and tribal area for this series of 123 tribes. The J-shaped curve takes the form $Y = aX^b$, where Y is the tribal area and X the mean annual rainfall and the constants for the fitted curve were

$$a = 7112.8 \quad \text{and} \quad b = 1.58451$$

The coefficient of curvilinear correlation in this case was found to be 0.81, and the variance explained by the correlation is 65 per cent of the total. Birdsell concluded that this high correlation between rainfall and density (assuming number of persons per tribe to be constant) indicates rigorous environmental determinism of population densities for Aborigines in Australia, and he added that there was no reason why other hunting and collecting populations, either from the Pleistocene or Recent periods, were not equally subject to similar environmental determinism.

In an attempt to understand the factors influencing population densities in tribes excluded from the basic series, Birdsell has extended his analysis to coastal, island, and riverine tribes. He calculated area ratios based on the deviation in observed tribal area from that predicted by the formula for the mean annual rainfall in the region. An *area ratio* of 0.5, for example, indicates the tribal area is only one half that calculated from the mean annual rainfall. Looked at from the point of view of density of population this may mean that the *density ratio* is 2.0, assuming the size of the tribe is still 500, or it may mean that the population is only 250, giving the standard *density ratio* of 1.0.

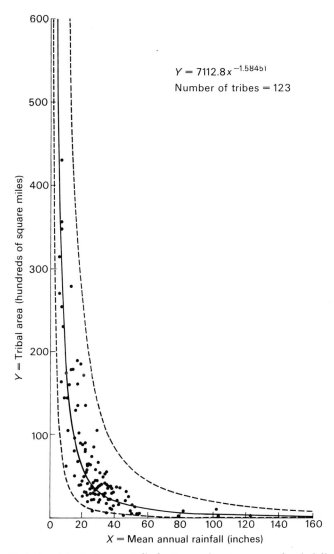

$$Y = 7112.8x^{-1.58451}$$

Number of tribes = 123

Fig. 3.3. Relationship between tribal area and mean annual rainfall for non-coastal tribes (from Birdsell).[17]

An important ecological factor affecting population density is what Birdsell calls 'unearned surface-water', that is rivers or fresh-water lakes which depend on water inflow from distant sources. The Murray River, for example, rises in a relatively high rainfall area, but flows for much of its length through a region of 25 to 40 cm of rain per year. The further downstream one goes the greater

the dependence on water from a distance and the greater are the
'unearned' ecological resources. When the *area ratios* for tribes along
the Murray River are plotted against distance from the mouth of
the river (Fig. 3.4) a striking change is observed, from values around
1.5 in the upper reaches down to approximately 0.03 for tribes
near the river-mouth. Since there is evidence that the number of
persons in these lower river tribes may have exceeded the standard
500, the *density ratios* of course would be even greater than that
suggested on the basis of area alone.

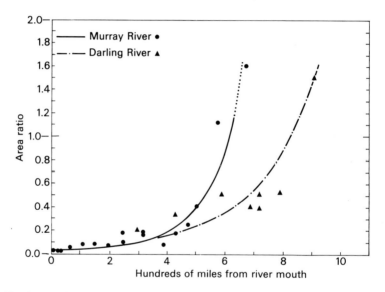

Fig. 3.4. Tribal area-ratios and distance from mouth of the River Murray
(from Birdsell).[17]

The problems posed by populations living on islands and along
coasts are more difficult. Birdsell concludes, since *density ratios*
for these populations can be as high as 4.6 for those living wholly or
partly on islands, that marine food-resources significantly alter the
ecology of Aboriginal populations. For coastal tribes, *density ratios*
vary from less than 1.0 for tribes along the coast of the Australian
Bight or the coast of central Queensland, to values of 2.5 or more for
tropical coastal areas. For these very different coastal environments
there is not enough information on resources and the factors affecting their availability to provide a simple relationship between them
and the population density. Certainly mean annual rainfall by itself
is a poor predictor in these situations.

The importance of coastal areas for Aboriginal populations has been stressed by Rhys Jones[4] for populations in Tasmania. The population distribution within the occupied area of Tasmania was far from uniform. The island was the home of nine tribal groups, and with respect to population density varied from 1 person per 20 km^2 for the Big River and North tribes to 1 person per 6 km^2 for the coastal North-West and South-East tribes, who were able to exploit more favoured environments. Tribal territories varied considerably in area, ranging from 2500 to 8000 km^2 but the length of coastline

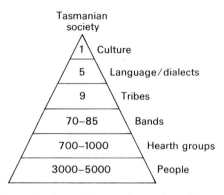

Fig. 3.5. Organization of Tasmanian society (from Jones).[4]

available to each tribe was even more variable, being zero for the Ben Lomond and Big River tribe and reaching 550 km for the South-East tribe. Jones points out that even tribes with no coastline of their own gained seasonal access to some portion of coast by agreement with neighbouring tribes. The analysis of the Tasmanian case by Jones makes clear the difficulty of determining the exact relationship between land and people. He distinguishes three broad categories among the tribes: the North-West, South-West, and South-East tribes were maritime groups, deriving the major part of their subsistence from the coast and possessing only a narrow hinterland. These tribes therefore had a relatively lower density of persons per km of coastline but higher density if related to the total area of land available to them. The Oyster Bay, North-East, and possibly the North tribes had not only a reasonable length of coastline but also a large area of hinterland. Population densities in these cases, both for length of coast and total area, had intermediate values. Finally, the third group of tribes, Big River, Ben Lomond, and North Midlands, could claim little or no coastline of their own. Their population density on an area basis was consequently relatively low, but if their population is

Table 3.3. Population densities in Tasmania (adapted from Jones)[4]

Tribe	Area (km^2)	Length of coast including islands (km)	No. of bands	Population	Mean No. of persons	
					per km^2 of land	per km of coast
North-West	3367	547	9–10	400–500	0.13	0.82
South-West	2849	450	6	200–350	0.10	0.61
South-East	3108	547	9	400–500	0.14	0.82
Oyster Bay	8547	515	15	600–800	0.08	1.40
Big River	7770	242†	7– 8	300–400	0.05	1.45
North	4662	113†	5– 6	200–300	0.05	2.21
North Midlands	6734	160†	10?	400–500?	0.07	2.81
Ben Lomond	2590	?	4?	150–200	0.07	?
North-East	5696	258	10	400–500	0.08	1.74
Total for Tasmania	69 000	2415	75–80	3000–5000	0.06	1.66

†Seasonal access to coast. The **Big River** tribe had lake shoreline.

related to the shorter coastline available to them — which in the case of the North Midland tribe whose territory included the Tamar estuary amounted to about 160 km — the density per km of coast was the highest for any of the tribes.

For mainland Australia Norman Tindale[13] has recently explored some of the ecological variables affecting tribal distribution and densities. Basing his conclusions on fifty years of detailed observation in all parts of the continent, Tindale draws attention to the smaller size of populations and the smaller areas occupied by them in regions with richer food resources, along coasts, on islands, and near the mouths of rivers. These smaller tribal units have each developed in response to a special local ecological association. At the other extreme large loose associations, which some consider were tribes, are also a response to special ecological factors. Most of them lived in the desert–grassland fringe and were dependent on natural grains as a major source of food. Tindale suggests that there was a broad belt of grassland country where it was possible to sustain populations up to several thousand persons. In these cases there was sufficient stability of food resources to make possible a network of communication between groups spread over relatively big areas. Tindale believes that the ability of all members of the tribe to communicate regularly is an important factor in stabilizing the tribe. There is a case, he argues, for distinguishing between these predominantly grain-eaters and the predominantly meat-eating peoples, the hunters of the more arid areas, whose tribal population more commonly approximated 450 to 500 people.

The most striking example of large associations, or what in some cases have been described as confederacies or nations, occurred in the region drained by the Darling River. In his early listing of tribal populations Krzywicki gave the population of the Kamilaroi in 1845 as 6000–7000 persons, and the tribe occupied a territory of approximately 75 000 km². A population of several thousands has been ascribed also to the Wangaibon, with a territory almost the same as the Kamilaroi, whilst the Wiradjuri is considered to have been one of the largest tribal groupings in the region, occupying nearly 100 000 km². Tindale notes that there were many hordes, with recognizable dialect differences in some cases, among the Wiradjuri and he believes that the maintenance of a cycle of ceremonies held in different parts of the tribal territory and involving a regular movement of people around the territory assisted in giving coherence to this widely scattered tribe.

The role of other cultural factors enabling such large groupings to maintain a sense of tribal unity has been discussed by Birdsell[19] in a

recent defence of his concept of a basic demographic unit. He argues
that the statistical tendency is for a local band or horde to have a
modal population size of 25 in desert regions, being somewhat larger
(50 to 100) in the better-watered coastal regions in the south-east
and north of the Continent. For tribes, he states that the statistical
tendency is to approximate 500 persons for the basic series of 123
tribes which he selected in his earlier investigations. However, it is
important to note that of the 123 tribes included in Birdsell's list, six
had fewer than 200 and 15 had more than 900 persons, and that the
standard deviation is 300 persons. So that even within this relatively
homogeneous ecological zone there is a range of tribal size of
considerable magnitude. It must be emphasized also that this basic
series of 123 tribes is less than 30 per cent of the tribes in Australia.
The remaining 70 per cent were excluded by Birdsell because in some
cases ecological factors distorted the basic relationship between the
size of tribal area and population density, or in other cases because
cultural variables produced undue deviations in the size of the tribal
population as compared to the assumed constant of 500 persons per
tribe.

Tribe and boundary

We have noted earlier that the concept of tribe implies some kind of
unity binding its members together into a more or less homogeneous
group, which distinguishes it from neighbouring groups. Since the
Australian tribe is also made up of land-holding local groups, the
total of these constitutes the tribal territory. A great deal of argument has centred around whether Aborigines recognized the limits of
such tribal territories in a clear-cut way, or whether the whole concept of a tribe is one which has been imposed by outside observers
wanting to equate the Australian situation with that prevailing in
Africa or America. What seems clear now is that no rigid definition
of a tribe is applicable for all parts of the continent.

Some anthropologists consider that a tribe can be equated with
a language unit. In the western and central desert regions, however,
there are dialect chains running for long distances without sharp
breaks at tribal boundaries; and Ronald Berndt[20] has discussed
the difficulty of identifying the 'tribe' in the Western Desert area.
Similar situations are found in other regions. In north Queensland,
for example, Dixon[21] states that some neighbouring tribes speak quite
different languages, but that for others the tribal boundary merely
separates groups speaking dialects of the same language.

What then constitutes the boundary between tribes? Dixon believes that at least two types of boundary separate local groups who recognize themselves as belonging to one tribe or another. One type of boundary is found where the tribe is centred on a river, and the boundary lies, imprecisely defined, in the relatively infertile land on either side. The other type is where the boundary lies along a geographical feature, such as the crest of a line of hills. The former type of boundary, lying somewhere in infertile country, whether flat or mountainous, appears to be more common in Australia.

Local descent groups, which are the land-owning units, reside for a major portion of their time in their own territory, but they may also move into the territory of other local descent groups. Indeed, there are great advantages in a tribe's including within its territory different kinds of vegetational zone. The tribe can then move around its territory according to the season, choosing to live at any particular time in an area which is climatically more pleasant and offers more abundant food. Thus among the Ydinijdi the 'tablelands' local group would descend to the coast when the 'rickety' nut was ripe on the small hills in the coastal country, whilst at another season when the black pine nuts were ripe on the tablelands, all the local groups would move into the mountains. Such cyclical movements were common in regions with marked seasonal changes: similar seasonal movements have been described by Hiatt for groups of Gidjingali in northern Arnhem Land.

In the arid interior movement of local groups was more irregular, being dictated by the vagaries of drought, sometimes extending over many years, alternating with varying periods of plenty. After good rain the local groups spread out to obtain maximum utilization of the sudden increase both in plants and the animals which come to feed on them. In times of drought the presence of a permanent source of water becomes paramount, but this alone would not be adequate for large concentrations of people since the surrounding food resources would be quickly exhausted. At such times affiliations with groups outside the tribe become important in allowing camps to be established in 'foreign' territory where conditions might be more favourable.

Land productivity, the number of people, language, and other aspects of culture, all interact to demarcate the limits of territory belonging to either a local group or to a tribe. When resources are plentiful, population increases, the population becomes more sedentary, the area's boundaries are more rigidly defined, and particular stones, crests, or other distinctive natural features become the recognized limit beyond which a person may not pass. As tribal area increases, and seasonal movement over large areas becomes a regular pattern of life, physiographic features such as a change in vegetation pattern, or a line of hills, constitute a recognized boundary. As tribal areas increase still further the edges become more blurred and the tribal boundary frequently becomes a series of overlapping areas at the periphery of the territories of the local descent groups. In Australia such peripheral areas sometimes included sacred sites belonging to one local descent group, but were recognized as areas that could be hunted over by members of another local descent group.

We can pursue this scenario further. The distinctiveness of each constellation of local descent groups, which have more in common amongst themselves than with other constellations, will be exaggerated as languages became more differentiated. When mobility is reduced, as in regions where food is plentiful, this process leads to fragmentation and also to a further increase in the number of linguistic divisions. In this situation a constellation of local descent groups may increase in size and become large enough to consider themselves independent of their neighbours. Eventually as dialect differences become accentuated, this new community comes to be considered as a tribal group.

There can be no simple answer, therefore, to the question of what constitutes a tribe in Australia. Each locality developed its own ecologically balanced community, ranging from a distinctive unit as small as 100 to 200 people, through varying constellations of local groups which were in a dynamic state of tension with neighbouring constellations. At the upper limit these became loose confederacies of several thousand persons. The land, with its ecological determinants, provided one set of controlling factors: culture, including technological innovation, provided another. The final result can be interpreted fully only in this biosocial framework which, in traditional Aboriginal Australia, as in other parts of the world, was extremely complex.

4

HUNTING AND GATHERING

There is no evidence that the deliberate cultivation of plants or the husbandry of animals was practised in any part of Australia before Europeans intruded into the continent. But there is growing evidence that Aborigines were aware of the effects of several activities in promoting increased yields from crops on which they depended. The most significant of these was setting fire to tracts of land to promote better growth in the next season or to stimulate the germination of the seeds of plants which were adapted to fire in the Australian environment.[1]

Rhys Jones has dubbed the Aborigines 'firestick farmers',[2] and they were indeed incipient farmers as well as highly skilled hunters and gatherers. Even as gatherers they took care not to exhaust their resources. For example, in Arnhem Land, when gathering yams they dug a hole beside the plant and cut off the basal part of the tuber, but left sufficient of the root to allow it to grow again. In this way they ensured their food supply for the next season. We recognize now, therefore, that although the Aborigines were hunters and gatherers, the manner in which they satisfied their food needs was broadly adapted to the ecology of each region and that, in addition, they used their technology to take advantage of certain features of that ecology.

There are some accounts which describe the hunting and food-gathering activities of a few groups still living in a traditionally oriented way. Unfortunately these reports are limited to a few parts of the continent, but they can be supplemented by the observations of early settlers and explorers, and from archaeological records, to enable a reconstruction to be made of the diversity of forms which the food quest took in different places.

Hunters by the seashore

On the northern shore of Arnhem Land live a group of Gidjingali-
speaking people, the Anbarra, who have recently moved back from
settlement life to their own territory. They are still dependent on
certain items of food such as flour, sugar, rice, and porridge from the
nearby store, but much of their vegetable food is collected and all
of their flesh food is derived from hunting. Betty Meehan and Rhys
Jones lived with the Anbarra for nearly a year and made a detailed
record of their daily activities in the quest for food; and their study
provides a valuable insight about traditional life on the Arnhem Land
coast.[3]

The Anbarra's country is small, a mere 50 km², though they have
access to a further 180 km² belonging to neighbouring groups.
Despite its small area it comprises a number of different types of
productive land; mangrove swamp, patches of jungle, freshwater
pools in stream-beds, grassy plains, and beach front.

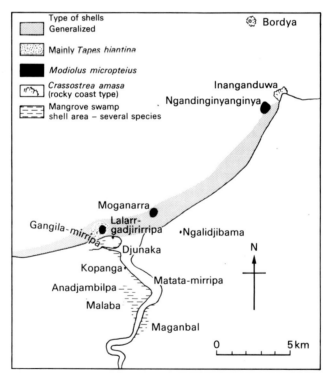

Fig. 4.1. Shell-gathering sites used by the Anbarra at the mouth of the Blythe
River, near Maningrida, Arnhem Land (from Meehan).[3]

Their flesh food consists mainly of fish and shellfish with additions of fresh- and salt-water turtles and birds, wallabies, snakes, and lizards. In addition to the store foods they also collect yams, water chestnuts, and many varieties of wild fruits; and these are supplemented with eggs and wild honey when available.

Women play a prominent part in providing food for the community, a total of about 35 people. In the first year of Meehan's study, shellfish belonging to 29 species were an important component of the diet, though 95 per cent of the total was made up of only five species of bivalve, and 61 per cent of the total was contributed by a single species, *Tapes hiantina*. Shellfish were collected from several habitats: open-sea sandy areas, open-sea mud banks, and stretches of mangrove; and *Tapes hiantina* came almost exclusively from the first of these habitats.

Women and children collected shellfish on most days if the camp was near the shore, but the frequency of shellfish-collecting days fell to only one in three when the camp moved to within 3.5 km of the mangrove beds, which were difficult of access. Men also collected shellfish at times, but frequently they were engaged in hunting or fishing, and then collected shellfish only incidentally. When they were collecting deliberately, however, the men's contribution was significant, with an average of 11 kg per trip compared with 8.5 kg per trip for the women and girls.

Shell-gathering was a relaxed affair. The shells were found by sifting through the wet sand with fingers or a simple tool, even when the sand was covered with up to 50 cm of water. From time to time the gatherers moved to areas with a better supply of shells. Fresh shellfish were cooked by being placed, lips down, in sand; and then a small, fast fire was made on top of the hinges. When the fire had burnt out, the ashes were swept away and the cooked shells placed on a bundle of fresh grass until cool enough to be eaten. On ceremonial occasions, when a large number of shells was required, they were cooked in steam ovens consisting of very hot empty shells, green branches, and bark.

The Anbarra exploit all the usable parts of the their environment, which is divided into a number of distinct ecological zones each yielding particular types of plant- and animal-foods. Among the latter are included wallabies from the edges of the open woodland and kangaroos and emus in the deeper woodland. Among the tall grass of the black-soil plains there are goannas and long-necked terrapins, which dig holes to survive in during the dry season, from which they are dug out as the season proceeds. Small rats (*Rattus colletti*) are also caught for a brief period. In the freshwater swamps

Fig. 4.2. Washing shellfish collected from open sea-beds.

and lagoons there are many fish adapted to changing salinities, including the perch-like barramundi (*Lates calcarifer*), several catfish, some mullets and smaller fish such as the herring (*Megalops cyprinoides*) and the Archer fish (*Toxotes jaculator*). The swamps also yield several species of birds such as magpie geese, brolga, ibis, jabira, and ducks.

Goanna lizards are recovered from burrows in the old inland dunes; and in the thicker monsoonal jungle patches there are more goannas as well as wallabies, snakes, and birds such as jungle fowl. In the Mangrove zone along the edges of the estuarine river and its inlets there is a wide variety of fish, many of which can be caught in traps and by spearing as the tide recedes. Some 20 species of fish, including mullets and stingray, are caught in the shallows of the open sea. Further out to sea, salt-water turtles and deep-sea fish such as mackerel are hunted from dug-out canoes.

During one month when weights were recorded, the 35 Anbarra were each consuming an average of 0.65 kg total weight of shellfish per day, or about 683 kg for the entire group during the month. In addition, during the same month the group consumed 500 kg of fish,

Fig. 4.3. Setting a fish-trap — Arnhem Land.

shark, and stingrays, hunted by the men; 86 kg of salt-water turtle and lizards; 50 kg of crustacea; 10 kg of land-mammals; 7 kg of birds and their eggs; and 1 kg of mangrove worms. Their varied protein diet was supplemented not only with carbohydrate foods from the store but also with 160 kg of carbohydrate vegetable food, belonging

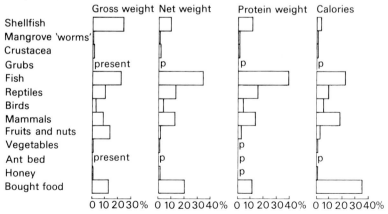

Fig. 4.4. Percentage contribution of various foods to the Anbarra diet during a one-month period (from Meehan).[3]

to six species. In addition they had 6 kg of wild honey, six different types of fruits, and three sweet grasses, as well as 230 kg of watermelon and 2 kg of earth from the nests of two species of termite.

From the size of shell middens at many places along the coast, particularly in the tropical north, it is clear that shellfish have been an important part of the Aboriginal diet over long periods of time. What is equally important, however, is that the Aboriginal food-collecting strategy was readily adaptable to changes in the environment. This was demonstrated in a striking manner by the Anbarra during the year following the study reported above. The next monsoon was exceptionally heavy and excess fresh water flooded into the area of the shell beds, destroying all but a few of the *Diyama*, and many of the other shellfish species. During that wet season the Anbarra changed their diet to fish, land animals, birds, and vegetable foods — the latter having matured earlier than usual because of the prolonged rains of the preceding year. The Anbarra were aware that similar disasters had overtaken their shell-beds in the past, and that in time the beds would return to their former productivity. Fortunately, despite the removal of one of their major and favourite items of diet, the resources of their Arnhem Land coastal habitats were sufficiently varied to allow a temporary adaptation without imposing real stress on the Anbarra population.

Whilst Betty Meehan's studies revealed the importance of sea-food for coastal groups in Arnhem Land, other detailed observations indicate the extent of plant exploitation in the same region. A total of 85 varieties of plants were used as sources of food in Arnhem Land, and Jack Golson[4] has published a list of genera and species, comparing them with forms present elsewhere in Australia and also with Malaysian species. He found that a significant number of Arnhem Land species were identical with, or similar to, species in Malaysia; and he points out that the earliest colonists on north Australian coasts would have found familiar food plants, as well as a rich supply of sea-foods. Moving further south, either along the coast or into the more arid interior, would have necessitated dietary adaptations to utilize unfamiliar species. It is particularly significant that many plants listed by Golson as food-sources in the more arid country were not utilized in Arnhem Land, even though the plants grow in that region.

Exploitation of particular food-plants in Arnhem Land was a seasonal activity. Margaret McArthur[5] carried out a nutritional survey during the American–Australian Scientific Expedition to Arnhem Land in 1948, which provided a valuable account of the foods utilized and methods of food preparation in four camps where traditional hunting and gathering was used again during the time the survey was carried out.

During the first half of the dry season, from late April until July, the main bulk of the vegetable part of the diet was provided by root vegetables and underground stems. The roots of water lillies, ranging in size up to 4 cm in diameter, as well as the roots of rushes and sedges, were either roasted or, in some cases, eaten raw.

The tubers of many varieties of yam (e.g. *Dioscorea bulbifera*) were eaten (yams were also an important food-source in many other parts of the continent). In Arnhem Land the tubers of long yams (*D. transversa*) grow up to 76 cm in length and up to 4 cm in diameter. They were eaten after cooking. However, the smallest round yam (*D. sativa* or the 'cheeky' yam) must be leached to remove toxic substances. They were cooked first and then the yams were sliced with bone or shell knives, placed in string bags, and left in a stream overnight, the length of time depending on the amount of yam and the volume and flow of water.

During the later part of the dry season, from the end of July to November, the most important part of the vegetable diet was the fruit of the burrawong or cycad (*Cycas media*). Like the 'cheeky' yam the cycad 'nut' also contains a toxic substance. After extraction, the kernels were sliced, placed between layers of fronds from the cycad, and laid out in rectangular enclosures in a stream. After two days, the kernels were pounded into a coarse meal from which the juice was squeezed out, and the meal was washed again several times before being pressed into cakes and cooked in hot ashes.

In western Arnhem Land wild rice (*Oryza* spp) was an important seed food. Other food plants exploited were the seeds and pods of tamarind trees (introduced by Macassan trepangers who had visited the Arnhem Land coast for several centuries), the nuts of the pandanus palm (*Pandanus spiralis*), and the seeds of several species of Kurrajong (*Brachychiton* spp and *Sterculia caudata*). They ate also, either raw or roasted, the growing shoot of palms, such as the fan or cabbage palm, and the fresh stems or the immature seed capsules of water lillies.

Margaret McArthur reports that many fruits, including wild grapes, figs, plums, and love-apples were eaten in abundance when in season, as is true for the Anbarra. In addition, the gum of certain species of trees or shrubs was eaten either raw or after boiling in water for a few minutes. Honey from the native stingless bee was avidly sought after, and children especially sucked the nectar from flowers such as banksias and grevilleas.

N. H. Scarlett[6] has recently studied the relative distribution of

plant-food resources in north-eastern Arnhem Land. The area has a
varied ecology ranging from mangrove forest, through a freshwater
swamp complex, tall open forest, and mixed woodland, to true monsoon forest. Mangrove forest is the poorest resource area for vegetables, with only a limited number of seed species available at all
times and a small number of fruits during the wet season. The freshwater swamp complex adds to this with a large number of root
species available through most of the year. Open forest and woodland is the richest plant community, offering an abundance of fruit,
particularly in the wet season, and with plenty of roots, supplemented during the latter part of the dry season, when roots are not
available, with a supply of seed. Monsoon forest is also a relatively
rich resource area, with fruit available at all times, but with a more
limited supply of roots and seeds than in the open forests and woodland.

Rhys Jones in his joint studies with Betty Meehan has recorded
the seasonal exploitation of the food resources available to the
Anbarra.[2] As noted earlier, collecting shellfish, utilizing some 30
species, was an activity carried out during all times of the year.
Similarly fishing with spear, hook, and net, utilizing a total of 70
species, also took place throughout the year, supplemented by fish-
traps from March to August. Hunting on land for species of wallaby,
goanna, and freshwater terrapin took place mainly from July through
to the end of December, whilst salt-water turtle eggs were obtained
from January through to June. Vegetable foods were collected
mainly through the dry season: water lilies from March to June,
yams from March to August, cycads from May to September, and
spike rush from April to October. Honey was collected chiefly from
May to July, and intermittently at other times except during the
wettest part of the year.

In contrast to the coastal dwelling Anbarra, an inland group of
Rittarnga in eastern Arnhem Land has been studied by Nicolas
Peterson,[7] though not in quite such detail as the observations by
Betty Meehan and Rhys Jones on the Anbarra. The general conclusions, however, indicate the wide utilization of resources in the
different ecological zones and a striking seasonal variation in the
species exploited.

We see, therefore, that the Arnhem Land peoples on the north
coast had a good supply of food which, although changing with the
season, was varied and ample for their dietary needs. Their daily
requirements were satisfied by a food quest of an average four to
five hours a day by the adult men and women, aided by the lesser
activity of the children. Further, not all species, particularly of

edible plants, were utilized as food. This fact itself highlights the importance of social factors in determining the level and type of economic activity in any particular community. When food is readily available density of population increases, but not to a point where nutritional stress imposes restraints on further growth. On the contrary, the Arnhem Land example demonstrates that other factors must have intervened to channel much of the energy of the group in other directions. It is of significance, perhaps, that many aspects of Aboriginal cultural life, painting and carving, song and dance, were more elaborate in Arnhem Land than elsewhere.

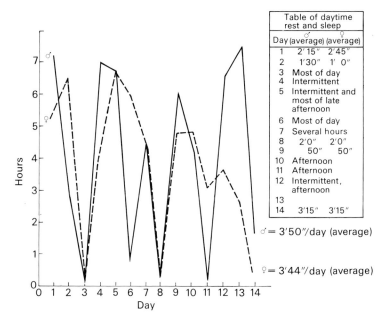

Table of daytime rest and sleep		
Day	♂ (average)	♀ (average)
1	2′ 15″	2′ 45″
2	1′30″	1′ 0″
3	Most of day	
4	Intermittent	
5	Intermittent and most of late afternoon	
6	Most of day	
7	Several hours	
8	2′0″	2′0″
9	50″	50″
10	Afternoon	
11	Afternoon	
12	Intermittent, afternoon	
13		
14	3′15″	3′15″

♂ = 3′50″/day (average)

♀ = 3′44″/day (average)

Fig. 4.5. Sahlin's construction from the data of McCarthy and McArthur of number of hours per day spent collecting food for one Arnhem Land community.[8]

Although the coasts of north Australia provided rich and varied resources for human exploitation, the marine environment also was important in other parts of the continent. As a contrast to her studies in Arnhem Land, Betty Meehan has investigated the diet of the Tasmanians, but her investigations in Tasmania had to depend upon a different strategy.[9] Instead of direct observation, as was possible for the Anbarra, she used records and diaries of early explorers, settlers, and government officials, supplemented by archaeological evidence from sites all over the island to carefully reconstruct a detailed picture of the Tasmanian diet.

We have noted already that all parts of Tasmania were occupied, except for the mountainous and rain-forest area of the west. Within the occupied areas, small groups varying in size from 2 to 70, but averaging about 20 persons, ranged over their territories to follow seasonally available foods and to fulfil social and ceremonial responsibilities. Well defined paths through the rain forest connected occupied areas in the north-west and north-east, and other paths existed along the coasts and in the inland areas of the east. Mobility was enhanced by rafts, which were used everywhere except along the north-east coast to cross rivers or to visit offshore islands. Sometimes groups made special trips to collect young birds, eggs, young seals, gum, or other foods not normally available to them.

The Tasmanians' diet indicates that they exploited, with one notable exception, practically every food-source present. The notable exception is the absence of bony fish in the diet of people in any part of the island. In Chapter 2 we drew attention to the sudden disappearance of fish bones from the archaeological record in Tasmania about 3000 years ago, and the observations of early explorers and settlers confirm that, not only did the Tasmanians not eat fish, but rejected it when offered. Other sea foods, however, were part of the diet of all people in Tasmania and included seals, crustacea, and marine molluscs (mussels, scallops, mutton fish, oysters, barnacles, sea snails, and whelks). Sources of other flesh foods included many species of marsupial (kangaroos, wallabies, native cats, possums, wombats, and marsupial rats and mice), the spiny anteater (*Tachyglossus setosus*), together with various species of sea birds, freshwater and land birds, and their eggs. Reptiles, insects, or their larvae did not appear to be important as items of diet.

Vegetable foods consisted of the roots of the fern *Pteris esculenta*, tree ferns, various fungi, pig-face (*Mesembryanthemum*), the native potato (*Solanum lacianatum*), the grass tree (*Xanthorrhoea australis*), gum from some species of Acacia, and certain seaweeds. However, vegetable foods seem to have been less important in the Tasmanian diet than in other parts of Australia.

The equipment used in obtaining and preparing food in Tasmania was also less elaborate than in many other parts of Australia. It consisted of simple spears, heavy sticks, wooden spatulae, baskets, ropes, water-containers, bird-traps, and stone tools as well as water craft used in transport. As elsewhere in Australia, the more staple items in the diet were supplied by the women. They collected the shellfish, crustacea, and vegetables, caught possums and small seals, fetched water and wood, as well as doing most of the cooking. The men's hunting provided larger, but more uncertain, items in the diet: kangaroos and wallabies, wombats, and large seals.

Neither the archaeological record nor early observations on food habits suggest any regional variation in the total content of the Tasmanian diet, though there were differences in the contribution of various items of food. Seal-meat, for example, played a bigger part in the diet in the north-west and north-east. But even on the coast a large part of the diet consisted of land foods: wallabies and wombats, fern roots, and native potatoes. There is no strong evidence, either, of marked seasonal migrations between the coast and the interior, although individual groups from time to time did go inland or come to the coast to obtain other foods or raw materials. What is of significance in the Tasmanian food economy, however, is the use of fire for modifying the environment. As noted earlier this practice of deliberately firing the bush was an important factor significantly altering the environment in other parts of Australia. In Tasmania the practice appears to have been widespread, and along the west coast the Tasmanians burnt areas of rain forest where it came down to the shore. This not only increased the area of their relatively restricted west-coast zone, but the resultant sedgeland was more productive of food than the unburnt temperate Tasmanian rain forest.

A riverine environment

High population densities along river systems, particularly in their lower reaches, indicate that they provided very favourable environments. Though there are no careful quantitative studies of the diets for a riverine Aboriginal community, the reports of the nineteenth-century explorers, Eyre, Mitchell, and Sturt, and of other recorders such as Beveridge, confirm that there was at most times a large quantity and variety of food available.[10]

In the south-east of Australia the rivers themselves supplied many species of fish and crustacea, the large freshwater crayfish being abundant at certain times of the year. In the estuarine regions these freshwater animals were replaced with marine forms, and shellfish became a prominent part of the diet. Nowhere, however, was the river the sole source of food. Large and small marsupials, such as kangaroos and wallabies, koalas, flying squirrels, bandicoots, marsupial rats, and echidnas, and also snakes, lizards, waterfowl, and birds such as scrub-turkey and emus were hunted and trapped. These were supplemented with insects or their larvae and with wild honey.

Vegetable foods were similarly varied. Reeds and bullrush roots were cut into slices and lightly roasted before eating. Yams and water

lilies were either cooked or eaten raw. Many fruits were collected,
including quandong (*Fusanus* spp), sloes, wild orange and lemon
(*Capparis* and *Cannthium*), emu apple (*Eremophila longifolium*),
and the fruit of pig-face (*Mesembryanthemum*). The seeds of barley
grass, of Acacias, and other plants were ground, made into cakes, and
baked. The shoots and leaves of the kurrajong tree and the grass tree
(*Xanthorrea* sp), pig-weed, rushes, various kinds of cress, and native
cabbage were eaten raw. The roots of some Eucalyptus trees and
Hakea were sucked, or dried and stored, and the gum from Acacia
species and *Eucalyptus mannifera* and of the sandalwood *Myoporum
platycarpum* was collected and eaten.

Although the food-collecting activities of men and women also
differed in the riverine areas, there was some overlap. The women
were mainly responsible for collecting shellfish, crustacea, young fish
fry, frogs, small land animals, and vegetable foods. The men con-
centrated mainly on the larger fish and land animals such as kangaroos and emus. At times highly sophisticated techniques were
employed. In swampy areas weirs were built across outlets to trap
fish as they moved back to the main stream and elaborate stone traps
were also set across the main stream. When river levels fell during the
summer shallow pools were scoured with weirs made of bough and
grass to concentrate the fish in small pools where poisonous plants
were used to kill them.

Some fish and crayfish were speared, others were trapped in nets,
either seine nets, oval-framed, or bow nets. Seine nets were sometimes up to 300 m long, about 1.5 m wide, and with a mesh about
7–8 cm. They were buoyed with grass floats and weighted with
stones.

Nets were used also for trapping land animals like kangaroos and
emus, as well as smaller birds. Nineteenth-century reports state that
water-birds were trapped by nets strung across water courses. Duck
hunting was a communal activity, the women driving the ducks
downstream: the men threw boomerangs to imitate the flights of a
bird or imitated the calls of hawks to lure the ducks into the nets.
Simple canoes made from a single piece of bark were a valuable
adjunct to fishing and in hunting wildfowl and for collecting eggs
in the reed-swamps.

Riverine environments appear to have offered abundant sources
of food, but there were also marked seasonal fluctuations in supply
and the economic activities of the tribe were adjusted accordingly.
Harry Allen has outlined this seasonal variation for the large Bagundji
tribe, who occupied an area on either side of the Darling River.[11]
The river was most productive when there was an inflow of fresh

water or floods during spring and summer resulting in abundance of fish, crustacea, molluscs, water-birds, and aquatic plants. At the other extreme, when the lowest water temperatures coincided with low flow rates during the winter, productivity of the river was low. Fish became more scarce, water plants died back, many animals went into a form of semi-hibernation, and water-birds migrated to other areas. The plains country away from the river, however, probably showed no such marked seasonal fluctuation. If sufficient rain fell some plant foods were available all year round. A limiting factor in the plains country was the inaccessibility of fresh water in summer and in this season travelling Aborigines carried water in kangaroo-skin bags or dug out the roots of water-storing plants.

Spring and summer saw a congregation of people along the river banks and lagoons, gathering water plants, fishing, trapping birds, and collecting seed. During winter the population split into smaller groups which spread out across the entire expanse of Bagundji territory. Mammal foods replaced fish and shellfish, smaller forms were dug out of burrows, and wallabies, kangaroos, or emus were caught in nets or traps. A variety of fruits and tubers were collected and seeds obtained from various species of Acacia, salt bushes (*Chenopodium*), and flax plants (*Linum*).

A grasslands economy

Although the collection of seed was widespread across the continent, it was a predominant activity in the more arid areas, and became highly specialized in the wide belt of grasslands which sweep across the north and down through the east of the continent (Fig. 4.6). As noted above, seed gathering was a major activity for the Bagundji in the Darling River basin, although in the Murray River area tubers were the main vegetable staple.

Early in the last century, Mitchell observed as he travelled down the Darling River that grass had been gathered and piled into heaps. Sometimes the heaped grass (native millet, or *Panicum* sp) was burnt and the seed collected from the ground. But storing the green grass in heaps also allowed the seed to be kept fresh for several months, so that a supply was available during the leaner period of the year. Threshing was done by pounding with a log in a round hole, or by trampling on the seed in a hole: dust and dirt were separated by shaking the grain in long bark dishes and the separated seed was stored in skin bags. Reports from other places suggest that storage of seed was not uncommon. Howitt, for example, reported in 1862 a store of *Portulaca* seed wrapped in grass and coated with mud,

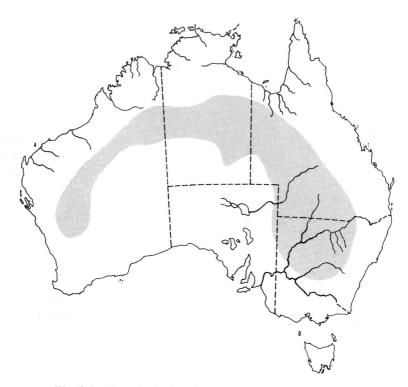

Fig. 4.6. The principal native grassland areas of Australia.

and more recently in central Australia nearly 1000 kg of grain was found stored in wooden dishes.

Grindstones used for grinding seed have been found in many areas, and are still in use in some places. Norman Tindale has filmed the grinding and preparation of cakes made from seeds and in his *Aboriginal tribes of Australia* he gives a valuable account of these activities.[12] Tindale makes an important distinction between the dry milling of Acacia seed, the pulping of fruits or the cracking of the hard seeds of kurrajong and quandong kernels, and the wet milling of grass-seed. Certainly in the more favoured grassland areas there were extensive tracts of grasses for harvesting and one report from south-west Queensland speaks of Aborigines reaping areas of 1000 acres of *Panicum,* using stone knives to cut the stalks. Tindale argues that the extractive efficiency of the wet-milled grass-seed economy was greater than that of one based on the hard seeds derived from the shrublands. This greater efficiency is one of the determinants of the far larger populations among some of the tribes in the grassland areas.

Fig. 4.7. Girl pounding seed — Arnhem Land.

A desert life

The most sparsely populated parts of Australia were its more arid areas, stretching westwards from the centre toward the central coast of Western Australia and south to the treeless Karst formation of the Nullarbor Plain. In order to survive in this region small groups of people wandered for most of the year over large tracts of country. Their tool-kit was simple, like that of the Tasmanians, and they often had to work hard to gather sufficient food. Rain, on which plant and animal life depended, occurred at irregular intervals, and skill in hunting and intimate knowledge of the habits of each species was essential for survival.

Richard Gould[13] has described a day's quest for food among a group of Bidjandjadjara-speaking people in the Western Desert during the 1960s. The extended family group consisted of five adults and three adolescent and five pre-adolescent children, the latter ranging from about 4 to 11 years old. They camped in sandhill country near dependable waterholes, and their main concern was the hunting of larger animals, the collection of smaller mammals or reptiles, and the gathering of fruits, seeds, and other edible plant-foods.

Hunting for larger animals was the chief role of the adult males.

Fig. 4.8. A 'modern' Wurly — Western Desert.

Gould describes the attempt on one day by the two adult men to spear an emu. A hide had been constructed of bush near a creek-bed about a mile away from the camp. First, the two men dug a small hole in the creek-bed until it was filled with water seeping in from beneath the surface. The hunters then waited in their hide, about 6 metres away from the soakhole, motionless for several hours until, finally, an emu appeared and cautiously approached the soakhole. Spears were fitted into the spear throwers. They remained poised until, when the bird was about ten metres away, one of the men rose smoothly to his feet and hurled his spear. The force of his throw was so great that the spear-shaft snapped, the spear missed its target, and the bird, now alerted, dashed away. With no chance of another emu coming that day, the men returned to camp, managing only to track down and dig out of its burrow a small goanna lizard weighing about 2.4 kg. Fortunately, attempts to catch emus were not always so unsuccessful and the older man had killed five emus in the previous three months. This was, however, an unusually successful period which might not have been repeated for several years.

While the two adult males were patiently waiting for the emu, the women and children had set off with their digging sticks and carrying-bowls. After walking 8 to 10 kilometres they found taliwanti plants on top of a large sandhill. While one of the group continued on, carrying a firestick, the remaining women pulled off the leaves and long strips of bark which were packed into one of the wooden bowls and left in the shade of a small bush. Later they saw a smoke signal some distance away. This indicated that the woman who had gone on alone had found a useful supply of food and the party moved off to join her. When they arrived they found there was not only a good patch of 'ngaru' (a fruit like small green tomatoes which is one of the staples in the diet of desert people) but also some bushes containing dried kampurarpa fruit. This latter, when ripe, also resembles small green tomatoes, but when dried in the sun looks like large raisins hanging from the bush. In the dessicated state they are edible and much appreciated. The four women picked the ripe ngaru and shook the dried kampurarpa fruit on to the ground, filling their wooden bowls. Whilst the women were collecting the children were chasing lizards and occasionally helping their mothers pick the fruit. Later they ate some of the fruit while waiting for their mothers to finish collecting. In less than an hour the women and children collected between 16 and 18 kg of fruit, and then, with their bowls full, they started their journey back to camp. Walking quickly, they stopped only to collect the bowl of taliwanti leaves and bark, and arrived back in camp just after noon.

The goanna, which had been caught by the two men, was now roasted and shared out among the group according to custom. A portion of shredded meat and bone eventually was given to every member of the group, making less than a mouthful each.

Later in the afternoon the women began preparing the ngaru and kampurarpa. The dried kampurarpa fruits were mashed with water on the stone grinding-slab, the paste made being scraped together and moulded into balls about 25 cm in diameter. In this form the paste keeps almost indefinitely.

Some of the ngaru fruit was eaten fresh, but the remainder was cleaned and the husks dried in the coals of a small fire. Sometimes it is dried in the sun, but after either method of drying it can be stored and may be left in caches in trees for hunters who have to travel long distances away from camp in search of game. When used for eating on the same day, however, the ngaru is mixed with water, ground, and formed into balls similar to those prepared from the kampurarpa fruit. When the food was ready, just before dark, it was shared out, the children coming in to devour handfuls of kampurarpa and ngaru paste.

Gould's account of one day's hunting and gathering activity in the desert dramatically illustrates the effort needed to ensure enough food each day for this small group of people. His observations over

80   HUNTING AND GATHERING

a longer period of time were that the major portion of the diet of
the Bidjandjadjara was vegetable food, made up mainly from at least
eight staples, such as nagaru and kampurarpa, which ripen at different times of the year and in different places (Fig. 4.9). Other foods
such as the yarnguli berry or sugar from the flower of the shrub
Grevillea eriostachya supplement and add variety to the basic staples.

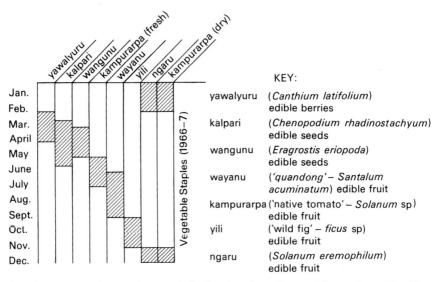

KEY:

yawalyuru (*Canthium latifolium*)
                edible berries

kalpari   (*Chenopodium rhadinostachyum*)
                edible seeds

wangunu   (*Eragrostis eriopoda*)
                edible seeds

wayanu   ('*quandong*' – *Santalum
                acuminatum*) edible fruit

kampurarpa ('native tomato' – *Solanum* sp)
                edible fruit

yili   ('wild fig' – *ficus* sp)
                edible fruit

ngaru   (*Solanum eremophilum*)
                edible fruit

Fig. 4.9. Approximate time periods for ripening of vegetable staples utilized by
desert Aborigines. By selecting different species food is available throughout the
year (from Gould).[14]

A similar account of dependence on vegetable food has been given
for a group of desert dwellers by Donald Thomson.[15] In *Bindibu
country* he describes finding large reserves of vegetable food on top
of brushwood shelters, some of it desiccated. Other dried food
material from a species of *Solanum* was impaled carefully on twigs
and Thomson was impressed that so much preserved food remained
in what was a drought year. The limiting factor was, of course, water
and the people from this camp had been forced to move further
away because the water-hole had dried up completely. He agrees with
Gould in his observations that although the hunting activities of the
men are more spectacular when they are successful, the women
provide the main food supply at most times of the year. In addition
to gathering fruits and seeds, they track and capture small reptiles
and mammals, dig out the fat wood-boring larvae of *Cremoplates
edulis*, known as 'witchetty grubs', and, at certain times of the year,

they also harvest truffles, a fungus called 'mulbo', digging them out of firm sand at the base of the dunes.

To the list of vegetable foods important to desert people given by Gould should be added the Yala or desert yam. Sweeney[16] in reviewing the food-sources of the Walbiri tribe in the north of central Australia, states that it is one of the most valuable of foods available to them and that it can be harvested at any time of the year. In good seasons, or in soakage areas where there is sufficient surface-moisture, the yala plant produces surface runners and sends down roots on which tubers form about 50 cm below the surface. In drought periods no surface runners are produced, and tubers, which may require several seasons to mature, are produced on underground roots 100 cm or more below the surface. These deep tubers are discovered by small cracks in the surface soil and are dug out by the women with digging sticks and their wooden carrying bowls used as shovels.

Animal food is much harder to get in the desert. Large animals such as emus and kangaroos are trapped or run-down successfully sometimes, but the greatest proportion of animal food comes from various lizards, more rarely from snakes and edible insect larvae. These sources have been supplemented since the time of contact, as in other parts of the continent, with small mammals, particularly rabbits and feral domestic cats. Curiously, there are few reports of the dog being used as food. Although large numbers of dogs are found in nearly all Aboriginal camps, their chief function, at least during cold nights in the desert, seems to be in helping to keep people warm whilst sleeping.

Times of feast

Seasonal fluctuations in food supply were common in all localities and an abundance of food at times when seed was ripening in the grasslands or during the summer following floods in the Darling River region made possible large gatherings of people in these areas. In addition to these seasonal fluctuations in the normal food supply, there were also some special foods whose supply reached unusual levels from time to time which were exploited by peoples with access to them.

One such unusual food was the fruit of the bunya bunya tree (*Araucaria bidwilli*) in south-west Queensland. This tree bears fruit once in three years, and its nut-like seed was much relished. When the trees were fruiting people travelled long distances to them and the abundance of fruit was so great that the tribes in whose areas the trees were found did not object to the presence of strangers in their territory.

Another unusual food which, when being exploited, resulted in large gatherings of people, was the adult of the bogong moth (*Agrotis infusa*).[17] Each year in summer the adults of this species move from the hotter, drier areas to the north and east into the cooler mountains of the southern uplands. Here on the higher peaks they congregate in vast number, covering rock surfaces from which they can be knocked down easily.

Records from the last century reveal that there was a seasonal movement of tribes in the neighbouring areas resulting in large

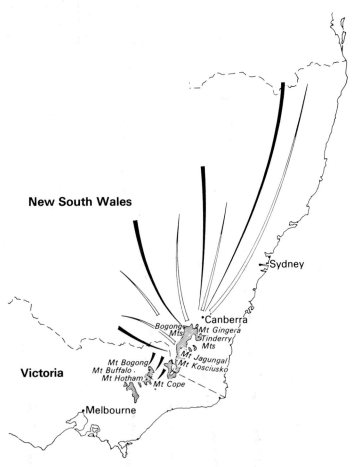

Fig. 4.10. Seasonal migrations of the bogong moth in eastern Australia.[17]

gatherings of people at campsites near the main concentration of moths. Women collected vegetable foods around the camps while men hunted the moths, either suffocating them with smoke, knocking them down with sticks on to sheets of bark, or catching them with nets in rock shelters. The moths were cooked by placing them in heated sand from which the fire had been removed, and were either eaten at once or ground into a paste and made into cakes.

The moth feasts lasted for several weeks and not only added a valuable supplement to the diet of the local population, but also provided an opportunity for social communication between larger groups of people and opportunities for trade between tribes. Articles such as possum-skin rugs, baskets, and bags were exchanged for spears, shields, and stone implements, and thus contributed not only to the exchange of ideas, but also to a wider base for the local economy.

The food equation for traditional diets

There is no complete account of the energy balance or of the adequacy of the diet in terms of essential components for any group of Aborigines living completely on a traditional diet and following a wholly traditional life-style. Such an undertaking is no longer possible, but there have been some limited studies both of the composition of traditional foods and of the quantities consumed to enable an approximate estimate of nutritional adequacy in pre-contact time to be made.

Long lists of foods utilized in various parts of the continent have been prepared by several investigators. Nicolas Peterson[7] points out, however, that many of the foods listed were eaten infrequently and only those that were staple components of the diet, that is those which accounted for at least 50 per cent of the total diet, are of importance for determining the major inputs into the food equation. In the arid areas, for example, there are up to 100 listed edible plant species but only about twelve staples. These vegetable staples include the root stocks of *Ipomoea costata* and *Vigna lanceolata*, the fruits of various Solanaceae and of *Ficus* and *Santalum*, the seeds of several Acacia and of herbs and grasses such as *Fimbristylis*, *Panicum*, *Portulaca*, and *Eragrostis*.

At certain times of the year the grubs of various moths of the family Cossidae were an important and valuable addition to the diet in arid areas, particularly in terms of animal protein and fat. But the main meat staples appear to have been lizards and snakes, together possibly with smaller marsupials and rodents, the larger game such as emus, kangaroos, and wallabies being more irregular and making an uncertain addition to the diet. The studies of Gould among the Bidjandjadjara and of Meggitt[18] among the Walbiri indicate that 70 to 80 per cent of the diet of these arid-area people was vegetable but no precise quantification has been carried out. Peterson, however, gives the results of analysis of some of the staples and these figures have been summarized in Table 4.1.

Table 4.1. Food values for selected staples in the diet of Aborigines in arid regions

Food		Protein (g/100g)	Fat (g/100g)	Carbo-hydrate (g/100g)	Kilojoules	Calcium	Vitamin C (mg/100g)
Acacia spp	seed	22	14	42	1665	92	—
Eragrostis	seed	17	0.6	71	1500	40	—
Ficus	fruit	6	2.4	—	—	4000	—
Ipomoea	root	2	0.8	52	955	19	—
Panicum	seed	15	5	63	1490	16	—
Portulaca	seed	20	16	52	1790	46	—
Solanum spp	fruit, fresh	2	0.9	17	365	82	34
Cossidae larvae		50	47	—	—	—	—

The high proportion of vegetable foods in the diet of people in the centre is not a universal feature of the dietary pattern of Aborigines in other places. Betty Meehan's study of the Anbarra referred to earlier is one of the best carried out so far and has provided quantitative values for this Arnhem Land community. Measuring the quantity of the plant-foods consumed, including all the gathered fruit and vegetables as well as the flour, sugar, and rice purchased from the store, she found that 'vegetable' foods contributed only 31 per cent of the total gross weight of food available. If the 'vegetable' foods were considered as sources of energy they contributed a bigger proportion of the total, but still only 57 per cent.

In the north of Australia some quantification of energy-intake has been made for the Arnhem Land region. The study by Margaret McArthur outlined on pages 68–9 made measurements of food-intake over short periods of time for adults and children at four localities where gathering and hunting was the chief means of obtaining food. By adjusting the calculated nutritional content of the food consumed for the lower average weights of the people studied and comparing these with the recommended daily allowance she was able to derive the figures given in Table 4.2. The energy-intake was close to the recommended daily requirement when an average level of physical activity was used as the basis for comparison. The intake of protein

Table 4.2. Percentage of recommended dietary allowances for
Arnhem Land groups living a traditional life in 1948

Locality	Kilojoules	Protein	Iron	Calcium	Vitamin C
Hemple Bay	116	444	80	128	394
Bickerton Is.	74	172	135	41	234
Port Bradshaw	79	300	131	490	220
Fish Creek	104	544	33	355	47

was substantially above the recommended daily allowance, as was the intake of iron at two, and of calcium and ascorbic acid at three of the localities studied.

Betty Meehan has made a similar quantification of food intake in the course of her observations on the Anbarra people with whom she lived near Maningrida. During a period of one month each person consumed an average of 0.5 kg of carbohydrate food obtained from the nearby store, 0.4 kg of gathered vegetable food, and 0.6 kg net weight of hunted and gathered flesh foods. Using tables of food equivalents this represents an approximate energy level of 10 000 kJ per person per day. This value is significantly above that obtained by Margaret McArthur for any of the four groups studied by her. None of Margaret McArthur's groups, however, included store items in their diet, and they had returned to hunting and gathering only for the purposes of the study. They may have lacked, therefore, some of the proficiency and persistence characteristic of earlier times and for this reason Margaret McArthur's estimates of energy intake may have been below the true values.

In a more recent assessment of the nutritional adequacy of traditional diets Margaret McArthur has pointed to difficulties inherent in studies of this kind. Not only were traditional foods seasonal in their occurrence and sometimes subject to longer-term fluctuations in times of drought, flood, or hurricane, but the energy requirements for daily activities of Aborigines living a traditional life-style in the varied environments in Australia is unknown. Nor do we know the efficiency of utilization of the various components of the diet.

In many areas traditional Aboriginal diets provided a higher proportion of calories from vegetable sources than from fat, and for this reason the diet was bulky. Consequently young children would find it difficult to obtain sufficient energy, and this resulted in their having lower average weights than children on a diet with a high proportion of refined carbohydrate. On the other hand most traditinal food was either eaten fresh or after little cooking; and this would have retained many of the important vitamins.

The contribution of animal protein to the diet varied markedly from region to region, as well as seasonally. In the arid areas 70–80 per cent of the bulk of food was vegetable. On the Arnhem Land coast 50 per cent or more of the bulk of food was provided by fishing and hunting in the first half of the dry season, but later in the year, in an inland camp at the end of the dry season, vegetables accounted for less than 10 per cent of the food, fishing provided 20 per cent, and over 70 per cent came from hunting kangaroos.

Although Aborigines in Australia clearly exploited their traditional environment effectively, no simple answer can be given to the question of what were the determinants in the food equation. Climatic and other ecological variables obviously controlled the type and quantity of plant- and animal-foods available. Seasonality and longer-term fluctuations in abundance of food conditioned human movements and the levels of technological development affected their extractive efficiencies in different regions. Roger Lawrence[19] in discussions on economy and habitat in Australia has stressed the dangers of assuming that the environmental stimulus resulted in the techniques with which the environment was exploited. He points out that preferences, as well as technological ability, affect the choice of plants used for food in any given habitat. For example, in arid areas in seasons of abundance Aborigines showed preferences for particular foods from among those available to them; and we have drawn attention already to the taboo on eating fish which operated in Tasmania for the last 3000 years.

Lawrence points out also that not all tribes in coastal areas had a coastal economy and he cites the Lama-lama group at the southern end of Princess Charlotte Bay in north Queensland. There people lived among the mangrove-lined estuaries of the area but had an economy more like that of an inland tribe. Similarly, although the sea cow, or dugong, is widely distributed in northern waters of Australia, it is used as a major food-source by only a small number of tribes. Other tribes in Cape York possessing a suitable technology placed no undue emphasis on hunting dugong. Their adoption of additions to the technology of hunting through the use of the harpoon and the outrigger canoe was made use of therefore in some activities but not in others.

Lawrence analyses other aspects of the technological exploitation of the environment as shown by the material culture of various Aboriginal groups. There was a basic range of equipment common to all tribes which included spears and spear throwers, throwing sticks and digging sticks, brush-fence traps, and hand-held stone core tools or hafted axes. This basic tool-kit was elaborated in some places by the addition of outrigger canoes, harpoons, and bone fish-hooks, or the use of nets, snares, flails, switches, and fish poisons. Many of these additions probably were due to diffusion from outside contacts.

Although the basic tools of Aborigines were similar everywhere, individual items varied considerably in design. Some of this variation was undoubtedly influenced by the raw materials available. In coastal regions, for example, shell and bone was frequently substituted for stone, but trading of objects resulted, as well, in moving objects into areas where the raw materials for their manufacture did not exist. For example, shell and bone implements often occurred in regions where stone was available. Though some elaboration of design may have reflected environmental adaptation in the first instance, the design frequently spread outside the original area, and it is difficult therefore to see the design of elements in the material culture of any one group as being determined completely by the environment.

Food-gathering and hunting is undoubtedly an economic activity conditioned by environmental factors such as climate, soils, topography, and access to water. But it is also modified by cultural factors and can be understood fully only in relation to the interplay of forces, both historical and contemporary, which condition human behaviour in any one locality.

5

PHYSICAL UNITY
AND DIVERGENCE

Aborigines have lived in Australia for at least 40 000 years. The original colonists must have come from Sundaland, the south-east-Asian area which extended at that time close to the Australian–New Guinea land-mass. We must ask now if modern Aborigines are descended from these first colonists only or if there were two or more later migrations which contributed distinctive physical or genetic traits which can still be recognized.

The suggestion that modern Aborigines are all descended from a single wave of migrants was made in the last century, being first stated explicitly by E. M. Curr. Since then it has been supported strongly by many physical anthropologists. In general terms the argument accepts the existence of differences among modern populations of Aborigines in traits such as stature, head shape, and hair form, as well as in genetically controlled characteristics in blood, but considers that such differences arose as a result either of selection by physical factors such as climate in various parts of the continent, or through the operation of factors included under the general heading of random genetic drift. (Of course there may have been a combination of selection and drift to produce the diversity observed today.)

The alternative view that Australia was populated as a result of two or more waves of migrants was also stated in the last century. Topinard, for example, noted what seemed to be major differences between the Aborigines in Tasmania and those on the mainland of Australia. This theory of dual or multiple origins has also found support among other physical anthropologists most notably Joseph Birdsell.

In the late 1940s Birdsell[1] put forward a tri-hybrid theory to explain the origin and diversity of physical traits among Aborigines. He has modified his original proposal only slightly over the intervening thirty years, and his concept can be summarized briefly as:

(a) A first colonization by 'Oceanic Negritos'. These were people of short stature, having dark skin, pedomorphic features of the face and skull, and tight, spirally-curled hair. Living descendants of the original Oceanic Negritos survive in the Andaman Islands, and in modified form in Malaysia (Semang). At the time of European contact groups showing affinities with these people were present in the rain-forest areas of north Queensland and in Tasmania. Since the Queensland groups were centred on Lake Barrine, Birdsell refers to them as 'Barrineans'.

(b) The second wave of migrants to reach Australia displaced the Oceanic Negritos in all areas except Tasmania and the Queensland rain forests. Birdsell calls people of this second wave 'Murrayian' since they were represented in the historical period only in a few marginal areas, notably the Murray River watershed. These people were of short, stocky build and were characterized by an abundance of body hair. Birdsell considers the Murrayians had affinities with the Amurian people in eastern Siberia, of whom the Ainu of Sakhalin and Hokkaido are living representatives.

(c) The third wave of migrants, which are typified now by Aboriginal populations around the Gulf of Carpentaria, arrived during the terminal stage of the last glaciation. These 'Carpentarians' displaced the Murrayians in all parts of the country except the marginal areas of the south-east and south-west. They did not reach Tasmania.

(d) Surviving populations in the historical period frequently reveal features suggesting that gene flow had occurred between the remnants of earlier migrations and the succeeding wave of colonists. The largest proportion of these historical populations across the continent, however, were predominantly Carpentarians.

It is this latter point which now makes it difficult to evaluate Birdsell's trihybrid hypothesis completely. The Tasmanian Aborigines of full-descent are extinct and the rain-forest Oceanic Negritos in north Queensland have been reduced in number and are merged with the surrounding Aboriginal populations. Similarly only a handful of full-descent Aborigines remain from the once populous areas of the south-east and south-west. The main body of data which has been collected from living Aborigines, therefore, relates to areas populated by descendants of Birdsell's Carpentarians. In this and the succeeding chapter we shall see that neither the living Aborigines nor, where data from skeletal remains is available, their antecedents, are or were homogeneous.

A generalized picture

No stereotype picture of an Aborigine can give a true representation, for variability of form is as marked among people in Australia as in other human groups. However, while not forgetting the extent of variation between individuals, there are some generalizations which can be made about Aboriginal physical traits.[2]

Skin colour is best described as medium to dark brown, being darker among populations in the north and lighter in the south and south-east. But although there are many observations about skin colour in different parts of the continent, no reflectance values using a photo-electric reflectometer have been published.

Hair form varies from completely straight through every grade of waviness to deep curl. Curliness is more common in males than females and it is more common in the north than in the south. Body hair in males is variable both in distribution and density. Although copious body hair appears to be more prevalent in the south and is claimed to be one of the principal traits of the Murrayians in the south-east, it is not a universal feature there. Moreover, some individuals with heavy beards and body hair occur also in central areas and elsewhere.

Hair colour is typically dark-brown to black, though in most parts of the continent many people, particularly the young, have lighter-brown or even reddish hair. Of special interest is the widespread distribution of blonde hair, which has its highest frequency in the centre and Western Desert, and occurs with diminishing frequency as one moves away from these areas. Blonde hair is present in some desert populations in the majority of children up to 10 years of age. After that age hair among boys darkens rapidly. Blondeness may persist into adulthood in a few males and in a larger proportion of females. In persons with blonde hair the eyes have the normal dark pigmentation.

Complete albinism is rare. A case from central Australia was reported nearly 50 years ago by Basedow on hearsay evidence, but more recently a well documented case has been recorded in north Australia.[3] The scalp hair and skin in this case was uniformly de-pigmented, but the eyes were brown in colour. Despite the presence of pigment in the eyes, however, strabismus was present, as in cases of total albinism among Europeans.

Although there is considerable variation in body build, for Aborigines living a traditional life the body tends to be slender with long thin legs and slender hands and feet. Women have the same bodily proportions. Slenderness is frequently replaced by excessive fat in

Fig. 5.1. (a) adult male, Kimberley; (b) Ranjbarngu girl; (c) adult male, Western Desert; (d) adult female showing 'blondness', Western Desert.

those leading a sedentary life with a high carbohydrate diet. Such conditions are common in many present-day Aboriginal settlements.

The stature of Aborigines varies considerably, there being both short and tall people present in every population. All the early observers agreed that, in general, Aborigines were about the same height as Europeans. The range is from about 150 to 180 cm although statures outside these limits have been reported (from 130 cm in central Australia to an individual of 211 cm in north Queensland). Males have a mean stature of about 170 cm and females about 157 cm.

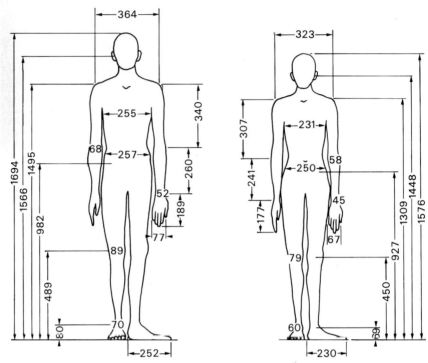

Fig. 5.2. Mean values in mm for (a) male and (b) female adult Rembarranga (from Prokopec).[4]

Figure 5.2 gives mean values for a number of body measurements for adult male and female members of the Rembarranga tribe, measured in south-eastern Arnhem Land by Czech anthropologists in 1969. The values given for the Rembarranga are typical of those found elsewhere in Arnhem Land.[4]

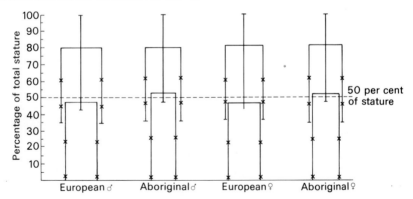

Fig. 5.3. Relative proportions of body length in Aborigines and Europeans (from Abbie).[2]

One characteristic, noted in nearly all investigations, is the relatively longer extremities in Aborigines compared with those in Europeans. According to Abbie, at the time of birth Aboriginal babies have a relative sitting height of over 60 per cent which is similar to that in European babies. The relative sitting height drops gradually until in the fifth or sixth year it falls below 50 per cent and by about age 10 it stabilizes at 46–47 per cent. This growth pattern, illustrated in Fig. 5.3, is the same in both sexes.

Variations on the theme

Anthropometric measurements have been recorded for populations in many parts of the country and over a range of time from early in the last century to the present. They show not only that in any one population there is a wide range of values, but also that mean values differ in various populations. Table 5.1 gives some of the values for mean stature in adult males found by several investigators. One of the earliest reports was by the French explorer, Peron, who measured a small number of Aborigines in Tasmania and found them comparable to Europeans. In the middle of the last century Robinson measured 23 adult Tasmanians and they ranged from 155 to 171 cm in height. Although many were short in stature, others were comparable in height to Aborigines in other parts of Australia.

Mean values for stature are somewhat higher in the north of Australia than in the south, but even in a narrower geographical range there are significant differences. Stature of males on Melville and Bathurst Islands, and at Roper River, for example, is less than in north-west Arnhem Land.

How much of this variation, either in traits such as stature, or in ratios of measurements such as relative sitting height, is innate or how much is due to environmental variation is still difficult to assess. There is good evidence that there has been quite a rapid temporal change in some of the measurements and this will be discussed in more detail in Chapter 7. One must exercise caution therefore in accepting differences in stature, or other body measurements, as indicating differing genetic backgrounds. Even ratios of measurements, while more stable than the linear values, are subject to modification under environmental pressures. Both linear measurements and ratios also change with age. This makes comparisons difficult if the ages of the individuals measured is not comparable.

Table 5.1. Adult stature in cm for male Aborigines in various parts
          of Australia

Group and/or locality	No. measured	Mean	SD	Range	Date of measurement	Reference
Arnhem Land						
N.E.	77	167.0	5.64	155–178	1930s	(1)
N.W.	98	169.6	5.94	155–187	1930s	(1)
Tiwi (Melville and						
Bathurst Is.)	28	166.8	4.56	155–175	1930s	(1)
Victoria River	28	169.3	6.10	155–181	1930s	(1)
Roper River	8	166.5	–	152–178	1930s	(1)
S.W.	41	167.9	8.0	151–182	1950	(2)
Rembarranga	38	169.4	5.6	–	1969	(3)
Central						
Walbiri						
(Yuendumu)	22	169.8	5.5	159–80	1950s	(4)
(Young adults)	26	173.0	5.8	–	1960s	(5)
Aranda	42	165.6	–	–	1920s	(6)
New South Wales and Victoria						
Kamilaroi (Brewarrina)	12	168.7	–	–	1920s	(7)
'Murrayians'	44	164.7	–	–	1938–9	(8)
Queensland						
'Barrineans'	95	157.8	–	–	1938–9	(8)
South Australia						
Ooldea	9	166.2	–	166–187	1926	(9)
Yalata	38	163.3	–	146–174	1958	(10)

References: (1) W. W. Howells, *Papers Peabody Museum Harvard University* **16**, 1–97 (1937); (2) N. W. G. Macintosh, *Oceania* **28**, 208–15 (1952); (3) M. Prokopec, *J. Hum. Evol.* **6**, 371–91 (1977); (4) A. A. Abbie, *Oceania* **27**, 220–43 (1956); (5) T. Brown and M. J. Barrett, *Med. J. Aust.* **2**, 29–33 (1971); (6) T. D. Campbell and C. J. Hackett, *Trans. R. Soc. S. Aust.* **51**, 65–70 (1927); (7) G. Taylor and F. Jardine, *Proc. R. Soc. N.S.W.* **58**, 268–94 (1924); (8) J. B. Birdsell, *Archaeol. phys. Anthropol. Oceania* **2**, 100–55 (1967); (9) T. D. Campbell and A. J. Lewis, *Trans. R. Soc. S. Aust.* **50**, 183–91 (1926); (10) A. A. Abbie, in *Aboriginal Man in South and Central Australia* (ed. B. C. Cotton) Pt. 1, 9–45 (1966).

Non-metrical features

Because of the difficulties in interpreting results of differences in linear measurements, or their derived ratios, some physical anthropologists have given attention to non-metrical morphological traits. Studies on contemporary Aborigines have included such characteristics as the frequency of various types of hair form, variation in the amount of skin pigmentation, presence or absence of fourth molar teeth, and excessive hair growth (hypertrichosis) of the ears. These studies have been supplemented by observations on the frequency of minor variants which can be detected in the skeleton. Work on minor skeletal variants in animals indicates a major hereditary component in their control. There have been several studies of such variants in human skeletons and the results have been used to estimate the degree of relatedness between populations.

Since archaeologists find that skulls survive better than the post-cranial skeleton, many of these studies have been confined to the metrical or non-metrical features of crania in museum collections. Frank Fenner,[5] in one such study of the non-metrical traits of more than 1100 crania, distinguished three types of Aboriginal skull. The first of these he called a southern type, which comprised skulls from South Australia, the south of the Northern Territory, Victoria, New South Wales, and southern Queensland. The second type came from coastal areas in the Northern Territory and the third type from a large area of Queensland.

Earlier workers using metrical traits had also distinguished different skull types in Australia.[6] Hrdlicka, for example, noted differences between skulls from the Northern Territory, Queensland, and South Australia. Morant distinguished only two types, while Wagner considered the southern skulls different, but he thought the Northern Territory and Queensland skulls resembled each other more than they did the southern type. Wagner also noted similarity between Queensland skulls and those from New Caledonia and commented, 'the geographical proximity of Queensland and Melanesia has played a certain role and that not one but various racial elements have left their mark on the indigenous populations of the northern part of Australia'. Towards the end of the last century W. Turner suggested that differences in skull measurements indicated a multi-racial origin of the Aborigines. Along the southern seaboard Turner considered there may have been intermixture with people such as the Tasmanians whose heads were not so long and narrow. As mentioned in Chapter 2, Loring Brace has recently put forward similar views based on a cline in tooth sizes across Australia.

Macintosh and Larnach[7] more recently re-examined crania from coastal districts in New South Wales and Queensland and compared them with cranial material from various parts of New Guinea and from other ethnic groups. They standardized the way in which a score can be given to each cranium on the basis of observations on 20 different non-metrical traits. Their results show that the scores for Aboriginal crania enable them to be distinguished readily from Caucasoid or Mongoloid crania. By contrast, comparison of New South Wales crania, as a group, with those from Queensland, show them to be very similar. Further, crania which come from the Cairns rain-forest area have the same mean score as that for skulls from the whole of Queensland. This latter point is important since it indicates that skulls from the area occupied by Birdsell's Barrineans cannot be differentiated in this way from other Queensland skulls.

Macintosh and Larnach also compared Aboriginal crania with crania from New Guinea, and for this comparison they used a reduced list of twelve traits. The scores obtained in Australia show a south-to-north change, or cline in values, with the scores for Aboriginal crania becoming closer to the scores for New Guinea as one

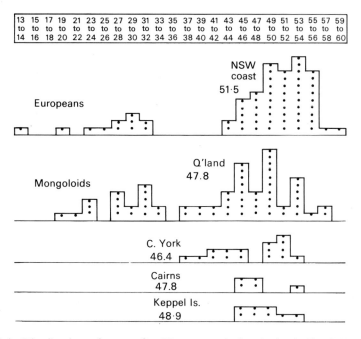

Fig. 5.4. Distribution of scores for 20 non-metrical traits in skulls of Aborigines from New South Wales coast, Queensland, Cape York, Cairns rain forest, and Keppel Island, compared with skulls from Europeans and Mongoloids (after Macintosh and Larnach).[7]

moves along the coast from New South Wales through Queensland to Cape York in the north. But not all the variation noted in this study is clinal. One group of skulls from Keppel Island off the Queensland coast fall within the range for New South Wales in their mean score, but show distinctive frequencies for 6 of the 20 traits examined. These distinctive frequencies are due to micro-evolution in a relatively isolated island habitat.

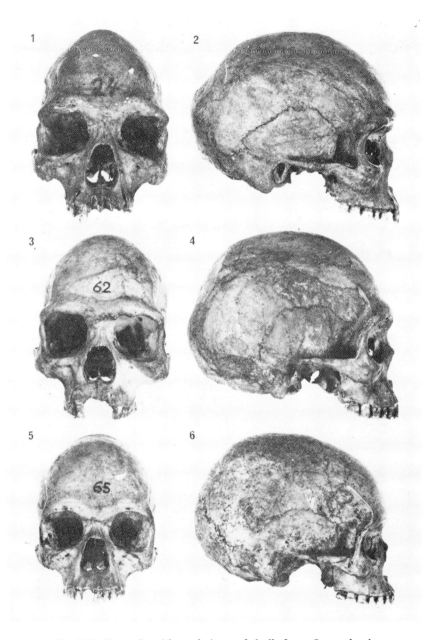

Fig. 5.5. Frontal and lateral views of skulls from Queensland.

Another detailed investigation of non-metrical cranial traits has been carried out by Kellock and Parsons.[8] Their work on more than 1200 crania from many parts of Australia recorded the presence or absence of 30 minor variants, such as suture lines between cranial bones, sutural bones or ossicles, foramina and canals. Many of the skulls in their series were the same as those examined earlier by Fenner and the majority of the skulls came from localities in the south-eastern portion of the continent: New South Wales, Victoria, and South Australia. A significant number of the Victorian and South Australian specimens were recovered from sites in the Murray River Valley or from the coast at sites near the mouth of the Murray River.

Kellock and Parsons found considerable variation in the frequency of traits, but nearly 90 per cent of the variation is contributed by 10 of the 30 traits studied. When a mean measure of difference based on these 10 traits is calculated it is found that the differences between States can be arranged in approximately linear order. The Northern Territory is most extreme from South Australia, with Queensland mid-way between these extremes. New South Wales and Victoria are together very close to South Australia, whilst Western Australia is between Queensland and Northern Australia. Kellock and Parsons argue that their results support Fenner's earlier suggestion that non-metrical skull traits distinguish distinctive populations in different parts of the continent.

They divided their series into three broad areas to maximize the differences. The first area consists of the south-east corner, the second a broad belt running in a sweep from Cape York through central Queensland and across to the southern part of Western Australia, and the third the Northern Territory and the remaining portion of Western Australia. Unfortunately the sampling within these broad areas is so patchy that the identification of the factors which might be significant in controlling the observed variation in skull traits is likely to be extremely difficult.

Another comparison of populations using non-metrical traits has been made by Richards and Telfer.[8] They restricted their observations to seven distinctive non-metrical characters of teeth recorded from dental casts for living populations at Kalumburu in the Kimberley and Yuendumu and Haast's Bluff in central Australia and from museum collections for populations from Anson Bay, near Darwin and the Lower Murray area of South Australia. Surprisingly, their results show a close similarity between the Lower Murray series and Kalumburu, with both of these being different from the two central Australian series. The tooth traits for the Anson Bay series place them somewhat closer to the central Australians than to either Kalumburu or the Lower Murray. Richards and Telfer also compared the Aboriginal teeth with series representing Caucasians and Mongoloid populations. The Aboriginal populations are more similar to Mongoloid than Caucasoid teeth, and this is most striking for the Anson Bay series. They believe this latter relationship is due to previous population admixture in the Anson Bay area.

Patterns on fingers and hands

The pattern of whorls and loops, ridges and creases on the fingers and hands, as well as on the toes and soles of the feet, is determined during foetal development and remains constant during life. There is a strong genetic component in what determines particular patterns. Thus identical twins have very similar dermatoglyphic patterns, but ordinary siblings are less similar. Husbands and wives are no more alike than other people in the general population, but each of them is still closer to their children than they are to unrelated persons. This combination of high heritability and lack of modification by the environment as well as the ease with which they can be recorded has made the study of dermatoglyphic patterns a valuable tool for characterizing populations around the world.

There have been several studies of fingerprints in Aborigines, but palm-prints have not been examined so frequently and will not be discussed here. One measure of fingerprint patterns is the 'Pattern Intensity Index' which is the mean of the total number of triradii on the fingers of both hands in the persons surveyed. A triradius is the junction area between loops and whorls, and there may be 0, 1, or 2 on each finger. The maximum value for any one person, therefore, is 20. When the number of triradii for each person is totalled and the total divided by the number of persons in the sample the result is the Pattern Intensity Index for that population. As shown in Fig. 5.6, Aborigines have relatively high values for the Pattern Intensity Index. They are similar in this respect to other Western Pacific peoples, for both Melanesians and Micronesians have Pattern Intensity Index values extending beyond the upper limit for Europeans.

There are marked differences of the Pattern Intensity Index between populations in different parts of Australia, and Parsons and his colleagues have analysed these in some detail.[9] Genetic isolation clearly pays an important part in differentiating populations in terms of their fingerprint patterns. The Tiwi of Bathurst Island, for example, have the lowest Pattern Intensity Index in Australia,

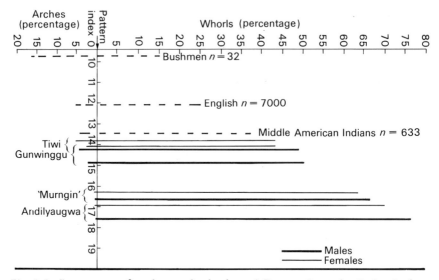

Fig. 5.6. Percentage of arches and whorls and Pattern Intensity Index in four
Arnhem Land tribes compared with Bushmen, American Indians, and English
(after Parsons and White 1976).[9]

whereas one of the highest values is found in the population of
Groote Eylandt, in the Gulf of Carpentaria. Parsons and White have
also analysed fingerprints from persons belonging to dialect groups in
north-east Arnhem Land. They find the biggest difference in dermatoglyphic patterns between dialect groups separated by low ranges
of hills — topographical features which, they believe, reduce the
amount of gene flow. In contrast to this, the dermatoglyphic traits
of the three dialect groups along the western tribal border are not
significantly different from those among their immediate tribal
neighbours, the Rembarranga.

White has shown also a marked differentiation between populations on the basis of the total ridge count but there is some overlap
between geographical regions. Highest values, approximately 190,
are found in north-east Arnhem Land, with low values in the range
135-65 in central Australia. However, northern populations such as
the Tiwi of Bathurst Island and the Nunggubuyu in eastern Arnhem
Land also fall within this central Australian range.

More complex methods of analysis

During recent years statistical techniques have been developed which
make possible the combining of data for many different traits into

a single index. Such an index can then be used to compare populations, the difference between any two being referred to as the
'distance' between them.

When comparisons are based on continuously variable traits, such
as stature, one of the more commonly used indices is the D^2 statistic
developed by the Indian statistician, Mahalanobis. Similar multivariate methods have been devised for use with discrete traits such
as blood groups, and these will be referred to in the discussion of
genetic distance in the next chapter.

Mahalanobis D^2 values have been calculated from measurements
on collections of Aboriginal skulls by several workers. Margetts and
Freedman,[10] for example, have recently compared skulls from
various places in Western Australia with skulls from three areas in
New South Wales, on the other side of the continent. The D^2 values
indicate that the northernmost samples from both States are closest
to one another, with D^2 distances increasing with geographical
distance along the coast in a southerly direction. Margetts and
Freedman believe these results indicate that the original populations

Table 5.2. Mahalanobis D^2 values for morphological distances
between skulls in various parts of Western Australia
and New South Wales (Margetts and Freedman)[10]

| | Western Australia | | | | New South Wales | | |
	Northern	Central	Southern	Eastern	Northern	Central	Southern
Western Australia							
Northern	—	2.33	3.72	5.17	2.30	5.60	6.67
Central		—	5.26	7.79	2.88	6.32	8.99
Southern			—	7.11	5.98	7.12	7.79
Eastern				—	7.81	12.53	12.83
New South Wales							
Northern					—	2.10	3.01
Central						—	2.59
Southern							—

migrated down both the east and west coasts, the central and
southern samples of the two coasts being longer separated in time
than the northern samples and therefore showing progressively
greater D^2 distances. Skulls from the Western Desert area of Western
Australia were sharply distinguished from all other samples. This may
be due to their long-term isolation under harsher environmental
conditions which has led, through a process of selection, to a modification of skull traits.

A similar type of analysis has been completed by Michael Pietrusewsky of the University of Hawaii.[11] He utilized measurements on male crania which could be assigned to twelve areas in Australia. The comparability of some of his groupings, with those in other studies, is unfortunately not very good. Pietrusewsky has put all skulls from Western Australia in his series, a total of only 13, into one group. In contrast, Margetts and Freedman organized 105 skulls in Western Australia into three coastal groups and one desert inland group. At the other extreme another of Pietrusewsky's groups comprises 36 crania from a single site excavated at Swanport, a few miles south-west of the City of Adelaide. Pietrusewsky included, also for comparative purposes, measurements on skulls from four localities in New Guinea and from three prehistoric sites in Australia, Kow Swamp in Victoria, Roonka in South Australia, and Broadbeach in Queensland.

Several clusters of skull types emerge from Pietrusewsky's analysis. One cluster is formed of skulls from Arnhem Land, from Queensland (excluding Cape York), and coastal New South Wales. Another is made up of skulls from the Murray River basin and other parts of Victoria and South Australia, with the Swanport skulls being a little distinctive from the others. The small sample of Western Australian skulls is even more distinctive than the Swanport collection. Whether this is due to the inclusion, in his small Western Australian series, of skulls from desert areas with those from other parts of the State is not clear. Finally, a small collection of 17 skulls from Cape York and 12 from the Torres Strait Islands form a cluster with the series from the New Guinea Papuan Gulf area. This latter group also clusters with other New Guinean collections from the Sepik River area in Papua New Guinea and from the Schouten Islands and the south coast in Indonesian West New Guinea. The group most clearly separated from all the above clusters in Pietrusewsky's analysis are the 33 skulls from all parts of Tasmania. They are closest to the Swanport and other southern Australian mainland series and are very clearly separated from the north Australian and New Guinea series.

Comparison of skeletal material from prehistoric sites presents even greater problems than for more recent sites. Not only are sample sizes smaller in most cases but the material is often damaged so that measurements cannot be made so precisely as can be done for relatively recent, intact material. Pietrusewsky, however, was able to utilize 9 skulls from Kow Swamp dated from 9000 to 13 000 years BP, 29 from Roonka, ranging from the recent historic period to 8000 BP, and 26 from Broadbeach with a time depth from the historic to 1300 BP. Inclusion of skull measurements from these prehistoric sites shows that the Roonka series is close to Swanport and the other southern Australian series, Broadbeach is close to south-east Queensland and coastal New South Wales. The robust skulls from Kow Swamp, however, are very distinctive, being separated by a high D^2 distance from any other series in Australia or New Guinea.

Another comparison of Aboriginal skulls with populations outside Australia has been made by the Japanese osteologist Bin Yamaguchi.[12] He was especially interested in Birdsell's hypothesis that the Murrayian element among the Aborigines was closely related to the Amurian, the living representatives of which are the Ainu of northern Japan. Using the D^2 statistic, Yamaguchi compared the skulls of two groups of Aborigines in Australia and a series from Tasmania with three sub-groups of Ainu, similar series from modern Japanese, Dayaks from Borneo, Hindu and tribal populations in the subcontinent of India, Melanesians from New Britain and New Caledonia, Maori in New Zealand and a prehistoric series of Jomon from Japan. The Aborigines cluster with the two Melanesian populations but are quite distinct from any of the other populations. Ainu, on the other hand, cluster with the prehistoric Japanese population, the Jomon, as well as with another Mongoloid population, the New Zealand Maori. Both the Aboriginal–Melanesian cluster and the Ainu–Jomon–Maori cluster are approximately equidistant from Hindu and tribal cluster in India, but the Ainu–Jomon–Maori cluster is closer to the modern Japanese and Dayaks than these are to the Aborigines and Melanesians. In all of these comparisons the Tasmanians maintain an isolated situation, somewhere midway between the other clusters.

Although Yamaguchi did not find a primary relationship between the skull series of Aborigines and Ainu he did not rule out the possibility of such a relationship between the ancestors of both groups in the far distant past. Both these groups, he concluded, could have been derived from a generalized upper Palaeolithic or Mesolithic common population in Asia. These two groups, however, went their own separate ways, the one to long-term isolation in Australia, the other to have frequent contacts with other Mongoloid populations in north-east Asia. To increase the differences further both groups, of course, may have been moulded by different selective pressures in their contrasting environments.

Do the results obtained through the use of the Mahalanobis D^2 statistic receive any support from other multivariate statistical techniques? One such method is called discriminant function analysis which enables an assessment to be made of the contribution to the total variation of each of the variables. It is possible, then, to select those variables which are responsible for the largest amount of variation. If two such variables are selected, the distance between the populations can be plotted in a two-dimensional diagram, and if three variables are selected the diagram can be shown in three dimensions. Inclusion of more variables makes it impossible to plot the results in diagrammatic form.

In a recent study Eugene Giles[13] has applied discriminant function analysis to measurements of skulls from Australia and neighbouring areas.

Eight Australian skull series, including Tasmanians, were compared with each other and with series from the Torres Straits Islands, and

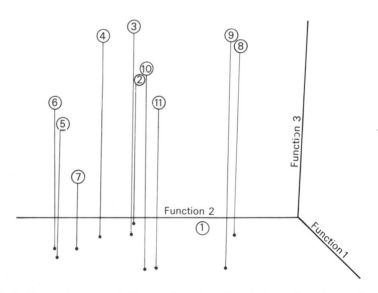

Fig. 5.7. Three-dimensional diagram based on discriminant function analysis of measurements in eight series of Aboriginal skulls and series from Torres Strait Islands, New Guinea, and New Britain (after Giles).[13]

from New Guinea and New Britain, the latter almost certainly coming from villages inhabited now by Tolais. The first three discriminant functions accounted for nearly 80 per cent of the total variance, and since these can be plotted in three dimensions the relationships between the populations are illustrated in Fig. 5.7. There are three clusters and one isolated population. Curiously, the latter is the Swanport series from South Australia. As noted earlier, in Pietrusewsky's analysis this clusters closely with the other series in the southern Australian area. Of the other clusters distinguished by Giles, one represents three populations in the Arnhem Land area, the second comprises populations from the Murray River basin, coastal New South Wales, and Queensland, together with the New Guinea series and the Tolais of New Britain. The third tight little cluster consists of the Tasmanians and the Torres Strait Islanders.

The most extensive comparisons between populations in Australia and other parts of the world using multivariate techniques have been made by William Howells.[14] In one of these studies Howells used measurements of living persons belonging to 151 local populations in Australia and the Pacific. The statistical analysis enabled Howells to select three functions based on these measurements which, together, accounted for 86 per cent of the total variation and these functions were used to calculate distances between the populations. This was followed by a clustering process. The two populations with the smallest distance between them are selected first, and these two are joined together. The mean values for this pair are then taken and put back with all the other populations and a new set of distances calculated and the pair with the shortest distance between them is again selected and joined together. In this way a network is built up step by step until all the populations have been joined together into a tree, or dendrogram.

When Howells had completed this analysis it showed that several clear-cut clusters were formed out of his 151 populations. Of interest here is that the 28 Australian populations included in the analysis all fall into one cluster which also contains some populations in northern New Caledonia, the Loyalty Islands, and western and northern New Britain.

Howells has carried out a similar analysis using measurements from skull series rather than from living people. For Aborigines, Howells chose a series of skulls from South Australia and the majority of these were from the Swanport site. The Tasmanian skull series is essentially the one used in the other studies discussed earlier, and the Tolais from New Britain included by Howells as representative of Island Melanesia are the same as the series used by Giles.

In the discriminant analyses carried out by Howells, the three south-west Pacific series together with Aborigines, Tasmanians, and Tolais, remain as a cluster readily distinguishable from populations in other parts of the world. Within this cluster the Tasmanians are closer to the Tolais, in terms of morphological distance, than they are to the southern Australians. This is different from the result obtained by Giles which shows the Tasmanians are very close to the

Torres Straits Islanders and not clustered with the Tolais. One of the problems associated with multiple discriminant analysis, however, is that the introduction of new populations into the series being examined may lead to a rearrangement of the clusters when the new information is taken into account. What is less easy to explain is the observation by Pietrusewsky, using the Mahalonobis D^2 statistic to measure morphological distance, that the Tasmanian skull series is very close to the southern Australian series and not to the New Guineans. Pietrusewsky, however, did not include the Tolais in his comparisons.

Whatever the exact ordering of relationships between Tasmanians, Melanesians, and Australian Aborigines, the morphological distances between any of them is small compared to the distances between them and any other clusters. Figures 5.8 and 5.9 show these relationships for some of the other series used by Howells. In the first of these Howells included in his analysis several African populations (Zulu, Dogon, Teita, and Bushmen), Andaman Islanders, three American Indian groups, Eskimos and the Buriats from Siberia, and representative Caucasoid populations. Comparing male skulls only (although measurements on female skulls where available show the

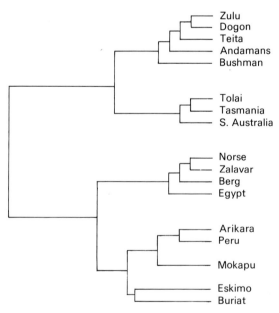

Fig. 5.8. Clustering of major populations based on multivariate analysis of skulls (from Howells).[14]

same relationship) there are two major branches of the dendrogram, one which includes the Caucasoid and Mongoloid populations, the other with the African, Andamanese, and south-west Pacific populations. This does not mean that the skull characteristics of the African and south-west Pacific populations are the same, for both groups form separate clusters, the skulls from the Andamans falling neatly into the African cluster.

Howells points out that an examination of the separate factors which emerge from the multiple discriminant analysis reveals that although some traits, such as narrowness of the cranial vault, relate Africans to south-west Pacific populations, unlike the latter, Africans are narrower in the base of the skull as well. The south-west Pacific skulls are distinguished from the Africans also by narrowness of the interorbital space and by a marked subnasal prominence in the midline profile of the skull. Another important difference in the

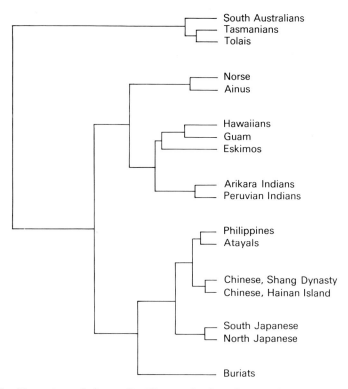

Fig. 5.9. Clustering of circum-Pacific peoples based on multivariate analysis of skulls (from Howells).[14]

south-west Pacific skulls, in contrast to those of Africans, is that the frontal profile is flat, and the malars project further forward and are larger.

The other set of comparisons made by Howells involves not only the south-west Pacific skull series, but additional Pacific and circum-Pacific populations. Again the device of constructing a dendrogram has been used to visualize the relationships more easily. The Australians, Tasmanians, and the Tolais emerge as a cluster on one of the main branches of the tree, quite distinct from all the other Pacific and circum-Pacific populations. These in turn form several clusters. One large cluster includes Hawaians, Guamanians, Eskimos, and South-American Indians. Another comprises a general series from the Philippines, a tribal population in Formosa (the Atayal), a recent series of Chinese skulls from Hainan Island, and an older series from the An Yang tombs dating from the Shang Dynasty, and two series of recent Japanese skulls, one from Hokkaido and one from northern Kyushu. The Buriats of Siberia, whilst falling into this main cluster, stand a little apart from the other groups.

To complete his detailed statistical analyses Howells draws some conclusions and issues some cautions. First, he warns that we do not know the real meaning of cranial differences between two populations, nor do we understand the apparent long-term persistence of certain skull traits in a population. Because of this lack of understanding it is difficult to determine precisely the genetic relationships between populations long separated in time and space on the basis of skull measurements. Secondly, Howells queries whether it is legitimate to use the distances calculated from discriminant, or other, analyses to join or differentiate populations which have no immediate or obvious connections — for example, Melanesians and Africans. Howells points out that Melanesians are often classed as Oceanic Negroids on the basis of skin colour and hair form. By the same reasoning this would have included the Tasmanians if they were Negritos. His multivariate analysis of the skull measurements of Aborigines, Tolais, and Tasmanians, convinces him, however, that these three groups have a common cranial morphology which sets them off from Africans. The traits which they appear to share with Africans, he believes, are more likely to be convergent adaptations.

Can one then use skull morphology to determine the original homeland, or homelands, of the Australian Aborigines? Despite considerable variation in skull traits within Australia, Howells sees the basic morphological pattern, including the Tasmanian, as similar to that of Melanesians. Measurements on one prehistoric skull from Keilor ally it with the Tasmania–Melanesian complex, and examination of meagre prehistoric skeletal evidence from Indonesia also points to an early occupation of those islands by people with similar 'Melanesian' traits. Other skulls in Indonesia do not have these traits, nor do any of the skulls in south-east Asia.

6

DIFFERENTIATION: TIME, SPACE, AND CULTURE

Human populations spread over a wide geographical area must inevitably undergo differentiation both in cultural and genetic terms, but this is the end result of a complex and dynamic process. The greater the barriers which prevent the movement of people between one sub-population and its neighbours, the more rapidly will this differentiation proceed. Its extent and direction will depend on many factors and here we will explore some of these as they operate in Australian Aboriginal populations.

At the genetic level we can visualize micro-differentiation as the result of a series of interlocking networks of genetic relationships interrupted by boundaries of varying sharpness formed by physical or cultural barriers to gene flow. Differentiation is further determined by the appearance of new mutations, the selection of beneficial genotypes for particular environments, or through the operation of chance in determining the reproduction or survival of certain genes.

The local endogamous group, or tribe, is the basic unit for population genetic study. Not that the tribe is itself a genetically uniform surface. It is composed of families whose constellation of genes is reshuffled and shared with those in other families on the basis of social regulations which control the exchange of mates, together with other factors which facilitate or make difficult reproductive relationships between adults in the group. Neville White and Peter Parsons,[1] as discussed in the previous chapter, have shown how such marriage networks, influenced by physiographic features, lead to genetic differentiation in populations in north-east Arnhem Land.

Genetic exchange is inhibited at the edges of the local endogamous tribe. If this inhibition is absolute the neighbouring tribes will become more and more dissimilar as selection, chance events, and fresh mutations act through time. The rate of divergence will be slowed, however, if some gene flow occurs across the tribal boundaries. This gene flow need not be uniform in all directions. Thus an adjacent tribe on one side may have trade items, which leads to frequent interchange of visitors; another neighbouring tribe may not be so favoured, and lack of travel between the two may be reinforced by the development of mutual distrust, effectively preventing the establishment of any social or genetic interchange.

Few studies have been made on the rate of gene flow across Aboriginal tribal boundaries in Australia, but it is well established that inter-tribal marriages did occur. Norman Tindale has provided some estimates of this, showing a mean frequency of inter-tribal marriage of 15 per cent, but ranging from as low as 8 per cent between some tribes to over 20 per cent for others.[2]

Even where gene flow occurs across the tribal boundary it will not normally lead to a rapid spread of new traits in the host tribe. Any new constellation of genes will work its way through the interlocking network of the local groups at unequal speeds in different directions, until finally a portion of that constellation may pass on across a distant boundary into a tribe one step further removed.

In the previous chapter we outlined the chief physical characteristics of Aborigines and examined the way in which some of these traits, particularly differences in skulls, can be used to distinguish populations in various parts of the country or to reveal differences from or similarities to populations in other parts of the world. This type of analysis, however, has special problems, some of which have been noted already. We do not know to what extent environment can modify skull shape or other traits. Even where it is thought that environmental factors are not important, as for the presence or absence of non-metrical traits such as foramina in bones, the exact genetic control of the trait is not known. What is more, skulls for many populations are not available in sufficient numbers to allow the statistical evaluation which would give the fine tuning we would like when considering differences between tribes or when we wish to match observed differences with population genetic theories. To do this we need data on traits under genetic control which are not affected by environmental factors and which can be collected from a large number of people in all the localities of interest. These conditions are best met by the genes which control various factors detectable in samples of blood. Such genes are called *genetic markers*.

Blood genetic markers

Studies of blood genetic markers among Aborigines have been carried out intensively during the last half century. Historically, these studies first focused attention on factors on the surface of the red cells. The best known of these are the ABO blood groups, of importance for blood transfusions, but many other blood-group systems are now known. The serum protein groups, detectable in the fluid portion of the blood were the next series of blood genetic markers to receive attention. Finally, recent studies have been concerned with genetically controlled differences in enzymes present in blood cells.

(i) *Blood groups*[3]

One of the most striking features of the ABO blood group distribution in Aborigines, noted by early investigators and now fully confirmed, is that only blood groups O and A are found over most of the continent. The only exception is a relatively small area bordering the southern and south-eastern shores of the Gulf of Carpentaria, and in one small population in this area, on Bentinck Island, in the Gulf of Carpentaria, the A group has been lost and only groups O and B are present. The highest values of the *A* gene are found in central Australia and these high values extend into parts of Western Australia. The subgroup A_2 is not present in Aborigines. Very high values of the *O* gene, between 85 and 96 per cent, are found in and around Cape York and the islands of the Gulf of Carpentaria.

Aborigines are distinctive also in the distribution of the MNSs blood groups. No S-positive persons have been detected and values of the *N* gene in general are high, ranging, in most populations, from 65 to 80 per cent, and reaching 100 per cent for one group in the Western Desert. Conversely near the south-western corner of the Gulf of Carpentaria and on Bentinck and Mornington Islands, the *N* gene has its lowest frequency in Australia, approximately 50 per cent.

As is true for many non-European populations the Rh negative gene (*cde*) of the Rhesus blood group system is not present among Aborigines and most of the variation between populations is found among the four alleles R^o(cDe), R^1(CDe), R^2(cDE) and R^z(CDE). The range of variation for each of these alleles is considerable: R^o from 0 to 43 per cent, R^1 from 44 to 94 per cent, R^2 from 5 to 44 per cent, and R^z from 0 to 26 per cent. Birdsell has used the marked variation in rhesus blood group genes between tribal populations in Western Australia to support the concept of a sharp interface between tribes inhibiting the flow of genes across the boundary (see p. 118).

Several other blood group systems have been studied, but less intensively than the ABO, Rh, and MNSs systems. The most interesting of these results are for the Diego system. The Di^a gene, which is a marker for Mongoloid populations, has not been detected except in one individual. In this case there is good evidence to suggest that the

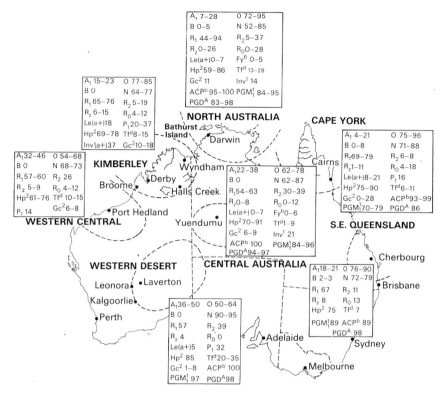

Fig. 6.1. Ranges of gene frequency for some blood genetic markers in Aborigines of full descent.

gene was introduced recently by an Asian working in the locality. For the P blood group system the *P¹* frequencies are generally in the range 20 to 50 per cent, and in the Lewis system *Leᵃ* is absent in many tribes and occurs in less than 10 per cent in most of the others. The Kidd system appears to be variable but so far has been little studied.

(ii) *Leucocyte antigens*

Specific groups on the surface of white cells, as well as other tissues, are also detectable by serological methods. These so-called human leucocyte antigens (HLA) are complex genetically, being controlled by at least four loci (A, B, C, and D). They are the subject of intensive study at present because of their importance in tissue transplantation and for susceptibility to some diseases. In addition, since there are many alleles at each HLA locus, they are useful genetic markers which can be used for discriminating between populations.

HLA types have been determined for only a few populations of Aborigines.[4] The results obtained so far indicate that, for the HLA-A and HLA-B loci at least, not only do Aborigines have distinctive gene frequencies, but different populations are also readily distinguishable. Since the HLA loci are important from the medical point of view it is hoped that further detailed studies will be carried out.

(iii) Serum protein groups[5]

Four serum protein systems show marked variation in gene frequencies across Australia. In the case of the haemoglobin-binding protein, haptoglobin, two alleles Hp^1 and Hp^2 are present, with frequencies of Hp^2 in general being very high by world standards. There are relatively few persons with no haptoglobin detectable in their serum (HpO) and so far only three persons with the unusual Hp 'Johnson' type have been detected, all in central Australia.

Data for the iron-binding serum protein, transferrin, show that all Aboriginal populations are characterized by the presence of an electrophoretically slow-moving variant, D_1. This is present also in nearly all Melanesian populations, and this variant, both in Aborigines and Melanesians, cannot be distinguished in amino acid composition from the D_1 transferrin found in black African populations. The frequency of the transferrin D_1 gene in Australia fluctuates markedly, reaching a value of over 30 per cent at Yalata in South Australia, and falling to low values in Cape York, where there is a range of 2 to 11 per cent. A very low value of 2 per cent occurs at Edward River, on the west coast of Cape York. Here the D_1 variant has been replaced by an electrophoretically fast B variant, unique to this area and representing a local mutation still confined to the population in which it arose.

A third serum protein system of interest is known as the group specific component (Gc). The Gc system is polymorphic in all human populations, with varying frequencies of the two genes Gc^1 and Gc^2. Some Aboriginal populations have a third Gc gene, Gc^{Ab}. This was discovered first in Cape York, and it is present in Arnhem Land and in the Kimberley, but has only a low frequency in central Australia. Gc^{Ab} has now been found widespread in New Guinea and in other Melanesian populations in the Pacific. Recently Michael McDermid in Canberra and Hartwig Cleve at Cornell Medical School in New York looked carefully at the protein produced by Gc^{Ab} and also that produced by black Africans: they were not able to discriminate between the two, or between the proteins produced by the Aboriginal and Melanesian Gc^{Ab} variants.[6]

The fourth serum protein system of importance controls genetic variation in the gamma globulin groups. Several loci are involved in this control. They are designated as Gm, Km, and Am. Only the Gm and Km loci have been studied extensively among Aboriginal populations, but there are already indications of variability at the Am locus which will merit much fuller investigation.

The Gm locus has many complex genes called haplotypes and for this reason, as is true also for the HLA loci discussed earlier, it is an extremely useful tool for discriminating between populations. A simplified picture for Australia is obtained by considering the frequencies of just three of these haplotypes.[7] The first haplotype, $Gm^{za;g}$ has a range of values from approximately 50 to 85 per cent, except for one very low value of 9 per cent on Bentinck Island. The second, $Gm^{zax;g}$, ranges from 7 to 38 per cent, whilst the third haplotype, $Gm^{za;b}$, ranges from less than 1 to 30 per cent, with Bentinck Island again being exceptional with the high value of 91 per cent.

The Km locus appears to be much more stable. For the Km^1 gene frequencies vary from 14 to 38 per cent. In general the lower values are found in central Australia and the higher ones in Cape York, with an exceptionally high value of 83 per cent occurring on Bentinck Island.

(iv) Red-cell enzymes[5]

More than twenty red-cell enzyme systems have been studied so far in Aboriginal communities. Many of these reveal either no variation or only sporadic variants. Among these are superoxide dismutase, the lactate and malate dehydrogenases, phosphoglycerate kinase, phosphohexase isomerase, and some of the peptidases. Other red-cell enzyme systems, however, have proved to be extremely variable and take their place beside the blood group and serum protein systems in helping to discriminate between populations.

For instance, in the red cell acid phosphatase system, the ACP_1^A gene is present in north Queensland, Arnhem Land, and the Kimberley, but it is absent in the Western Desert and central Australia. For the 6-phosphogluconate dehydrogenase system (PGD), the common variant gene PGD^c ranges in frequency from 2 to 15 per cent. In addition, there is a unique gene, PGD^{Elcho}, found in Arnhem Land and in the Kimberley area of Western Australia. Another unique gene, $PepB^6$, in the Peptidase B system is localized almost completely among the Nunggubuyu speakers in eastern Arnhem Land. A few other examples of it have been found on the fringes of Arnhem Land and also again at several localities in the Kimberley on the north-west coast of Western Australia. Its presence here, as in the case of PGD^{Elcho}, may be due to recent movement of Aborigines around the coast. However, $PepB^6$ occurs in two other populations outside Australia: on the Asmat coast in Western New Guinea and among the Aboriginal tribes of Western Malaysia.

A specific variant at the PGM_2 locus in the phosphoglucomutase system occurs among the Walbiri tribe in the northern part of central Australia, and the only examples so far found elsewhere are in the Kimberley to the north-west.

Perhaps the most striking of all the localized red-cell enzyme variants are the recently discovered unique variants of carbonic anhydrase (CA). This zinc-containing enzyme exists in two molecular forms, CA1 and CA2, each controlled by a separate genetic locus. In most human populations variants at either of these CA loci occur only sporadically or with very low frequency. The only exceptions so far are the occurrence of the CA_2^2 gene in black Africans, and other variants CA_1 and CA_2 genes among Parsis in Bombay. Three different unique CA genes have been found in Aborigines, two at the CA1 and one at the CA2 locus.[8] One of these, CA_1^{10}, is found only in a limited area of Arnhem Land and must represent a relatively recent mutation. However, the $CA_1^{9\text{Aust}}$ and CA_2^4 genes occur in nearly all Aboriginal populations studied so far. Frequencies for both genes range from 0 to 8 per cent, with the highest frequencies occurring in central Australia. So far no examples have been detected on the northern Arnhem Land coast, nor do any of these genes occur in New Guinea or elsewhere in the world. This suggests that $CA_1^{9\text{Aust}}$ and CA_2^4 both occurred as mutations in central Australia and have been spreading out from their point of origin. They have now reached the Kimberley area in the west and Cape York in the east, but have not, so far, reached and established themselves in the north of Arnhem Land.

Genes and microevolution

The blood genetic marker data indicate that small-scale evolutionary changes have taken place among Aborigines in Australia.

The structure of marriage relationships outlined in Chapter 3, despite variations in detail in various localities, emphasizes the relative smallness and isolation of the gene pool. Furthermore, despite the fact that there are few significant topographical barriers in Australia, such as wide rivers or high mountains, social barriers and geographical

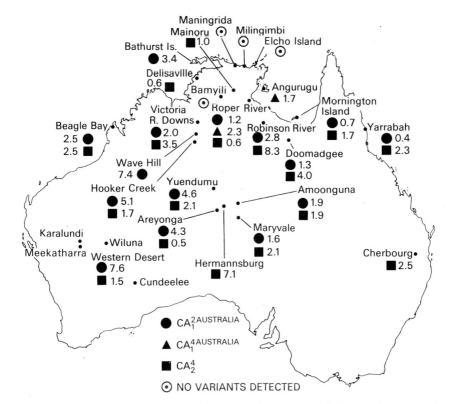

Fig. 6.2. Percentage distribution of genes unique to Aborigines at the two loci controlling the enzymes for carbonic anhydrase 1 and carbonic anhydrase 2.

separation have provided sufficient impediment to the movement of genes to allow genetic differentiation of local populations. This has taken place in spite of a mean rate of intertribal marriage of 15 per cent as found by Tindale which represents a gene flow of 7.5 per cent per generation across tribal boundaries.

The distinctiveness of tribes is demonstrated by significant changes in gene frequency as one moves from one tribe (or locality) to a neighbouring one. It is shown also by the occurrence, sometimes at the relatively high frequency of 5 to 10 per cent, of a unique marker gene, such as $PepB^6$ in the Walbiri, localized in one particular population. Tribal boundaries, however, are not inviolate, and this is indicated by the existence of clines of gene frequency and by the spread into more than one tribe of specific marker genes. For example PGD^{Elcho} spreads across tribal boundaries in Arnhem Land and Kimberley: Gc^{Ab}, $Gm^{za:b}$, and ACP_1^A are both found across the north of Australia but only Gc^{Ab} is found, at low frequency, in the centre. Conversely, the highest frequencies of $CA_1^{9\text{Aust}}$ and CA_2^4 occur in the centre, and have spread out from there into Western Australia and Queensland but have not yet penetrated into the northern part of Arnhem Land.

Clearly, specific blood genetic markers are of great value in investigating gene flow. Consideration of the distribution of these marker genes as well as of variation in the frequencies of more common genes enables us to say something about the spatial differentiation as well as the origin of Aborigines. A recent study by J. B. Birdsell[9] used extensive blood group data provided by Roy Simmons for 28 tribes in Western Australia. Birdsell and his colleagues plotted the frequencies of genes in three blood-group systems, ABO, MNSs, and Rh, for each of these tribes, and they examined the differences in frequency between pairs of neighbouring tribes, a total of 49 comparisons for each gene. One of the most striking results is the very wide range in frequencies over the total series of 28 tribes. This range approaches, and in some cases exceeds, that found in the whole of Europe and Asia. When the differences between neighbouring tribes are examined, however, the transitions are found to be fairly smooth, with increasing difference in gene frequency as geographical distance increases. These transitions are good examples of genetic clines. But there are some striking exceptions to these smooth transitions, the best example being for the Rh gene R^z. In many of the tribes the frequency of R^z ranges from zero to 10 per cent, but there are three tribes in which it reaches the values of 19, 20, and 25 per cent respectively, the differences with neighbouring tribes ranging from 14 to 22 per cent. Birdsell believes these, and similar marked differences between neighbouring tribes, are the result of founder effects, that is, where the present tribal population has come from a very small founding population. The smoother clines across the tribal surface he interprets as due to unknown selection processes.

Instead of considering changes in the frequency of genes one at a time, we can combine the information available at all genetic loci to provide a measure of genetic 'distance' between populations. This is a statistical technique analogous to the Mahalonobis D^2 distance for measuring morphological differentiation between populations which was discussed in the previous chapter. Several statistical methods for measuring genetic distance have been devised during the last few years, but despite their differing theoretical approach to the problem, in practice they yield essentially the same information.

Together with two Indian colleagues, V. Balakrishnan and L. D. Sanghvi, I have applied these techniques to investigate tribal differentiation in the Northern Territory of Australia.[10] Our first analysis focused attention on five tribal populations in the southern part of the Northern Territory: the Aranda, Walbiri, Luridja, Bidjandjadjara, and Pintubi. In Table 6.1 the genetic distance values are given, based on data for nine genetic loci, the values being standardized so that the maximum distance is scaled to 100. If one then carries out a cluster analysis to construct a dendrogram it becomes clear that three of these populations, Luridja, Bidjandjadjara, and Pintubi, are genetically more similar to one another than to Aranda and Walbiri, which themselves are genetically well differentiated.

Table 6.1. Standardized values for genetic distances between five central Australian tribes. Maximum distance scaled to 100

	Aranda	Bidjandjadjara	Luridja	Pintubi	Walbiri
Aranda	—	87.6	77.2	100.0	83.0
Bidjandjadjara		—	47.6	66.7	82.1
Luridja			—	57.9	78.8
Pintubi				—	91.5
Walbiri					—

Although these five tribes are each genetically distinct, the differences between them do not appear to be so great if the focus of attention is enlarged to include tribes in the north of the Northern Territory. When this is done, as shown in Fig. 6.3, the variability between four of the central tribes is compressed (Pintubi were omitted because of lack of some data). Somewhat more of the variation is taken up by four tribes in Arnhem Land: the Malag, Nunggubuyu, Ranjbarngu, and Gunwinggu, and approximately one half of the variability is used up in accommodating the Tiwi, a population living on Bathurst and Melville Islands some 30 km off the west Arnhem Land coast. The main interest in this result is the suggestion that an island provides an effective barrier to gene flow and leads to greater genetic differentiation than is the case for tribes who have no great physical barrier along their boundaries.

Other implications of these results are that genetic differentiation increases as tribes become more distantly separated geographically and that since the central tribes occupy a climatically different zone from those in the north, the differentiation may also be a function of climate, operating through some selective process. Both these possibilities were tested by estimating the correlation between genetic distance and either geographic distance or some change in climatic conditions. When the estimated central points of tribal territories

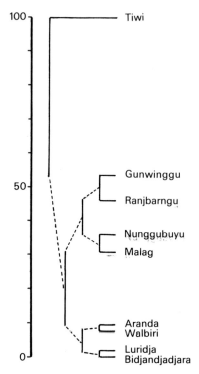

Fig. 6.3. Evolutionary relationship for 9 tribes in the Northern Territory based on distances calculated from the frequency of blood genetic markers.

were used to measure the geographical distances the correlation between geographical and genetic distance for the nine tribes in the Northern Territory is only 0.28. This low value is due, in part, to the highly aberrant position of the island population of the Tiwi. Although geographically not far distant from their neighbours, they are genetically very distinct. If the Tiwi are excluded the correlation coefficient rises to 0.41. Even so, although genetic distance does increase with geographic distance, obviously it is not the only contributor to the genetic variability.

In attempting to estimate the effect of climate on genetic distance the problem is to choose what factors are likely to be important. The description of climatic conditions in Australia given in Chapter 1 suggests that the variations over much of the continent are largely a function of latitude, with only small differences in a longitudinal direction. Genetic distances, therefore, were plotted against latitudinal and longitudinal differences. The correlation between genetic distance and lognitude is only 0.13, but for latitude it is 0.39, and this latter correlation is highly significant. When both sets of variables are considered simultaneously, difference in latitude is about four times as effective in predicting genetic difference than is longitude. Climatic factors therefore could easily account for at least some of the microevolutionary divergence observed among Aboriginal populations.

A question which needs answering at this juncture is whether there is some other measure of differentiation between tribes which might be used to compare with the observed genetic differentiation. To answer this it is necessary to digress briefly to discuss Aboriginal languages.

The diversity of language

When a population splits into two or more subgroups the original common language begins to change, each subgroup going along its own path of language development. Initially these variants of the parent language are mutually intelligible and are called dialects. If contact between the speakers of the different dialects is limited so that they do not regularly speak with members of the other subgroups, the dialects eventually become unintelligible. They will then have reached the status of separate languages.

In the early stages of language development it is easy to see that the languages were derived from a common parent language, as is the case, for instance, with German and Dutch among European languages. The longer the time of separation the fewer the similarities — witness, for example, the differences between German and French, or between either of these and Sanskrit, which is also a member of the Indo-European group of languages. Still longer separation makes it impossible to group the languages together into a 'family tree', for there are no longer any correspondences to give clues about former relationships.

There are three main ways in which languages change. First, the grammatical structure can alter — the verb, for example, may move from a positin in which it regularly follows the object to one at the end of the sentence. Secondly, the sounds can change, so that the same word gradually becomes modified by alteration of the consonants or vowels, and eventually becomes unrecognizable to a speaker of a related language. Thirdly, the vocabulary itself can change, a completely different word being substituted for one with the same meaning.

Changes in grammatical structure and in sounds are difficult to quantify, though they are very important in determining the relationship of one language to another. Alterations in vocabulary, on the other hand, can be counted; and this has focused attention on the use of lexico-statistics in language classification. According to the definition of Swadesh, languages which share over 80 per cent of words, or cognates, in a basic vocabulary list, are considered to be dialects. Those which share 28–80 per cent of cognates belong to separate languages of the same family; those which share 12–28 per cent cognates belong to separate families, whilst those which have 4–12 per cent of cognates in common belong to different stocks of the same language phylum.[11]

Ability to quantify the number of cognates which languages share has given rise to another field of study — that of the rate at which languages change, called glottochronology. This rests on the supposition that the length of time taken to replace cognates remains the same as that in languages whose history of divergence can be dated. Such studies have indicated that 19 per cent of cognates are replaced in a language in 1000 years. Of course, when two languages are being compared, each will have its own independent substitutions, so that they will have 19 per cent of 19 per cent, or 34 per cent of different cognates between them 1000 years after separation. If the rate of cognate substitution continues at a constant rate then two languages with a common ancestral mother tongue will be different in 72 per cent of original cognates at the end of three thousand years and in 88 per cent at the end of five thousand years. At the end of ten thousand years the languages will almost certainly not be recognized as belonging to the same stock, or even the same phylum.

Glottochronology has been criticized severely, because many factors influence the way and the rate at which languages change. For example, migrations and trade contacts with neighbouring or even distant populations cause some words to change more rapidly than others. In the case of Aboriginal languages in Australia, certain words become taboo after a death, and they are replaced, often by 'borrowing' from a neighbouring language. Such word 'borrowing' will tend to slow the rate of divergence between neighbouring languages. To counter these arguments the proponents of glottochronology claim that the list of words chosen for comparing the frequency of cognates is made up of basic items, common foods, parts of the body, etc. which are less subject to changes of a superficial or personal nature.

For want of a better quantitative measure of language divergence, but bearing in mind the possible limitations of glottochronology, we will consider firstly the classification of Aboriginal languages in

Australia, then examine the correspondence between linguistic and genetic divergence, and finally, using a time-scale based on glotto-chronology, see if this gives any useful insight into the rate of micro-evolutionary change as measured by genetic distance statistics.

Aboriginal languages in Australia are diverse, perhaps as many as 260 being spoken at the time of first settlement by Europeans 200 years ago. Several attempts have been made to classify them, using either topological, comparative, or lexico-statistical criteria. Each method produces a different classification, although nearly all have some features in common. Since we are interested in comparing genetic patterns with cognate frequencies the classification used here is based on that given by Stephen Wurm, using a lexico-statistical approach.[12]

Australian languages belong to a single phylum which is quite distinctive, having no demonstrable relationship with any other language phyla (the now extinct Tasmanian languages probably belonged to another separate phylum). In addition to their distinctiveness from other languages in the world, Australian languages have another special feature. With the exception of languages in the north of Cape York, they appear to have been free from external influence for many thousands of years.

Over the continent as a whole, excluding Tasmania, many of the languages have many structural similarities despite having a low percentage of shared cognates. It is possible also to demonstrate dialect chains, where the nearest neighbours on either side are very similar but the languages at the extreme ends of the chain are very different, sharing perhaps less than 50 per cent of cognates. Linguists have noted other special features of Australian languages such as similarity in the sounds, or phonological system, between languages which are often only very remotely related. In addition, several broad categories based on structural features can be recognized — for example, languages using only suffixes and others using prefixes.

Using slightly different values of cognate frequencies from those adopted by Swadesh, Wurm classifies Australian languages into 26 families. Examination of the language map (Fig. 6.4) reveals another intriguing feature of the Australian linguistic situation. All but one of these families occur in the north of the Northern Territory, Western Australia, and north-west Queensland. The twenty-sixth family, called Pama-Nyungan, occupies seven-eighths of the continent, although this somewhat unbalanced distribution may not have represented the original situation. Wurm believes that the apparent uniformity of this large Pama-Nyungan family may be due to the rapid spread of a new language which superimposed itself on earlier,

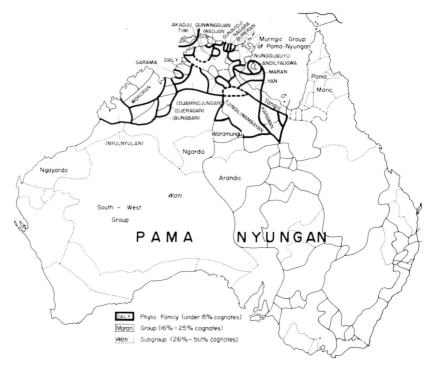

Fig. 6.4. Diversity of Aboriginal languages in Australia.

more diverse languages. This is in agreement with the views of Capell, whose earlier linguistic analysis laid much of the groundwork for modern linguistic studies in Australia.[13]

Capell recognized a small body of vocabulary that was spread over a wide area to which he referred as 'Common Australian'. The highest concentration, about 80 per cent, of these 'Common Australian' forms occurs in the arid areas of the centre and west of Western Australia and adjacent areas of the Northern Territory and South Australia. In much of the remainder of the continent only 40–50 per cent of these common forms are found, with values of less than 30 per cent across the north and in parts of south-eastern Australia. Except for this latter area and Cape York, the main part of the area which has a low percentage of 'Common Australian' forms is occupied by the twenty-five language families in Wurm's classification that do not belong to Pama-Nyungan.

The differing frequencies of 'Common Australian' in various parts of the continent, taken in conjunction with the non-uniform distribution of the twenty-six language families, has prompted linguists to speculate on the history of language development in Australia. Hale has suggested that the speakers of the earliest Australian languages entered the country somewhere west of the Gulf of Carpentaria and as people spread to other parts of the continent over many thousands of years their languages became greatly diversified. Capell's views of the manner in which 'Common Australian' spread have been adapted by Wurm and others to explain the present language pattern. The speakers of one of the original diverse languages, living in north-west Australia probably south of the Kimberley, began to move eastward and south, superimposing their language on those already present, thus introducing a greater uniformity than had been there before. This language modification did not affect the northern part of the continent. In this area highly diverse languages remained, except in north-east Arnhem Land where languages similar to those in the centre developed. At the extreme limit of their penetration the influence of 'Common Australian' was less strongly felt: here languages with marginal vocabularies persisted, reflecting earlier ties with languages whose speakers were sometimes on the other side of the continent.

Wurm argues that the spread of 'Common Australian' took place some 3000–4000 years ago. He points out that this corresponds with the time when new technical innovations, as reflected by the development of the small-tool tradition, was also spreading along paths similar to those followed by 'Common Australian'.

Genes and language

We have already noted that language differentiation is much greater in the north and north-west parts of Australia, 25 of the 26 families of Aboriginal languages being found in approximately one-eighth of the area of the continent. The remaining seven-eighths is the home of the languages belonging to the Pama-Nyungan family. Within this family, however, the distribution of languages is not uniform. Is this lack of uniformity reflected in the genetic differentiation of Pama–Nyungan speakers?

Five tribes in the southern part of the Northern Territory who were included in the study of genetic distance speak languages in the Pama–Nyungan family.[10] The Aranda speak a language which belongs to a separate group, Arandic, whilst the other four tribes speak languages which belong to the Nyungic group. Within this group the Walbiri language is differentiated somewhat more than the others, belonging to the Ngarga sub-group and the other three, Bidjandjadjara, Luridja, and Pintubi, speak languages belonging to a dialect chain in the Wati sub-group. Linguistically, therefore, the last three tribes are closest to one another, Walbiri and Aranda being more distinctive from these three and from each other. This is exactly the differentiation found by the genetic distance analysis as shown in Fig. 6.3. In other studies we have included another member of the Wati sub-group, a population from the Western Desert area of Western Australia. They also cluster with Bidjandjadjara, Luridja, and Pintubi, but are somewhat further away genetically than would be expected from their linguistic position at the end of the Wati dialect chain.

If the other Northern Territory populations are included in the linguistic–genetic distance comparisons again there is broad agreement. The Tiwi, as noted already, are genetically very distinctive, and this is true also of their language. C. R. Osborne[14] has commented that although it is clear from the deep structure, semantics, general morphological type and phonology that Tiwian is an Australian language it has almost no lexical cognates with any other Australian languages — not even with its closest neighbours. The distinctive position of Tiwian is drawn attention to also by R. M. W. Dixon in his most recent and comprehensive review, *The Languages of Australia*.[15]

The other four tribes in the Northern Territory for which genetic distances have been estimated show a poorer fit between genetic and linguistic differentiation. Gunwingguan is a large language family containing within it a separate language group, Ranjbarnic. Our genetic sampling included people who spoke both these languages, and in the genetic distance analysis these two emerged as a cluster. Two other tribes also cluster together in the genetic distance analysis, the Malag and Nunggubuyu, although linguistically they are quite distinctive. The Malag live in the north-east corner of Arnhem Land and speak a language belonging to the Murngic group of Pama–Nyungun. The Nunggubuyan language, on the other hand, belongs to a different family. Geographically these two tribes share a common boundary, and this proximity appears to have been more important genetically than their linguistic differences would suggest. However, it is important to note that the Malag, who are linguistically related to the tribes in the centre of Australia, are also closer to these central tribes in genetic distance than are any of the other Arnhem Land tribes.

The biggest discrepancies between language and genes occur when localities from a wider geographical range are brought into the analysis, especially when localities in Cape York are included. Languages in Cape York have been classified into a Pama–Maric group of the large Pama–Nyungan family. One might suspect, on this basis, that they would have their closest genetic affinities with other Pama–Nyungan speakers. Genetic distance estimates indicate, however, that Cape York populations are more closely related genetically to populations in Arnhem Land. This type of discrepancy may be due, in part at least, to inadequate understanding of the linguistic situation. Recent language studies in Cape York[16] suggest that the situation there is more complex than previously thought, and Wurm has proposed that it may come to resemble the linguistic complexity present in Arnhem Land. In fact, he points out that the 'Common Australian' element in the west of Cape York Peninsula is as low in frequency as in the southern part of Arnhem Land. Future studies, therefore, may help to redress the present discrepancy between the linguistic and genetic picture for this part of the continent.

Genetic relationships with populations outside Australia

When considering the differences and similarities between cranial traits in Aborigines and other populations we saw that morphological distances show Aborigines to be most closely related to Melanesians, both in New Guinea and other parts of Island Melanesia, but to be morphologically quite distinct from any of the other world populations. A similar set of relationships emerges from a study of the distribution of blood genetic markers.

There are certain genetic markers which demonstrate the Aboriginal–Melanesian bond clearly and hint at tenuous relationships with peoples in more distant parts of the world. But other specific markers indicate that the original Aboriginal–Melanesian ties must have been broken for some considerable time. The first category of markers includes the transferrin Tf^{D1} allele, which is widespread throughout Melanesia and Australia and the group specific component allele Gc^{Ab} which occurs in Melanesia and in northern parts of Australia. In addition, detailed study of the distribution of the gamma globulin groups allows us to deduce that there were old ties between New Guinea and Australia. For example, the allogroups $Gm^{za:n-:g}$ and $Gm^{zax:n-:g}$ are found in the central and Western Desert Aborigines and also at high frequency in the Highlands of New Guinea, and these allogroups may well have been the predominant Gm types in the original populations of these areas. At a later time $Gm^{za:n:b}$ was added in New Guinea and in the north of Australia. This addition was probably introduced by migrations of new populations into New Guinea and coastal areas in the north of Australia. On the basis of present frequencies of this allogroup in New Guinea, Arthur Steinberg and I calculated that north Australian populations

may have had up to 30 per cent gene admixture with outside populations.[17] These could have been either New Guinean or ones similar to
those which entered New Guinea, such as the speakers of the Austronesian languages which swept into the Western Pacific some 4000–
5000 years ago.

Although markers such as Tf^{DI}, or Gc^{Ab} indicate common genetic
ancestry in the past between Aborigines and Melanesians, there must
have also been a long period of relative isolation after the land-bridge
across Torres Strait was destroyed. Genetically this is shown by the
fact that many specific markers occur in New Guinea which are not
found in Australia: these include genes for variants of serum albumin
and for red cell enzymes such as phosphoglucomutase and phosphoglycerate kinase. Conversely, there are variants such as the red cell
enzyme variants PGD^{Elcho} or the carbonic anhydrase genes $CA_1^{9 \text{Aust}}$
and CA_2^4 which occur widely in Australia but which have never been
detected in New Guinea or other parts of Melanesia. The occurrence,
survival, and spread of these mutant genes in either New Guinean
or Australian populations, without gaining a foothold in the other
population, is confirmation of the length of the physical separation
between these two areas. It is consistent with the geological evidence
which indicates the drowning of the land-bridge across the Torres
Straits took place some 8000 years ago.

A similar picture to that provided by the distribution of specific
genetic markers is found if all the blood genetic data are subjected
to a multivariate genetic distance analysis, similar to that used to
study the genetic differentiation between tribes within Australia.
Bronya Keats has done this for 12 populations in Australia and 16
in New Guinea and Island Melanesia.[18] As is shown in Fig. 6.5, all
the Australian populations occur on one main branch of the tree,
whilst all the Melanesian populations are found on the other branch.
When the actual genetic distances are examined, however, it is clear
that the northern Australian populations are closest to the Motu-
speaking people around the Gulf of Papua and are also close to other
Austronesian-speaking people, the Manus and Usiai in the Admiralty
Islands and to the Fijians. The genetic distance analysis therefore
adds further support to the view that there are basic differences as
well as underlying similarities between the Aborigines and their immediate neighbours to the north.

Recently I have extended this genetic distance analysis to include
populations from other parts of the Pacific. Two Australian populations were chosen, one from the centre (Walbiri) and one from Arnhem
Land (Malag). They have been compared with several populations
outside Australia for which identical information is available.[19]

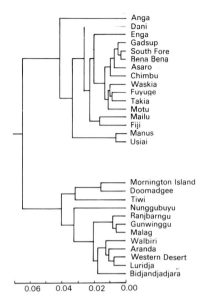

Fig. 6.5. Phylogenetic tree based on blood genetic traits of relationship between 12 Aboriginal and 16 New Guinea and Island Melanesian populations.

In Fig. 6.6 I have used a principal component analysis of the genetic distance to give a two-dimensional representation of the genetic relationships between the two Australian populations and twelve Pacific populations. Both the central and northern Australians are shown as remote from any of the other populations. As might be expected for people living on islands separated by large distances the other groups are also well scattered, but among them there is some pattern which relates broadly to geography. Starting in the north of the Pacific the Ainu occupy an isolated position. Then we move down to a proto-Malay group, the Batak, who live in Sumatra, and appearing near to them the Atayal, a tribal population in Taiwan. Next we find a group from the Western Carolines followed by Samoans and Rennelese, two somewhat more remote groups and both of Polynesian affiliation. Back toward the centre of the distribution are the Motu from the south coast of Papua New Guinea, who speak an Austronesian language related to Polynesian. The genetic neighbours of the Motu are people from the Tokelau Islands and Fiji, both of which are strongly Polynesian in culture. Then we have some more remote groups, the Banks Islanders and Eastern Caroline Islanders. These are in the wrong position in relation to our expectations on the basis of language and culture but

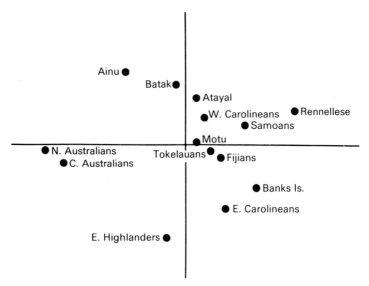

Fig. 6.6. Principal component analysis based on genetic-marker data showing relationship between north and central Australian Aborigines and 12 Western Pacific populations.

probably they have gone through a 'bottleneck', during which process their population was reduced drastically in size to expand again later from the few survivors, at some time in the past, which has altered their gene pool drastically. Finally, we come to the Eastern Highlands of New Guinea, remote from the others, but moving back in position towards the Australians.

Crude though this genetic analysis is, it does seem to emphasize yet again the distinctiveness of the Australian Aborigines and demonstrates that they have no close relationships with populations outside Australia. Their affinities, such as they are, lie with the New Guineans and with some of the other Pacific peoples not much further removed. But the lapse of 10 000 years or so has allowed the development in Australia of a group of completely different languages and genetic microevolution has produced a people adapted to their environment and genetically differentiated, not only from tribe to tribe within Australia, but also from their closest neighbours.

A diversion on proteins, language, and time

One of the problems facing the student of human evolution is how to measure the rate at which this evolution is taking place. When we are looking at changes which have taken place over a long period of time it is possible to look at fossils dug up from strata which have been dated by independent means, and work out the rate of skeletal change between the earliest and latest specimens available. Doing this for the evolution of the hominid line, for instance, gives a value for the increase in cranial capacity between Autralopithecus and modern man of about 0.5 cc per 1000 years. But when we are interested in the kind of evolutionary change which is made manifest by differences in the frequencies of genetic markers in blood there are no base-line data for comparison, since enzymes or serum protein systems cannot be determined for fossils. To overcome this difficulty it is necessary to make indirect estimates of the rate of change of blood genetic markers and compare these with the observed differences.

Most of the genetic differences detectable in the enzymes or other proteins present in blood are due to the substitution in the protein of one of its building blocks, or amino acids, by another amino acid. This altered protein originates as the result of a mutation in the gene controlling the production of that particular protein. Only the offspring who inherit this mutant gene will possess the new protein form, but gradually, in each succeeding generation, more individuals may get the gene for the altered protein, and after the lapse of many generations the altered form of the protein may replace the old form in the entire population. If the protein is one common to many different species of animal it can be purified from each species and its complete amino acid sequence determined. For example, the so-called β-chains of haemoglobin in man and horse have, out of a total of 146 amino acids, 121 in common but differ in 25 places on the chain. These differences, so the argument goes, have accumulated step by step through the chance occurrence of mutations affecting single amino acids and their subsequent spread and fixation in the population.

How long does it take for a single amino acid substitution to become fixed in the population in this way? If we take the example of the β-chain of haemoglobin in man and horse, we can estimate this from the length of time during which the ancestors of the horse and of man have been following their separate courses. Palaeontologists tell us that the ancestry of these two species parted company some 75 million years ago. However, the time during which these amino acid substitutions have occurred is of course 150 million years, since they have been taking place in both lines for 75 million years each. This means that for haemoglobin there has been, on average, one amino acid substitution every 6 million years.

Several proteins from a range of species have had their amino acid sequences determined, and the rates of amino acid substitution per site vary considerably. The number of amino acids in different proteins varies also. If an average is taken for proteins of different size and with different rates of change there is approximately one amino acid substitution per protein every 10 million years.

Within a single species, of course, evolution has not proceeded long enough for estimates of rates of change to be based on the number of amino acid substitutions which have become fixed in the population. Instead it is necessary to obtain a measure of how far mutations in any particular protein molecule have gone along the path towards fixation. This is measured by the frequency of variant genes at the locus controlling the production of that protein. If two populations differ in the frequency of a gene, the difference will be an indication of the time of separation between the populations. We can then take an average for as many genes as possible. If we do this for two separate populations the difference in these average frequencies is the genetic distance between the populations. Masatoshi Nei[20] has argued that, if the genetic distance between the populations is D, then a simple relationship holds between this distance and time, t. If we use the average rate of amino acid substitution given above then

$$D = \frac{2t}{10\ 000\ 000}.$$

If we estimate D using Nei's measure of genetic distance, which is based on the frequencies of electrophoretically detectable alleles at all loci examined, then t can be derived by simple substitution in this formula. Nei and Roychoudhury have done this for times of divergence between the major human ethnic groups.[21] The resultant times are 115 000 years between Africans and Europeans, 55 000 years between Europeans and East Asians and 120 000 years between Africans and East Asians. These values are consistent with some

Table 6.2. Time of separation in years between three major human populations based on the genetic model of Nei and Roychoudhury[20]

	Europeans	Black Africans	Japanese
Europeans	—	115 000	55 000
Black Africans		—	120 000

estimates which have been made for the divergence time between the major human races based on the fossil record.

When Nei's formula is used to calculate divergence time between populations in Australia and New Guinea or between populations within Australia, values are obtained which do not fit so well with what we know of the prehistory of these populations. For example, I have used Nei's formula to calculate when the peoples of the Western Desert in Australia diverged from the Enga in the Western Highlands of New Guinea, and when the Tiwi of Bathurst Island diverged from the Western Desert people. The times which result are 127 000 and 47 000 years respectively. That is to say, if Nei is right, these local populations began to differentiate from one another at the same time as the major differentiations between Africans, Europeans, and East Asians were taking place. Nei himself conceded recently that small populations, such as those we are concerned with in Australia and New Guinea, do not obey the rules in the same way as do large continental populations such as Europeans, Africans, and East Asians.

Having considered how the biological 'clock', based on the rate of amino-acid substitution, can be used to estimate divergence time between human populations, and having found that there are problems in obtaining satisfactory estimates for small populations, let us turn now to see how linguistic studies may be used to calibrate time of separation between groups and how this relates to genetic distance data. If languages change at a constant rate, as discussed on p. 122, two languages diverging from a common ancestral form will share only 66 per cent of cognates at the end of 1000 years, 28 per cent after 3000, and 12 per cent after 5000 years. Using cognate frequencies for New Guinea populations Booth and Taylor have shown these correlate best with a method of calculating genetic distance developed by Luca Cavalli-Sforza. When they use glottochronology to calibrate these genetic distance values, the time in years is obtained by multiplying the genetic distance value by 100 000. Having calibrated the distance values for New Guinea populations with known differences in cognate frequencies, they then use this calibration to estimate the time of separation for populations in other areas.[22]

Table 6.3 shows these results for the time of separation between some Australian and New Guinea populations. The times of separation obtained by this method are reasonable. For instance, the Malag of north-east Arnhem Land and the Western Desert population, both of which speak Pama-Nyungan languages, became separated 4400 years ago. The Tiwi of Bathurst Island became separated from the

Table 6.3. Time of separation in years estimated from genetic
distance values calibrated by glottochronology[21]

	Aborigines			New Guineans	
	Western Desert	Malag	Tiwi	Enga	Motu
Western Desert	—	4400	10 500	19 700	11 600
Malag		—	9 400	23 700	9800
Tiwi			—	21 600	9200
Enga				—	7200
Motu					—

Malag nearly 10 000 years ago, corresponding to a time when rising sea-levels began to make communication between the Tiwi and mainland tribes more difficult. The Malag were separated from the Motu around the Gulf of Papua at about the same time. The largest time intervals of about 20 000 years are between Aboriginal tribes and the Enga, in the Highlands of New Guinea. This is also a reasonable time depth since we would expect that populations at the extremes of the range would have already differentiated, even when the land-bridge between New Guinea and Australia was intact.

Of course, many people have argued that the rate at which languages change is not constant. This may well be true in Australia, where taboos on certain words after a death lead to rapid change by borrowing or the invention of new terms to replace the taboo words. However, although the time estimates based on glottochronology may not be the final answer to the problem of determining the rate of genetic differentiation, they do provide us, for the present, with estimates of the rate of evolutionary divergence consistent with the archaeological and geographical facts concerning populations in our area of interest.

7

GROWTH AND DEVELOPMENT

Aboriginal babies at birth weigh less than their white counterparts
and this is true whether the data for white babies are from northern
Europe, the United States, or Australia. As indicated by the mean
values in Table 7.1, the lower birth weight of the Aboriginal babies
appears to be a general phenomenon over the whole continent.

Bronya Keats[1] recently analysed the birth-weight data in some
detail. As is true for other ethnic groups around the world, male
Aboriginal babies are slightly heavier at birth than are females, with
males averaging 2.8–3.3 kg, the lightest weight being on Bathurst
Island and the heaviest on Mornington Island. The corresponding
figures for female babies at birth average 2.7–3.1, the lightest again
being on Bathurst Island, but equal with two other northern populations at Maningrida and Milingimbi, and with the heaviest also on
Mornington Island.

Babies born in the north of the Northern Territory, including
Bathurst Island, Milingimbi, and Maningrida, are smaller than those
in Queensland and in the Kimberley area in Western Australia: the
differences, however, are not great. More striking is the difference
between the birth-weight of babies born to parents who are both of
full Aboriginal descent compared to those born to parents one or
both of whom are part Aboriginal. The mean birth-weights for part-
Aboriginal babies are intermediate between those for the full-
Aboriginal babies and the value for white babies.

For a limited series Keats has shown that girl babies born to full
Aboriginal parents are significantly lighter in weight than girl babies
born to part Aboriginal parents, and this holds also if only the
mother is part Aboriginal. In the case of male babies, those born to
full Aboriginal parents are lighter in weight, but not significantly so,
than when either or both their parents are part Aboriginal. Keats
suggests that although the genes inherited from the mother play an

Table 7.1. Mean birth weight (kg) based on several sources

	Males	Females
Full-Aborigines		
Queensland		
various localities	3.0	2.9
Kowanyama	3.0	2.9
Mornington Island	3.3	3.1
Northern Territory		
North coastal	2.9	2.9
Bathurst Island	2.8	2.7
Maningrida	2.9	2.7
Milingimbi	3.1	2.7
Yuendumu	3.1	2.9
Ernabella	3.1	3.0
Santa Teresa	3.1	3.0
Western Australia		
various localities	3.0	3.0
Kimberley	3.1	3.0
United Kingdom		
whites (1966)	3.5	3.4
Part-Aborigines		
Queensland		
various localities	3.2	3.1
Kowanyama	3.3	2.9
Western Australia		
various localities	3.3	3.2
Kimberley	3.3	3.1

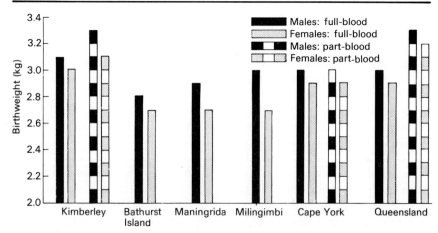

Fig. 7.1. Mean birth-weights for Aborigines of full and part descent across the north of Australia.[1]

important part in determining birth-weights of both male and female babies, the father's genes are important only for the male babies, a suggestion consistent with the view that some genes determining birth-weight are carried on the Y-chromosome.

Growth patterns of Aboriginal infants

Since the birth-weights of Aborigines are significantly lower than those for whites, but the final adult stature is very comparable in the two groups, there must be marked differences in the pattern of growth during the developmental period. This pattern of growth can be considered conveniently in two age-periods, the period of infancy up to 5 years of age and the remaining period of late infancy and adolescence.

Several workers have drawn attention to the similarity in the average growth curve for young Aboriginal infants and those for young infants in many developing countries in Asia, Africa, and the Americas. Figure 7.2 is based on data collected in the north of the Northern Territory by Ellen Kettle.[2] There is a rapid increase in weight during the first few months, but a slowing down in the rate of increase occurs at about 6 months of age. At 18 months of age there is a maximum difference of 3.5 kg between Aboriginal and white

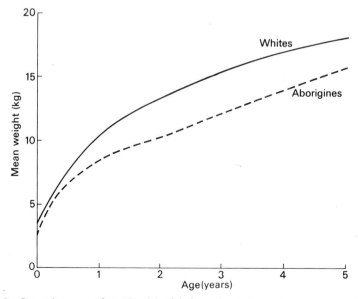

Fig. 7.2. Growth curves for Aboriginal infants in Arnhem Land compared with white Australians.[2]

Australian children, and this difference is maintained, on average, during the remaining pre-school years. Similar results were obtained by Bronya Keats for children up to 4 years of age in Queensland and the Northern Territory. Mean weights were lower at all ages for Aboriginal than for white Australian children, the differences being more marked for full Aboriginals than for part Aboriginals, particularly for boys. Girl part-Aboriginal children had growth curves very little different from those of full Aborigines in the same locality.

Weight is known to be more sensitive to environmental factors than some other measurements, but the differences between Aborigines and whites already noted for weight hold also for height and head circumference though the differences are not so large. Bronya Keats found that white children, after reaching a weight of 8–9 kg, tend to put on more weight relative to height than do Aboriginal children. Head circumference, on the other hand, levels off as weight increases, and the mean head circumference at a particular weight is not significantly different for the white and Aboriginal groups. Similarly, when height is compared with head circumference height increases at a faster rate, but again there are no significant differences between the groups. The major differences in the growth pattern of the white and Aboriginal groups then is related to a weight factor, whites on average being relatively heavier at any height.

Keats also fitted polynomials to the growth data for the Aboriginal and white children. The curves can be expressed in the form

$$Y = \alpha + \beta t + \gamma t^2$$

where α is the initial value, β the rate of growth, and γ the decrease in the rate of growth at any time t. For weight and height both the values of α and β are higher for the white children than for the Aborigines, but this is not so for head circumference. Differences between the growth curves of males and females can also be tested by comparing the sets of data generated from the polynomials. In Keats's data male and female growth curves for weight are significantly different only for white children. For growth in height the differences in the male and female curves are significant for part Aboriginal children at Kowanyama, in Cape York, as well as for white children, whilst for growth in head circumference sex differences are significant for full Aboriginal children in the Northern Territory, for full Aboriginals and part Aboriginals at Kowanyama, as well as for white children.

These mean values, of course, obscure striking differences in individual growth patterns. There is also another difficulty in interpreting the mean growth curves as the cohort under consideration becomes older. Infant mortality among Aborigines is very much higher than for white Australians, and lighter babies tend to become infected and to die more easily than heavier ones. As age advances, therefore, the mean growth curves represent results for the sturdier survivors. Because of this and the operation of similar factors it is difficult to determine to what extent the growth patterns represent innate differences in Aborigines.

If attention is focused just on the percentage of children who fall below the established standard for various growth indices it appears that a large number of Aboriginal children are suffering mild to moderate protein-calorie malnutrition. Table 7.2 gives the percentage of children in the Northern Territory who fall below the standard values for whites in weight, weight for height, and weight for head

Table 7.2. Proportion of Aboriginal children in the Northern Territory in different percentage classes of standards for white children (data from Keats)[2]

	80–100 per cent of standard	Less than 80 per cent of standard
Weight at six months		
males	94	6
females	79	21
Weight: 12–48 months		
males	75	25
females	57	43
Weight for height: 0–48 months		
males	96	4
females	93	7
Weight for head circumference: 0–48 months		
males	99	1
females	99	1
Height: 0–48 months		
males and females	100	0
Head circumference: 0–48 months		
males and females	100	0

circumference. For weight alone, at six months of age only six per cent of Aboriginal boy babies are less than 80 per cent of the white standards, but 21 per cent of girl babies are in this category. The situation becomes worse with increasing age: between 12 and 48 months 25 per cent of boys and 43 per cent of girls are less than 80 per cent of the weight of their white counterparts. To determine the sensitivity of weight alone we can look at two commonly used ratios of measurement, weight for height and weight for head circumference. For both of these ratios nearly all Aboriginal children are above 80 per cent of the white standards. As well, all Aboriginal children for the ages under consideration are above 80 per cent of white standards for both height and head circumference alone. Demonstratively, therefore, weight for age is the main indicator of different growth patterns in Aboriginal and white children. Since weight is readily modified by nutritional changes it seems likely that the difference between white and Aboriginal children could be abolished by improved nutrition of the Aborigines.

However, the difference between children with full or part Aboriginal parents suggests that genetic differences might still play some part in explaining the difference in growth pattern between white and Aboriginal children. Bronya Keats has attempted to analyse the genetic component of some of these differences by examining the data available at birth for children who are related, either as brothers or sisters or as cousins. The intraclass correlations are higher for birth-weight than for either birth length or head circumference at birth. Also the correlation in birth-weight is higher for pairs of brother than for either pairs of sisters or brothers and sisters. Her data are not adequate to control all the variables to enable a partitioning of the genetic and environmental factors but she concludes that genes carried on chromosomes inherited from the mother, and for male children on the Y-chromosome inherited from the father, do play a part in determining birth-weight. Similar careful studies on relatives followed over several years are needed to answer the question of the relative contribution of genetic and environmental factors to growth patterns after birth.

Growth in older children and adolescents

The dynamics of the growth process are best displayed by longitudinal studies: in these measurements are made at frequent intervals on the same individuals over the entire period under consideration. Though this has been done for several series of young infants, only one investigation approaches the requirements for a longitudinal growth study of older infants and adolescent Aborigines.

As part of a study of dental health and the functional relationships and patterns of growth and development of dental and craniofacial structures, Murray Barrett and Tasman Brown have recorded data on height, weight, and other metrical traits for members of the Walbiri tribe at Yuendumu in central Australia, investigations which were part of studies by research teams from the University of Adelaide at Yuendumu since the early 1950s: some measurements on Aborigines in central Australia were made twenty years earlier. Barrett and Brown's careful investigations, however, started in 1961, and during the next ten years they assembled growth data on nearly 300 individuals between four and 18 years of age. Not all of these were measured every year, but their data are mainly longitudinal.

Figure 7.3 shows the centile curves for growth in height for Walbiri boys. Growth is relatively steady up to 13, when boys show

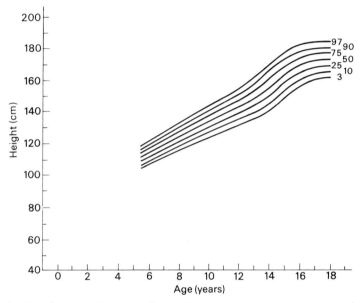

Fig. 7.3. Centile growth curves for male Aboriginal children and adolescents at Yuendumu.[4]

a marked adolescent growth spurt. The rate declines again between 15 and 16, and adult height is reached at 18 years of age.[3]

The adolescent growth spurt in girls at Yuendumu occurs 18-24 months earlier than in boys, and the girls achieve their adult stature by 17 years of age. From age 8 to 14 girls are, on average, taller than boys of the same age, but the position is reversed after 14 and in final stature the boys are approximately 10 cm taller than the girls. Magnitudes of peak growth in height are 9.8 cm per year in boys and 8.3 cm per year in girls, levels which are similar to those reported for whites.

The difference in the growth process between the sexes is demonstrated very clearly by studies on the timing of ossification events in bones of the hand and wrist. Brown and Barrett[4] have taken serial X-ray photographs on a large series at Yuendumu and in Fig. 7.4 the age at which ossification occurs in each of four bones is indicated in relation to the growth velocity curves for stature in the same series of girls and boys. Peak growth velocity occurs at 12 and nearly 14 years respectively, and the ossification process in the hand and wrist is complete by 16.5 years in girls and 17.3 years in boys with epiphyseal union of the radius.

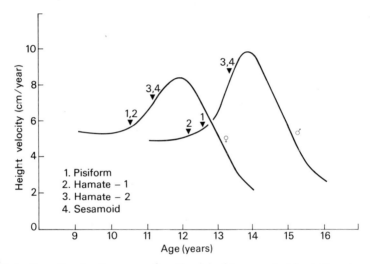

Fig. 7.4. Growth-velocity curves for Aboriginal boys and girls at Yuendumu and the time of ossification of bones in the hand and wrist.[4]

Estimates of what is called the *skeletal age* can be made by comparing X-ray photographs of the hand and wrist with published standard photographs, based either on studies of white American or English children of known age. For the Yuendumu children the average skeletal age lags behind that of the American children by nearly 6.5 months for boys and just over 4 months for girls. There is considerable variation in the rate at which skeletal maturation takes place in different individuals. This variation may be due to either genetic or environmental factors, but the Adelaide researchers believe that the skeletal age-lag in the Yuendumu children could be due almost entirely to nutritional factors.

Measurements of the face and skull show that the growth spurt of other parts of the skeleton proceeds at more or less the same time as for total height. For example, the age of peak growth velocities in boys is 13.7 years for height, and is almost the same for the anterior base of the cranium, length of the maxilla and mandible, and for total facial height. Only for upper facial height is the peak growth velocity achieved somewhat earlier, at 13.0 years. Serial records on the bones of the jaw and face obtained at Yuendumu are of great importance in revealing the plasticity of these structures and in helping to understand how changes in eating habits can affect the size and position of the teeth and jaw relative to other craniofacial features. Such studies have a bearing also on interpreting differences in fossil cranial material, particularly if it is suspected that dietary differences may have existed among the peoples whose skulls have been studied.

Body composition

The retardation in growth of Aboriginal children, which is most marked after 6 months of age for weight, but which occurs also for height, shows itself also in a retardation in the age at which skeletal maturation occurs. This difference in the growth pattern may show up, therefore, in other characteristics of the growing child. Total mass of the body is the sum of several components: chiefly bone, fat, protein, connective tissue, and intra- and extra-cellular water. We shall see later that Aborigines in the central desert area have an increased amount of extra-cellular water compared to whites, and that fat is a fluctuating component which causes variation in weight without meaning necessarily that there are major nutritional disturbances likely to affect health.

What is important is the amount of actively metabolizing tissue, or the cell mass. Donald Cheek recently stressed the importance of estimating cell mass in relation to body length as a measure of the nutritional status of the individual. Measuring the mass of cells is not easy in the living person, but use can be made of the fact, determined experimentally, that the ratio of intra-cellular water to protein in cells, in muscles and viscera is relatively constant. It is necessary therefore to measure the amount of intra-cellular water, and this can be done indirectly. In the field a small dose of deuterium oxide (D_2O) and sodium bromide (NaBr) is given by mouth and a sample of blood is taken one hour later. The total body water can be estimated from the amount of dilution of the D_2O, which is rapidly distributed into the cells as well as the space outside the cells. NaBr on the other hand remains outside the cells, so the dilution of the bromide leads to the estimation of the extra-cellular volume. By subtracting this from the estimated total body-water one is left with the intra-cellular water, which is directly proportional to the cell mass. Experimental evidence suggests that in calorie deficiency there is a proportional reduction in the ratio of intra-cellular water to body length, but there is a disproportional reduction in the intra-cellular water if there is a marked deficiency of protein.

In a study of a small number of Aborigines in the Kimberley area of Western Australia and at Alice Springs in the centre, Cheek and his colleagues[5] found a significant reduction for girls in the intra-cellular water (considered as a measure of cell mass) in relation to the cube of body length; there was a reduction also for boys in comparison with white standards, but the difference was not statistically significant for the boys. They believe the data for the boys indicates some reduction in protein reserves for some individuals, although reduced calorie intake may also be involved. The greatly reduced protein reserves found in girls, however, are of much greater concern, particularly for those who may become pregnant at 13 or 14 years of age.

Teeth

Many of the early observers commented on the quality and other attributes of the teeth of Aborigines. Once again it is researchers from the University of Adelaide who have provided us with the most extensive and detailed studies of these important parts of the body in living Aborigines. Many reports have been made on Aboriginal teeth in museum collections, for teeth are among the most durable parts of the skeleton and remain at sites of burial often after other bones have disintegrated. Comparison between the dentition of the living and of skeletal remains therefore is of considerable importance.

Compared to teeth in Europeans, Aboriginal teeth are large, and they have a number of features in the form of both the crown and the root which are found in skeletal material of considerable antiquity. This greater size is manifest in the mesiodistal and bucco-lingual crown tooth diameters, which are larger in Aborigines than in most other population groups both in the deciduous and permanent dentitions. Males have larger teeth than females and this is most marked for the permanent canines in the lower jaw. The mandibular or lower arch of Aborigines is large, a feature necessary to accommodate the larger teeth. The maxillary arch, into which are set the upper teeth, is also large.[6]

Unusual dental features as well as deformities have been reported in Aborigines. Among the former are occasional shovel-shaped

incisors; and diminutive and peg-shaped lateral incisors and canini-
form maxillary lateral incisors are not uncommon. Supernumerary
teeth in the incisor and premolar regions and also fourth molars are
seen sometimes and there is some evidence that the frequency of
the latter varies significantly in different parts of the continent.
Among the deformities, crowding of the teeth and other irregulari-
ties in tooth position have been observed not infrequently. More
severe malocclusions, however, display a relatively low incidence
compared with white populations.

Some deformities are deliberately induced, others are the result of
dietary habits. In many parts of the continent knocking out of a
tooth, or tooth evulsion, is part of the male initiation rites, although
in other areas, such as north-west Queensland, it is not a part of the
initiation ceremonies. In most instances an upper incisor, usually the
central, is the evulsed tooth. It was not universally practised in
central Australia, and Spencer and Gillen commenting on this
practice among the Aranda consider that it was 'partly a matter of
personal taste and fashion'.[7] Tooth evulsion appears to have increased in frequency in central Australia in recent years.

One characteristic feature of teeth, especially noticeable in
museum collections and also among older living Aborigines, is the
heavy wear, or attrition, of the biting surfaces of all teeth as well as
the contacting surfaces between adjacent teeth. The physical nature
of much traditional food demanded vigorous effort in mastication,
and since food was often cooked by throwing it on to the fire or
into hot sand or ashes, it had an abrasive quality which resulted in
continuous wear on the teeth. Cusps and surface grooves were
ground down almost to the gum line, and sometimes the pulp
chamber was exposed if the rate of wear exceeded the rate of secondary dentine deposition. Despite this heavy wear attrition, dental
caries was uncommon and is rarely seen in museum tooth collections.
It is rare also in Aborigines still living a more traditional existence.
However, heavy tooth wear often resulted in pathological conditions
such as jaw abscesses if the pulp was infected or degenerative arthritis
of the temporomandibular joint through abnormal stresses on the
joint mechanism.

Loring Brace,[8] in a recent study of the size of teeth, based on
measurements of museum material, draws attention to interesting
differences between localities in the north, centre, and south-east of
the continent. Teeth are smallest in Cape York and increase in size
roughly in proportion to the geographic distance away from this area.
Maximum size is found generally in the upper Murray Basin, but
lower values are found toward the coast and near the mouth of the

Murray, and also in the central desert area. An anomalous result is the very large size of teeth in the collection from Broadbeach, near the border of Queensland and New South Wales. Brace interprets this as an extension north-east of the robust skeletal material represented in the upper Murray Basin, and concludes that the persistence of large teeth in these areas is due to the survival of the original genetic element for large teeth in those regions most favourable to human habitation.

Temporal changes

In many parts of the world changes in life-style have been accompanied by changes in body build and physiological responses. Increase in average stature, one of the easiest traits to document, has been taking place during the last 100 years, but other changes have also been demonstrated in many different populations over the last few decades. These include a decrease of the age of menarche in girls, increased elevation of systolic blood pressure with age, as well as changes in the pattern of disease and the expectation of life. These changes are frequently attributed to alterations in environmental factors: nutrition, public health measures, pollution, and psychological stress. The possibility exists that some part of these changes may be due to the breakdown of genetic isolates leading to heterosis, but it is not easy to assess the importance of this effect in human populations.

Accurate records to determine whether similar temporal changes are occurring in Aborigines are not available for many of the traits, such as age of menarche, studied in other parts of the world. Limited information from some areas of Australia does indicate, however, that where changes in life-style are taking place the physiological response is comparable to that noted elsewhere. In the case of stature a direct comparison over a 35-year period can be made for central Australia. Several groups of Aborigines were measured in the area around Yuendumu between 1927 and 1933. Similar measurements were made in the 1950s and finally between 1961 and 1970 we have the longitudinal series of measurements referred to earlier and carried out by Barrett and Brown.[9] The difference in average height of young adults over the whole period is about 5.5 cm, corresponding to an increase in average height of 1.5 cm per decade. This increase is almost the same for young adult women, who remained about 10 cm shorter on average than men in the same age range in both the 1930s and 1960s. The increase in average height of older adults was not so great. In the 1960s older men were only 2.7 cm and older women only 1.2 cm taller than in the 1930s.

Table 7.3. Increase in stature of Aborigines in central Australia[9]

		Age (years)	Average height (cm)
Young adults	1930s	17–25	167.5
	1960s	17–23	173.0
Older adults	1930s	26–45+	168.0 ·
	1950s	22–65+	169.8
	1960s	30–60	171.1

The increase in average height of young Aboriginal adults is similar to that found in many other parts of the world, that is about 1.5 cm a decade between 1880 and 1950. But the increases elsewhere show variation in different age groups, being about 1.5 cm per decade in the 5–7 year age group, 2.5 cm per decade at adolescence, and 1 cm per decade for adults.

Barrett and Brown believe that nutritional changes are the most plausible explanation of the increase in average stature found in central Australians. The earlier measurements were made on groups still living a traditional life, gathering plants and hunting. There were times in the desert when adequate nutrition must have been difficult and they point out that two of the groups who were measured in 1931 had survived a great drought in the area during 1926–9. It is likely that many of the children and adolescents who survived had been through a period of severe food deprivation which could well have impaired their growth. By contrast the children and adolescents who had been living at the Yuendumu settlement since 1946 were sheltered from many of the effects of adverse seasons. The increased availability of food almost certainly has had an important impact on growth. It has been suggested that this could result just from an increase in carbohydrate intake, particularly sugar. Increased sugar intake, so the argument goes, leads to extra insulin production, and insulin is a growth-promoting factor. It is just such a dietary change which has taken place among Aborigines living in settlements. The relationship between increased sugar intake and growth stimulation remains to be clarified, however.

Changes in stature are reflected also in weight changes, and for the central Australian groups the young adults in the 1960s were 5.5 kg heavier than their counterparts in the 1930s. In Queensland some information is available on weight changes for young infants over a 20-year period at Cherbourg settlement, north of Brisbane, and at Palm Island, a government settlement near Townsville. At Cherbourg, between 1953 and 1972, the mean weights of male infants up to

2 years of age fell slightly, whilst female infants gained slightly. At
Palm Island the weights of both males and females fell during the 10-
year period 1963–72.

Few other changes of a temporal nature have been noted for
Aborigines, but some of these can be ascribed with certainty to
changes in the diet. The most striking example relates to dentition.
Decrease in the amount of tooth wear, which is one of the striking
features of teeth among older Aborigines, is an obvious consequence
of adopting a diet of highly processed and cooked food. Traditional
diets demanded a mechanism for chewing which could respond to
the stresses imposed on it by tough and gritty food. Tooth wear was
inevitable under these conditions and within limits was beneficial
to the system. Murray Barrett, reviewing the decrease in tooth wear
in Aborigines at the present time, points out that the new diets
require less chewing, but he considers that, contrary to what might
be expected, modern man's dentition and masticatory system are
now subject to greater stress. This greater stress is indicated by an
increase in the occurrence of malocclusions and oral dental diseases
in general.

Increase in dental disease is also apparent from surveys of the
dental health of Aborigines. Early surveys of the number of decayed,
missing, and filled (DMF) teeth showed that in central Australia the
proportion of persons with DMF teeth was 12, 19, and 57 per cent
for juveniles, adolescents, and adults respectively. Twenty years later,
in 1970, the figures were 22, 50, and 66 per cent for the same three
age groups. It is important to note that, despite the significant
increase in the incidence of caries in these Aborigines, the proportion
of subjects affected and the average number of teeth affected per
subject, especially among the young, is still lower than for other
Australian children. In some areas dental surveys of white children
up to 16 years of age have revealed caries in 95 per cent or more.

Mental and cognitive abilities

The earliest attempt to measure objectively the intelligence of
Aborigines was made by Stanley Porteus in 1915. In that year he
applied the 'maze' test he had recently developed, to Aborigines at
Point McLeay in South Australia and the results were published two
years later.[10] Porteus continued his interest in Aborigines over a
period of 50 years, both he and his colleagues testing people in many
parts of the continent with various modifications of the original
'maze' test. In all these tests Aborigines scored lower than whites.
There is much evidence, however, that scores on the 'maze' test

are strongly influenced by environmental factors and it is now well-established that the test score for Aborigines is higher in those who have had contact with white Australians, and this increase is proportional to the extent of contact.

Many attempts have been made to devise tests which are not influenced by cultural factors.[11] A so-called 'culture-free' test was developed for Australian conditions by McElwain and Kearney in Queensland 20 years ago. The test is non-verbal and non-representational and no object used in the test has an everyday use or meaning. Over one thousand Aboriginal children have been given the Queensland test. Again, as for the Porteus 'maze' test, the results indicate that Aboriginal children score lower than white Australians but the difference is inversely proportional to the amount of contact they have had with white Australian culture. Where contact with white Australians has been high, Aboriginal and white children have similar scores. The difference is larger in situations where contact has been moderate, and becomes greatest where contact has been low.

These results suggest, therefore, that the Queensland 'culture free' test is not as 'free' as its proponents thought. Indeed, more recently McElwain and Kearney have concluded it may be impossible to devise such a test since 'a person brings to the solution of any complex problem tactics which are determined in part at least by experiences peculiar to his social history'.

Some of the more interesting recent developments in the study of cognitive abilities have been in the application of tests based on concepts developed in Switzerland by Jean Piaget. Piaget's theory is that the normal child follows a regular progression in the development of the way in which he gets to know the world around him and handles the relationships which he perceives in it. The child passes first through a sensori-motor stage during the first 18 months. Next he passes to a pre-operational stage in which symbolic thinking begins, but which is characterized also by egocentrism and various forms of precausality. This lasts until 6 years of age. Between the ages of 6 and 12 the child goes through a gradual transition to achieve finally the stage of formal, propositional thinking. At this stage the individual is capable of productive, objective thought. He can suspend judgement, consider various aspects of a problem, and manipulate space, time, object, symbol, and causality within the context of his social setting.

Do all children go through these stages, and, if so, do they achieve the same level of maturation, on average, as the same age? Tests have been designed to measure the acquisition of skills needed to enable the final transition to the stage of formal, propositional thinking.

One such set of tests measures the acquisition of concepts of conservation of matter, that is weight, area, quantity, length, and number which, according to Piaget, occurs normally at about 9–11 years of age. Another set of tests measures ability to classify.

De Lemos[12] has used modifications of Piaget's tests for conservation in studies of Aboriginal children both in central Australia and in north-east Arnhem Land. The results give general support for Piaget's stages of development, determined of course on children in Europe, but the order in which development occurs is not the same. Unlike the findings in Europe, more Aboriginal children succeed on the test for weight than for quantity. Aboriginal children's ability to conserve the appreciation of area was achieved much later than conservation of quantity and length, although in Piaget's studies on European children they occur at the same age. De Lemos suggests that several factors could disturb the test scores, including the order in which the tests are presented. Of greater interest, however, is the observation that children of part-Aboriginal descent living at the same settlement as the full-descent Aboriginal children, achieve levels of development more similar to those of European children. Since de Lemos could find no obvious difference however between the environments of the part and full-descent children she believes genetic factors may play a part in explaining her results.

Other studies of Piaget's theory, however, reveal that environmental factors have a very marked effect on the developmental rate. De Lacey[13] found that the amount of contact with white Australian culture influenced the ability to classify, as measured by Piaget tests. This has been supported by the work of Dasen, on the development of logico-mathematical and spatial operations, although in this case the influence of white European contact only becomes statistically significant after age 10–11 years. Dasen and collaborators[14] extended their investigations of the effect of contact with white Australian culture to children of full- and part-Aboriginal descent who had been fostered or adopted into white Australian families living in the city of Adelaide. In all the tests the fostered and adopted Aboriginal children showed patterns of development closer to those of white children and, in some tests, the two groups were almost identical. Only for tests of conservation of weight and of quantity were the fostered and adopted children obviously different from the whites, although even on these tests they were very different from the patterns of development shown by non-adopted Aboriginal children in central Australia.

The effects of adoption or of living in a foster home became manifest in the response to Piaget-type tests after a short time, certainly within two years. We can conclude, therefore, that though Piaget's concepts on the way in which mental ability matures in the developing child has provided valuable insights into these processes they need to be evaluated and reinterpreted carefully in each group to which they are applied. Relevant to this is the application of what Berry has called ecological functionalism. For example, European children develop logico-mathematical concepts earlier than spatial concepts. However, since Aborigines traditionally live by hunting and food-gathering they need to develop spatial concepts earlier than logico-mathematical concepts. Tests need to be designed which measure an individual's cognitive ability in his own environment, and make possible cross-cultural comparison in both directions.

Judith Kearins[15] has adopted this approach during recent studies in Western Australia. She argues that for people living in the desert areas of Australia requirements for survival obviously include the development of sensory ability in vision and probably hearing, and a visual memory for patterns rather than fixed single elements, and she has developed a series of tests for these abilities. The tests were applied to Aboriginal adolescents from the Western Desert area attending High School in Kalgoorlie and to a group of white children matched for sex and age attending a High School in an outer suburb of Perth in Western Australia. She found that the Aboriginal children performed better than the white Australians in both the visual acuity and the visual memory tests and concluded that this type of evolutionary/ecological approach could be valuable in cross-cultural studies of cognitive abilities.

8

ADAPTING TO THE ENVIRONMENT

During recent years much attention has been given to understanding the balancing mechanisms which enable mammals to adjust to changes in their physical environment. The interactions between the many factors involved are frequently complex and it is difficult to study one in isolation without distorting the others. For primates the complexities are even more difficult to disentangle, and in the human case social culture adds another dimension to the complexity.

All of the factors which control biological responses interact with those which affect the behaviour of the individual or the social group. This is very evident for Aborigines. They construct shelters appropriate for the climatic conditions using the materials available in the local environment. Desert-living Aborigines, for example, construct summer shelters orientated east–west which at the top exclude the sun and at the bottom have open supports to allow wind – a constant feature of the desert climate – to pass through. To withstand the lower winter temperatures they make shelters under rock ledges or construct igloo-type houses from spinifex, with the small entrance facing away from the wind. Other behavioural adaptations to desert living include sleeping in shade during the middle part of the day, and during summer travelling at night rather than during the day. As well as this desert Aborigines remain near a waterhole during the hot part of the summer, and in the cooler months move about over wider areas, combining hunting in different places with congregating for ritual ceremonies.

There are several levels at which biological adaptation to the physical environment operates. The first of these involves short-term effects. Changes in the environment are monitored by the sensory system, and physiological and/or behavioural responses ensure that the body processes return to normal. Sometimes adjustment is almost immediate, but in other cases it takes several weeks or months, a type of change referred to as *acclimitization*. The second level of adaptation involves longer periods of adjustment which begin during the developmental period, before and after birth. There may be changes in structure, as for example in the responses of the respiratory and circulatory systems to life at high altitudes, or in the setting of hormonal and isoenzyme patterns which control cellular responses. There may be changes also in the level of response of the nervous system to pain, heat, and cold, a type of change known as *habituation*. The third level of adaptation, if the environmental challenge persists over long periods of time, may give rise to survival of better adapted phenotypes. This type of adaptive response is referred to as *genetic selection.*

Australian Aborigines, as we have noted in earlier chapters, expanded to occupy almost all the ecological zones on the continent, from the monsoonal tropics of the north to the cold temperate areas of the south-east and south-west. The initial exploitation of the coastal riverine environments occurred at least 40 000 years ago, which represents some 1500 to 2000 human generations. This is enough for some detectable genetic selection in response to environmental conditions to have occurred, particularly for traits which confer a high level of selective advantage. The arid interior, of course, was colonized much later and selection can have operated for only 350 to 500 generations in these areas. Even so, if selective pressure was high it is possible that some measurable changes have taken place.

Morphological adaptation

If genetic selection has taken place among Aborigines, little evidence of it has been collected. The most likely candidate among morphological traits is for body-build. Birdsell[1] measured 44 adult males, comprising most of the last surviving Aborigines of full descent from the south-east corner of Australia, and compared them with measurements made on adults from Arnhem Land and other places on the continent. The people from the colder south-east were shorter and heavier than those from Arnhem Land.

As well as the difference in body measurements the south-east Australians showed other features which differentiate them from Aborigines in other parts of Australia. Two of these features are of interest here: the degree of skin pigmentaion and the amount of body hair. For south-eastern Australians Birdsell measured the intensity of pigmentation in unexposed areas of the body using a standard colour chart. He found that the categories of red-brown and light-brown were present in 80 per cent of the people in the south-east but in only 5 per cent of those in the north. Birdsell also recorded the type of beard and the quantity and distribution of body hair. Among south-east Australians he found that nearly 90 per cent of males had a heavy beard and abundant body hair compared with 8 and 16 per cent respectively for these traits among people in Arnhem Land.

Birdsell believes the fact that there is a high proportion of persons in south-east Australia of short stature and heavy body build among whom the menfolk have abundant facial and body hair supports his view that these people are descended from immigrants of a different origin from the ancestors of Aborigines in the north. In his view the metrical traits and indices of the south-east Australians suggest a close affinity with the Ainu of Hokkaido. But it can be argued that these traits may represent the end result of genetic selection for life in a colder climate. Short, stocky build, heavy beard, and abundant body hair are all traits favourable to the conservation of body heat in the cold. Equally, the long thin extremities of Aborigines in the arid areas is a morphological adaptation to hot, dry climatic conditions.

Body temperature and metabolism

It is no longer possible to carry out studies of physiological adaptation in Aborigines of full descent from the colder south-east or south-west areas of Australia, to match the observations referred to in the previous section on morphological adaptations. A lot of attention has been devoted, however, to studies of Aborigines still living in the more arid areas and in the tropical north.

The stimulus for some of the early studies came from observations of the capacity of Aborigines to sleep unclothed during winter in the desert, conditions which are intolerable for Europeans.

Sir Stanton Hicks,[2] with collaborators from the University of Adelaide, were among the first to carry out measurements on body and skin temperature and on metabolic rate during August, the coldest month. In the early 1930s they established that when Aborigines sleep unclothed this does not result, as it does for whites, in an increased rate of metabolism. They concluded that Aborigines living under desert winter conditions have an effective vasoconstriction in surface layers of the body, particularly in the extremities, which permits lower skin temperatures (feet 17 °C) and conserves energy loss. However, they also stressed the importance of behavioural adaptations. The traditional arrangement for sleeping consists of a lightly constructed wind-break and one or more burning logs. Acacia and eucalyptus wood found in the arid regions will smoulder all night and produce sufficient radiant heat to reduce the gradient of body to skin temperature. The effectiveness of this behavioural adaptation was demonstrated subjectively by the physiologist Neil Crosby, who told me some years ago that he could sleep comfortably under conditions comparable to those experienced by desert Aborigines. Dogs are also used to help maintain body warmth.

A more objective evaluation of the factors involved was carried out by Scholander and Hammel and their collaborators during the

Fig. 8.1. Diagram of Aboriginal wind-break and fire for controlling heat-loss during sleep under desert conditions.

1950s.[3] They measured body temperatures and oxygen consumption for one or two adult male Aborigines at Areyonga, in central Australia.

The Aborigines constructed the windbreak and arranged the fires in the accustomed manner, in this case with a fire on either side and one or two men between. To keep the fires burning it was necessary for the men to wake up, restoke them, and then fall back to sleep, an activity which occurred 3–10 times during the night. The fires produced a big gradient in skin temperature: on the side distant from the fire the skin temperature often fell to 12–15 °C, whilst on the side nearest the fire it rose sometimes to 45 °C, a surface temperature which is painful to Europeans. Members of the research team slept under similar conditions but their skin temperatures were always higher than those of the Aborigines. Both groups, however, were able to spend the night on a basal oxygen consumption and without any apparent accumulated heat-debt which would have necessitated increased oxygen consumption in the morning.

To test whether Aborigines are better adapted to the extreme cold of desert nights, particularly during the winter, the experimental

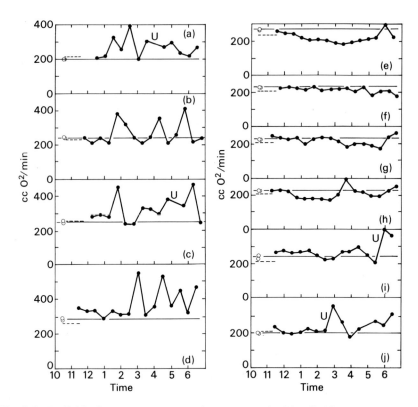

Fig. 8.2. Individual oxygen consumption curves of white (left) and Aboriginal (right) subjects in sleeping bags exposed from late evening (5–7 °C) to dawn (0–2 °C). u = urination.[3]

conditions were altered. The subjects slept in a blanket sleeping-bag sheltered by a thin windbreak on four sides but without fires. Air temperatures during the night fell to between 5° and 0 °C. Under these conditions the white members of the research team showed erratic elevation of their metabolism ranging from the basal rate to twice basal, the increased oxygen consumption being due to periods of restlessness and shivering. Under the same conditions the Aborigines slept with little disturbance and their metabolic rate remained steady, in some cases being even below the basal rate. When bouts of shivering did occur they were nearly always at the time of waking in the morning.

Both Aboriginal and white subjects had reduced rectal and skin temperatures, and toward morning when foot temperatures dropped to 15–17 °C, the whites found this distressingly cold. On the other hand, the Aborigines, despite the lack of metabolic compensation, which meant that foot temperatures fell even further, were able to sleep undisturbed. It is clear that an important adaptation of the desert Aborigine is habituation to extremes of skin temperatures, either through heating to 45 °C from a fire close to the body surface, or to below 15 °C in the foot through vasoconstriction and radiation to the night sky. Such temperatures in non-habituated Europeans caused extreme discomfort, and it seems that this is true also for non-habituated Aborigines. For example, in the tropic north Hammel and his associates and Morrison[4] found that even when the air temperature was above 26 °C their Aboriginal subjects insisted on some form of cover at night and were uncomfortable when skin temperatures started to fall.

In addition to adaptation by habituation to extremes of surface temperature there is another important physiological adaptation to cold in desert-living Aborigines. The studies of Scholander and Hammel confirmed earlier reports that Aborigines in the cold effectively reduce the supply of blood to the surface layers of the body. This restriction of blood-flow results in lower skin temperatures and makes unnecessary the increased metabolic activity that would otherwise be needed to compensate for the excessive heat loss. This vasoconstriction does not occur in Europeans even when acclimatized. Tests on a group of young Norwegians showed that after six weeks' exposure to sleeping with minimal covering in mountain areas and with night temperatures similar to those in central Australia (0°–5 °C) their body surface temperature remained relatively warm and their metabolic rate increased almost entirely as a result of shivering. Such a method of compensation, of course, wastes energy and is unlikely to be selected for genetically, particularly in areas where food is not abundant.

The earliest observations on the rate of oxygen consumption by Aborigines showed that in the desert areas their metabolic rate was relatively low. Subsequently Stanton Hicks and his colleagues and also Wardlaw and his associates concluded that, when corrected for the conditions under which the measurements were made, the

Aborigines' metabolic rate showed no essential departure from normal.[5] However, Hicks found that although the rate of oxygen consumption was within the accepted range, increased oxygen consumption following eating meat (the specific dynamic response) more rapidly reached higher values in Aborigines than in whites. Hicks suggested that such a response was a valuable adaptation in hunting people. No recent studies have been made to verify these observations or to check if the increased specific dynamic response may have become modified as a result of the changing dietary patterns among Aborigines during recent years.

Derek Roberts[6] has shown that there are marked differences in metabolic rates of people from different parts of the world. Chinese and Japanese have low, Europeans somewhat higher, and American Indians the highest rates of oxygen consumption. It is possible that the high rates of American Indians are due to the persistence of genes setting levels for higher metabolism which were selected for in their ancestors before they crossed the Bering land-bridge from their cold Siberian homeland. Within the Americas further differentiation has taken place in the rate of metabolic activity. American Indians and Eskimos in the extreme north have higher metabolic rates than do Indians in Central America. Rates in the extreme south, in Patagonia, are comparable to those in the north.

Though the climatic contrasts within Australia have not been as extreme as that between Siberia and the more temperate and tropical areas of the world, they may have been great enough to have produced some selective changes in the metabolic levels in Aborigines from the tropical north and the colder south-east and south-west parts of the continent. Unfortunately there have been no studies so far of metabolic rate in relation to the different climatic zones occupied by the Aborigines.

The need for water

In the view of Victor Macfarlane,[7] man is fundamentally a creature of the wet tropics. He lacks a thick covering of insulating fur, he has a high rate of sweating and water turnover, a low capacity for concentrating urine in the kidneys, and is capable of reproduction at all times of the year. All these traits are characteristic of animals which evolved in the tropics. During the evolution of modern man, however, the genus *Homo* spread across the world and eventually colonized areas ranging from the tundras and marginal glaciated areas of northern Europe and America to the deserts of Asia, Africa, and Australia. Macfarlane points out that *Homo sapiens* was sufficiently biologically rugged as well as cunning, to survive glaciations, the intervening wetter periods, and aridity. Although the time when man first began to use shelter, clothing, and fire is not certain, all were being used during the last glaciation from 60 000 to 12 000 years ago. These are important defences against cold, but one of the critical limiting factors for human survival is access to water. In a neutral environment a man denied access to water may survive for two weeks, but in a hot environment, in the sun, death will occur within a day if access to water is denied. This dependence on water has focused the attention of many physiologists on the way in which Aborigines in the desert metabolize this scarce commodity.

The most detailed of these studies has been carried out by Macfarlane himself, who suggests that the ancestors of the Aborigines spent most of their evolutionary life in southern Asia, and even after moving into Australia they colonized first the wetter coastal and riverine areas. When they moved finally into the more arid areas they took with them relatively high rates of water consumption and sweating, which still persist. With his research team Macfarlane has made observations on four different groups of Aborigines, three living in arid areas and one in central Arnhem Land. In the arid areas the range of air temperatures during the day was 34–42 °C, with low humidities, whilst in Arnhem Land the temperature range was 30–36 °C with the humidity at the time of maximum temperature between 40–70 per cent.

All the Aboriginal groups studied are able to drink water faster and to take in a larger volume than members of the research team, but this difference is more marked for desert-living groups than for those in Arnhem Land. The characteristic pattern in the desert areas is to take a large drink shortly after dawn and another in the evening. Even in cool weather the desert Aborigines drink 2 per cent of their body weight in 10–35 seconds (an average of 17 seconds per litre) whilst whites, in order to drink 2 per cent of their body weight, need 156 seconds (an average of 100 seconds per litre). Aboriginal children can also swallow large quantities of water rapidly.

The distribution of water in the body is different in whites and Aborigines. In unacculturated desert Aborigines the extra-cellular fluid volume averages 25–28 per cent of body weight compared to just under 20 per cent for whites. Total body water for desert Aborigines is 66 per cent and 69 per cent for Aborigines in Arnhem Land compared to 62 per cent of body weight for members of the research team. Thus there is relatively more extra-cellular volume and more total body-water available in the Aborigines.

Although body-water volume and water intake is greater in

Aborigines, there is also a higher rate of water turnover, which can be measured by heavy water dilution. This is manifest also in two ways: urine excretion and sweating. Overnight urine volumes for desert Aborigines frequently reaches 700 ml, with whites averaging 280 ml and rarely reaching 300 ml. The urinary osmotic pressures among the whites are greater than those of the Aborigines. For Aborigines in Arnhem Land the differences are not so great, but the urinary concentration is still lower and the volume greater than among members of the research team in the same environment.

Table 8.1. Body water content and rate of water turnover in various groups under differing climatic conditions (data from Macfarlane 1976)[7]

	Body-water (ml/kg)	Body solids‡ (%)	Water turnover† (ml/l/24 hr)
New Guinea			
Tropical island (hot)			
Melanesians	645	35.5	114
Europeans	600	40.0	70
Mountains (cool)			
Melanesians	731	26.9	66
Europeans	620	38.0	68
Arnhem Land			
Wet tropics			
Aboriginals	695	30.5	173
Europeans	618	38.2	130
Central Desert			
Aboriginals	660	34.0	143
Europeans	617	38.3	86

†Expressed as amount per litre of body water turned over daily, because of differing body solids content in the groups.
‡The body solids are proportional to the amount of fat stored.

When subjected to water deprivation during summer in the desert other interesting differences appear. For the tests both Aborigines and whites drank to satisfy their thirst between dawn and 7 a.m. and then took no further fluid until 5 p.m. During the course of the day two or three walks, each of 5 km, were taken in the sun across the desert with high ambient temperatures (35 °C+). The early morning urine flow rates of the Aborigines in the hot weather were above those of the whites. Sweating began in the Aborigines at about 9 a.m.

Table 8.2. Water-loss during one hour's walking in the desert sun (data from Macfarlane 1973)[7]

	Mean weight (kg)	Urine flow (ml/min)		
		Before	During	After
Morning 29–22 °C				
Europeans	82.1	0.4	0.3	0.4
Aborigines	60.3	2.6	1.3	0.9
Afternoon 34–23 °C				
Europeans	80.6	0.5	0.2	0.3
Aborigines	59.1	0.8	0.6	0.8

and the urine flow rates decreased slowly as dehydration progressed. The response of the whites to these conditions was more dramatic, with a rapid reduction of urine volume by 70–80 per cent.

In the Arnhem Land environment there were similar but smaller differences between the two groups. At the beginning of the day urine flow rates were about four times higher in Aborigines than in whites. During exposure to heat and exercise the flow rates were reduced in both groups but Aborigines still maintained a rate approximately twice that of the whites. When the exercise stopped flow-rates increased in the Aborigines, but water retention continued in the whites. The same pattern of response was observed among Aborigines in each of the four groups studied, though the difference between them and the members of the research team was least for the Arnhem Land Aborigines. Initially, rates of water excretion were high and although this was reduced during the periods of exercise during the heat of the day, after the exercise stopped there was still sufficient body-water left so that the urine flow rates increased again in the Aborigines: this did not occur in the whites.

Rates of sweating also showed important differences between the two groups. As measured by loss of body weight, desert Aborigines sweated at twice the rate of the whites during the periods of walking in the sun. Again the differences in Arnhem Land were smaller, the loss of body weight being only 15–32 per cent greater in the Aborigines.

More significant was the observation that Aborigines suppress sweating in a humid environment. Sweating was measured by collecting the moisture in a plastic bag placed around the arm. The sweat

Table 8.3. Effects of vigorous exercise under desert conditions (37 °C dry bulb, 23 °C wet bulb). 30 cm steps at 30 per minute for 5 minutes (data from Macfarlane 1973)[7]

	Before			Exercise	Recovery			
	Pulse rate	Blood pressure	Oral temperature		Pulse rate at 1 min 5 min		Blood pressure at 2 min	Oral temperature
Aborigines								
Average	87	99/69	36.8	5 minutes' stepping	132	94	116/71	36.7
Rise					45	7	17/2	−0.1
Europeans								
Average	85	138/91	37.0		142	101	181/81	37.0
Rise					57	16	43/−10	0

collected per hour was only about one-fifth the amount of the sweat collected from whites under the same conditions. This greater ability of Aborigines to suppress sweating was confirmed in tests carried out in the laboratory using Aborigines and part-Aborigines who had been away from either desert or tropical conditions for some time. It was found that sweat suppression was even faster and greater in extent among Aboriginal children.

The faculty of sweat suppression when the arm is placed in a humid environment could well explain the apparent contradiction between Macfarlane's studies and those of Wyndham and his collaborators in north Queensland.[8] The latter workers measured sweating rates in the saturated environment of plastic tents maintained at 32 °C. They found that Aborigines produced about 62 per cent of the amount of sweat produced by well-acclimatized Europeans under the same conditions. The investigators believe this represents an adaptation of survival value, since reduced sweating rates allow the conservation of body water and salt. Macfarlane's studies suggest, however, that when the humidity is high Aborigines have an efficient sweat-suppression mechanism. If the Queensland Aborigines were reinvestigated under conditions approximating more closely those found in the normal environment it is possible that their sweating rates would be similar to those found by Macfarlane for Aborigines in Arnhem Land.

Macfarlane concludes that there are at least three quantitative physiological differences between Aborigines and whites in handling water. Firstly, the ability to take in large volumes of water rapidly, secondly rapid excretion of water through the kidneys, and thirdly higher rates of sweating with rapid sweat suppression in a humid environment. Desert Aborigines survive the rigors of summer, he believes, by remaining near water sources and going without food rather than water. But they are able to go for longer periods without water than whites because they can take in large quantities of water, for which the extra-cellular space acts as a reservoir. This enables them to traverse considerable distances, either in the hunt, in food gathering, or in a search for another water-hole from which they can replenish their depleted store of body water.

Regulation of salt

An important function related to the use of water by the body is the mechanism for regulating the ionic concentration of the blood and tissues. This is achieved by changes in the salt content of sweat and the excretion of ions by the kidneys. Kuno showed, in classical studies on acclimitization by Europeans, that the excretion of salts in the sweat dropped to near zero during a period of several weeks after they moved from a temperate to a hot climate.[9] This capacity to acclimatize and reduce the loss of salt in the sweat probably explains the differences noted by Macfarlane in his Aboriginal and white subjects. The sodium excretion in the sweat of the least-acculturated of the Aboriginal desert groups was less than half that in the sweat of white members of the research team, but it approximated more closely the white values as the degree of contact with white Australian culture increased. However, there was no significant difference in Na^+ output in the sweat of whites and Arnhem Land Aborigines.

The renal responses of whites and Aborigines showed more marked differences. Aborigines with the least contact with white culture increased sodium and potassium excretion in the urine during exercise in the heat, whilst the whites reduced it under the same conditions to 30 per cent of the resting value. More acculturated Aborigines in the desert and in Arnhem Land had a salt retention pattern similar to that of whites during exercise in the heat. There were more individuals in this group, however, who maintained a salt excretion pattern similar to that of people who had minimal contact with white culture.

Macfarlane interprets these differences in renal patterns as a function of salt concentration of the sweat and the volume of extra-cellular fluid. If the volume of extra-cellular fluid, which can be drawn on for sweating, is large and salt concentration of the sweat is low, salt will be excreted in the urine to avoid its accumulation in the plasma. Since whites secrete twice the electrolyte concentration in their sweat compared to that which Aborigines produce, and whites have smaller amounts of water stored in the extra-cellular space, sweating will be accompanied by a loss of salt and a reduction in volume of water. These changes will be sufficient to mobilize hormonal salt retention by the kidneys and so reduce output. He points out also that one effect of contact with whites is to change dietary patterns and thereby increase the intake of salt. This will necessitate increased excretion of salt in the sweat. Under conditions of culture contact, therefore, Aborigines come to resemble whites more closely in their metabolic patterns, with consequential changes in the physiological handling of water and salt.

Blood pressure and cardiovascular function

Several studies have reported differences between Aborigines and whites for a number of other physiological or biochemical traits, and also noted that the differences are inversely proportional to the degree of contact with white Australian culture. The changes noted in response to acculturation include a rise in blood cholesterol, phospholipids, and mucoprotein, a change in the menstrual pattern of women, increased immunity to community diseases, and a rise in blood pressure.

Most observers have found that systolic blood pressures in Aborigines living a partially traditional life are lower than for whites and rise more slowly with age. One study, in Queensland, shows a contrary result, with higher mean systolic pressures in Aborigines, but falling toward the white levels with increasing contact with white Australian culture.[10] However, Nye reported 40 years ago that Aborigines in Queensland have low blood pressure.[11] This apparent contradiction may be due to differing salt levels, since other studies have shown a positive correlation between blood pressure and salt intake. This is relevant also in interpreting the blood pressures recorded for the hunter–gatherers studied by Macfarlane in central Australia. He estimated that the Aborigines obtained only 40 to 80 millequivalents of salt per day from their food, while the whites obtained between 180 and 300 meq. per day, these high values undoubtedly contributing to the elevated blood pressure in the whites.

As part of the studies on water metabolism in Aborigines, Macfarlane made tests on the cardiovascular response to exercise of men living in the hot environments in either the desert or Arnhem Land. During summer, desert Aborigines spend most of the day sleeping in the shade, but they are capable of vigorous exercise when hunting. This sometimes involves walking, running, or stalking for long periods of time, as well as carrying home the quarry if the hunt has been successful. Macfarlane's tests required a standard exercise of making 150 steps of height 30 cm. The results showed that resting systolic blood pressure was lower in Aborigines than in whites and that both the Aborigines' blood pressure and pulse rate rose less during exercise and recovery was quicker than in whites. On the other hand the diastolic blood pressure in whites was lower than in Aborigines during the recovery period, probably because of the greater vasodilation among the members of the research group. Resting blood pressure among the Arnhem Land Aborigines was higher and the rise during exercise greater than in the group of desert Aborigines, tested by Macfarlane, who had least contact with whites.

Several recent investigations have been concerned with the effects of urban life on blood pressure in Aborigines. Edwards and his collaborators[12] found mean systolic blood pressures for 40-year-old

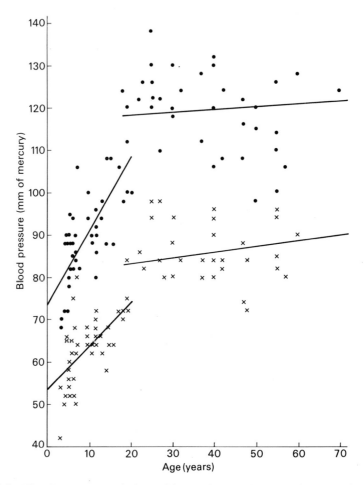

Fig. 8.3. Blood-pressure variation with age in Aboriginal males at Maningrida. Upper curves — systolic; lower curves — diastolic.

Aborigines in various parts of South Australia to be almost the same as those for white males and females of the same age in Tecumseh, Michigan. Hypertensive individuals were more common among the younger Aborigines (i.e. those less than 40 years of age) living in more urban situations, than among those still living a partly traditional life. They concluded that different life-styles could affect blood pressure and that no definite support could be found for a direct effect of ethnicity.

Blood pressure is known to be affected by many variables, including age, obesity, and diet, as well as by psychological stress. Most of the studies on Aborigines have not controlled all these factors and frequently the number of persons tested has been small, making it difficult to assess the significance of the effect of genetic and environmental components. Similar difficulties arise in the interpretation of many other physiological or biochemical differences between Aborigines and white Australians. Among such reported differences are higher levels in Aborigines for vitamin B_{12}, proteins, and urate levels in serum and taste-threshold for phenyl-thiocarbamide. Some of the reported differences are undoubtedly due to the presence of intestinal parasites, viral or other infectious agents, as well as inadequate diets in the Aboriginal subjects. When these factors approximate to the norms found in whites the observed differences may disappear.

Alcohol metabolism

A problem which has attracted considerable attention during the last decade is the rate at which alcohol is metabolized in different individuals or ethnic groups. The possibility that inherited differences exist for the physiological response to alcohol has been suggested as one reason why some people become disorientated more easily than others after taking alcoholic drinks. Other studies have placed emphasis on the importance of social and psychological factors in explaining these differences. Studies of alcohol metabolism received a fresh impetus when Fenna and his colleagues reported that blood-alcohol levels in Canadian whites fell significantly faster than in Eskimos and Canadian Indians after intravenous injection of standard doses of alcohol.[13] There was additional support for the possibility of a genetic basis for varying responses to alcohol in the discovery that Japanese have a very high frequency of a genetic variant of liver alcohol dehydrogenase. This fact, coupled with claims that Japanese do not tolerate alcohol as well as Europeans, suggested that persons carrying this genetic variant are unable to detoxicate ethanol as fast as those without the variant. However, more recent studies do not support this suggestion, and it is now believed that the control of alcohol metabolism is through the liver aldehyde dehydrogenase rather than the alcohol dehydrogenase.[14]

In a recent critical review of the experimental evidence relating to differences in alcohol metabolism Reed[15] has concluded that, with the exception of North American Indian groups, there is no difference between peoples in different parts of the world in their average ability to metabolize ethanol. This is the conclusion reached also by Marinovich and colleagues in a limited study of alcohol metabolism in Aborigines and whites in Western Australia.[16] The subjects were given, per kg of body weight, 1 ml of absolute ethanol mixed with water or fruit juice, and the blood-alcohol concentration was monitored over a period of several hours. The mean rate of fall of blood-alcohol level in mg per hour was 17.7 for whites and 18.1 for Aborigines, the difference between the means being non-significant, although among the Aborigines there was a much greater variation about the mean. However, many of the subjects in this study were not of full Aboriginal descent and the influence which this may have had on the result needs further investigation.

There is an urgent need for a more detailed study of alcohol metabolism among Aborigines and whites, taking into account the effects of sex and age, body composition, diet, and previous experiences of alcohol use. It may be relevant also that the universal ability of Aborigines to drink two litres of fluid in 30–40 seconds probably encourages the rapid ingestion of wine or beer, with a consequent rapid rise in circulating alcohol. Climatic and social factors which are relevant to understanding the response to drinking alcohol will also need to be taken into account if we are to achieve a better understanding of this important problem.

9

CHANGING PATTERNS OF HEALTH

The health and disease patterns of a community can be understood fully only in relation to the total ecological relationships within that community. These relationships range from the broad climatic and geographical factors which determine the distribution of disease vectors, through the physical factors such as housing, water supply, and sanitation, to the demographic and social factors which influence the interpersonal relationships between members of the group, and their response to challenges from within the group as well as from outside. In attempting to outline the health of Aborigines all these aspects are of importance. In addition it is necessary to add a dimension of time. What was the health of Aborigines in the past, how has it changed, and what causes can be found for the changes which have occurred?

When we look into the remote past we find there is almost no information on specific diseases which afflicted Aborigines before they had contact with people from outside the continent. In the absence of written records or of oral history about disease the only clues come from an examination of skeletons for evidence of pathological changes. Such studies in other parts of the world have provided valuable information about diseases in prehistoric communities, though the evidence is not always indisputable and many diseases, of course, even when they have a fatal outcome, do not always leave tell-tale marks on the skeleton.

Two recent studies[1] have been made on skeletal material in Australia. In the first of these, Sandison examined bones in museum collections, whilst in the second, Prokopec based his conclusions on the skeletons from the Roonka burials in South Australia. Sandison noted a number of minor congenital anomalies. Dental caries was rare, but the teeth were frequently worn down and pulp exposure and abscesses at the roots of the teeth were not uncommon. No examples of cutting holes in the skull were observed, but damage caused by blows with blunt objects was found in many cases. Healed fractures, particularly of the forearm, were also present and Sandison believes these were caused by warding off blows during fights. Similarly there was evidence of damage by sharp weapons, such as spears, in the region of the wrist and lower thigh. These sometimes resulted in purulent infection which left their mark on the bones in these parts.

Severe degenerative joint disease of the osteoarthritic type was also seen, disorders which, in the spine, sometimes led to bone fusion, or ankylosis. There were also occasional examples of 'boomerang' tibia, though without evidence of infection or malnutrition. This disorder is commonly attributed to infection with treponema, organisms responsible for syphilis and yaws. Indeed, Sandison found evidence for treponemal disease in skeletons from the Murray River area, supporting the view that a form of endemic syphilis or some other 'treponemid' disease was present in Australia before Europeans arrived. Of interest also is his finding that there is no evidence of leprosy in any of the bones which he examined, even in those which came from the tropical north.

The Roonka skeletons, of course, come from a single locality, but cover a time-span of at least 7000 years. Prokopec found evidence from Roonka similar to that noted by Sandison from other parts of the country. Damage to bones resulting from fights or blows was not uncommon, grinding wear on the teeth was well developed and there was clear evidence of diseases of the gums and oral cavity as well as tooth abscesses. Dental caries, however, was not present, except in teeth from the most recent burials, belonging to the period after contact with Europeans. Prokopec believes the number of child skeletons indicates that the expectation of life was relatively short. But those who survived into adulthood achieved a stature approximately the same as that for Aborigines living at present in the centre of Australia.

So these clues from bones enable us to say that in the period before contact with Europeans aggressiveness against individuals often involved damage to bones, that wound infection occurred, that skeletal abnormalities and joint diseases were present, and that some infections, such as those caused by treponemal organisms, were present and others, such as leprosy, were not.

The devastation of conquest

Whatever the standard of health among Aborigines may have been at the time when European settlement began, the impact of that settlement upon their health was dramatic and devastating.

The first evidence of this impact came only a year after the First Fleet dropped anchor in Sydney Cove in 1788. In April 1789 small-pox was raging among Aborigines in the Sydney area, and many deaths resulted. The origin of the epidemic is unknown, though it is reported that the surgeons with the Fleet had brought 'variolus matter in bottles'. Some authorities believe it was introduced by visiting French ships under the command of La Perouse early in 1788, others that it was brought by Malay trepangers to the north coast of Australia and crossed the continent from there. Whatever its source, this epidemic of smallpox spread rapidly and left traces of its presence in pock-marked survivors in New South Wales, Victoria, and South Australia. It was followed by another violent epidemic of the same disease which started in 1829-30 and con-tinued until 1845. There was a further epidemic in 1860-9, but by this latter date the Aboriginal populations of south-east Australia and elsewhere had been drastically reduced through the effects of introduced diseases, and also by the complete disruption of their natural balance with the environment.

The European settlement of the coastal fringe, which commenced in 1788, extended slowly into the interior and around the coast from 1820. Armed clashes occurred, tribal lands were occupied, many diseases took their toll, and the natural food of the survivors was destroyed. Many tribes vanished in one or two generations.

The demographic effects of disease were outlined by Basedow[2] in a review of the health of Aborigines in the early years of coloniza-tion, and in 1932 Basedow stated 'at the rate havoc is at present being wrought by civilization among the pureblooded section of the Aboriginal community, it will not be many years before the last of them have shared the unenviable lot of their Tasmanian brothers . . .'.

Indeed, it was in Tasmania that the impact of colonization had an irreversible effect, resulting in rapid decline and then extinction of the Aborigines. Rhys Jones[3] estimates that the Aboriginal population of Tasmania, which at the time of first contact was between 3000 and 5000 persons, declined between 1815 and 1830 at the rate of 10-15 per cent per annum, the last Tasmanian dying in 1876. A similar picture has been outlined by Diane Barwick for the Aborigines in Victoria. Of the 11 500 Aborigines estimated to have lived in that area in pre-contact days, only 2000 remained in 1863: all observers, she says, 'commented on the extraordinary mortality of the 1850's'.[4]

What happened in other parts of the continent is not documented so well, but the situation in the other areas settled by whites was

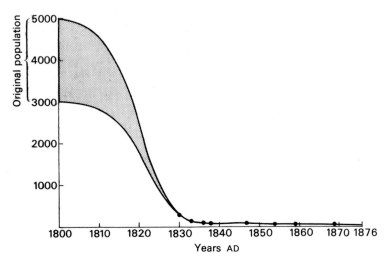

Fig. 9.1. Decline of the Tasmanian population of Aborigines of full descent (from Jones).[3]

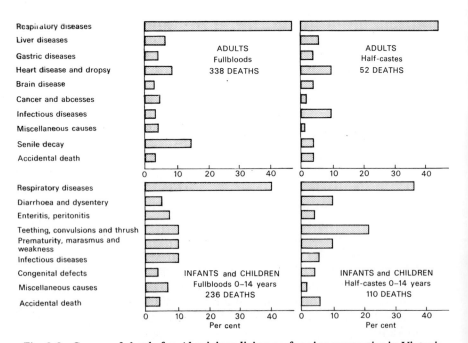

Fig. 9.2. Causes of death for Aborigines living on farming properties in Victoria in 1876–1912 (from Barwick).[4]

similar. For example, in the far west of New South Wales in the area around the town of Bourke there were approximately 3000 Aborigines in 1845. The number had fallen to 1000 in 1863 and to less than 100 in 1884.

Basedow considered disease to be a major factor in the population decline of the Aboriginal. He suggested that they were particularly susceptible to many diseases to which they had not been exposed before the arrival of Europeans, including measles, influenza, syphilis, gonorrhoea, typhoid fever, whooping cough, diphtheria, leprosy, tuberculosis, and hydatid. After their arrival these diseases took a heavy toll. It has been claimed that many Aborigines at Point Pearce station in South Australia died of Bright's disease, a severe kidney disorder. There were epidemics of typhoid fever at Barambah, Queensland, in 1915 and 1926, and at Point Pearce in South Australia in 1923. Measles epidemics were reported from Western Australia in 1867 and from Queensland and South Australia in late 1890. The 1867 epidemic was estimated to have carried off half the population and high rates of secondary infections, particularly pneumonia, were reported in other epidemics. Influenza was also a serious cause of death in 1860 and other epidemics occurred in 1875, 1891, 1901, 1908, 1911, 1915, and throughout Australia during the pandemic of 1919. In Queensland during the 1919 pandemic 67 out of 600 Aborigines died at Barambah and 31 out of 200 died at Taroom. It has been claimed that the mortality among Aborigines in all areas of the country from this influenza pandemic was 25 to 50 per cent, but there are no reliable records to confirm this high mortality.

Aborigines were considered to be more susceptible than Europeans to many other introduced diseases, including tuberculosis. The form of this latter disease in Aborigines was different from that experienced commonly by Europeans and it was a cause of great mortality. Nineteenth-century observers noted that this was true as well for syphilis and it is possible that this disease contributed significantly to the decimation of the Aboriginal tribes.

Present mortality and morbidity in children

The alienation of tribal lands reached its climax early in this century. Deprived of the freedom to hunt and gather freely in many areas the Aborigines drifted toward settlements where they had access not only to the assistance provided by religious orders but also to the detritus of European culture. In some cases new settlements were established in localities where formerly only a small number of persons could have survived by traditional means. In others shanty settlements grew on the fringes of small towns or groups of Aborigines congregated in the squalid inner suburbs of large cities.

Each of these situations has its own ecology: all are characterized by poverty, by lack of a stable economic base, and by the absence of that sense of community which could engender a pride in Aboriginal culture. This constellation produces a pattern of high morbidity and mortality. In children dietary imbalance is common and there is retardation of growth and a high incidence of intestinal infection, contagious skin disorders, and anaemia, as well as eye and ear infections which lead frequently to impairment of sight and hearing. This, in turn, gives rise to learning and behavioural problems which are aggravated by the inadequacies of the physical and social environment.

This general pattern is now well established in many parts of the continent. Data collected by workers at the Queensland Institute of Medical Research illustrate it in more detail.[5] Approximately three-fifths of the 25 000 Aborigines in Queensland are located in rural areas and about one-tenth are in the major urban centres. A large proportion of the rural Aboriginal population live on government-controlled settlements, some of them until recently under close supervision by Church Missions.

A survey of mortality and morbidity in Queensland settlements was carried out in 1967. Table 9.1 summarizes the major findings for mortality up to 4 years of age. The number of still births, of deaths

Table 9.1. Age-specific death rates for Aborigines in 10 Queensland communities (1962–7) compared with the rates for the total Queensland population (1967).

	Aboriginal communities (A)	Total population Queensland (T)	Ratio A/T
Still-birth rate (per 1000 live births)	45.0	10.7	4.2
Deaths of premature babies (per 1000 live births)	13.5	3.4	3.9
Deaths under 1 month (per 1000 live births)	46.0	12.1	3.8
Deaths under 1 year (per 1000 live births)	112	17.7	6.3
Deaths 1–4 years (per 1000 pop'n in age-group)	17.4	1.3	13.4

of babies and infants under one month of age, and the crude death rate for all ages are two to four times the rates in the general Queensland population. The contrast is most marked for the infant mortality rate (under 12 months of age) and for the toddler death rate (12 months to under 5 years). This latter rate is thirteen times that in the general Queensland population. David Jose has analysed the causes of infant death and finds that in 50 per cent of cases the causes are 'gastroenteritis' or 'pneumonia', giving a death rate per 1000 cases at risk for these two diseases 22 times greater for the Aboriginal children than for non-Aborigines. In 80 per cent of deaths due to these two disorders there is an abnormal loss of weight for at least one month prior to death, which suggests that protein-calorie malnutrition is a precipitating factor.

The infant deaths frequently occur in epidemic form following an influx of visitors to the settlements at holiday periods. The disease is nearly always rapid from the first signs of illness to death in 4-12 hours. Autopsies show an extensive infection in both the respiratory and gastrointestinal tracts. A similar picture emerges from study of the causes of death among older children. The death rate from 'gastroenteritis' and 'pneumonia' is more than 30 times greater among Aboriginal children at risk in this age group than for similarly aged non-Aboriginal children in Queensland. Other infections such as meningitis and cerebral abscess account for a further 28 per cent of deaths among the older children.

To complement the mortality statistics, patterns of morbidity were obtained for the children in six of the Queensland Aboriginal settlements. Jose and Welch[6] found that growth-retardation affects 50 per cent of Aboriginal children in the age range six months to three years, and that 16 per cent have severe growth retardation associated with anaemia and infections of the respiratory tract, skin, and bowel. Clinical and laboratory studies have detected deficiencies in iron, ascorbic acid, and in total calories; in addition, low serum levels of albumin, cholesterol, folate, and other vitamins are found frequently.

The primary precipitating causes are nutritional deficiencies in the mothers and inadequate infant feeding after weaning. This is followed by infections leading to intestinal malabsorption which further aggravates the growth retardation. A high proportion of the children dying from gastroenteritis or pneumonia also experienced ear infections severe enough to cause deafness and these children were also growth-retarded. Among those who survive, the growth-retarded children have poorer educational and employment records, which helps to perpetuate the cycle of deprivation.

Attention has been focused on the high infant and toddler mortality in Queensland, but correspondingly high rates among Aboriginal children have been reported from many other parts of Australia.[7] Table 9.2 gives comparative figures for infant mortality in three States for the years 1973–7. For Western Australia there are also detailed figures available for morbidity patterns. This is made possible because this State records the ethnic affiliation of patients entering its hospitals. Relevant figures are given in Table 9.3. The commonest cause of sickness demanding hospital attention is disease

Table 9.2. Aboriginal birth, still-birth, and infant-mortality rates, and comparable data for total Australian population

	1973	1974	1975	1976	1977
Crude birth rate					
(per 1000 population)					
Queensland	37.8	34.5	32.6	32.3	29.2
Western Australia	32.5	32.1	31.5	26.8	—
Northern Territory	35.9	34.4	36.0	32.8	32.6
Australia	18.5	18.0	16.9	16.4	16.1
Still-birth rate					
(per 1000 Aboriginal births)					
Queensland	21.5	42.1	20.6	25.4	39.8
Western Australia	—	—	17.0	20.2	—
Northern Territory	20.4	34.3	18.6	34.7	36.5
Australia	11.7	11.8	10.3	10.4	9.3
Infant mortality					
(per 1000 Aboriginal livebirths)					
Queensland	109.9	70.4	54.2	66.7	54.1
Northern Territory	79.7	55.6	50.1	52.8	74.6
Australia	16.5	16.1	14.3	13.8	12.5

of the respiratory system, followed by infective and parasitic disease, with an almost equal number of admissions for accidents, poisoning, and violence. Disorders of the blood, cancers, and congenital anomalies are relatively under-represented.

The relative importance of these morbidity patterns is indicated by comparing them with hospital admissions for white patients. For example, although Aborigines constitute about 4.0 per cent of children under the age of 16 in the Western Australian population, Aboriginal children admitted to a large paediatric hospital amounted to 12 per cent of all patients with gastroenteritis and dysentery, 56 per cent of patients with intestinal parasites, 27 per cent with nutritional disorders, 25 per cent of admissions for children with discharging ears, and 16 per cent for pneumonia. Not only were relatively more Aboriginal children admitted to hospital, but the duration of their stay was longer. Aboriginal infants with intestinal infections spent an average 23 days compared to 6 days for white infants. Comparable figures for other diseases are 21 days and compared to 14 days for intestinal parasites, 28 days compared to 16

Table. 9.3. Morbidity statistics for Aborigines in Western Australia. Discharge rate from hospital per 1000 population (1973)

Type of disorder	Aborigines (A)	Non-Aborigines (NA)	Ratio A/NA
Infective and parasitic	76.2	7.2	10.6
Neoplasms	3.5	8.1	0.4
Endocrine, nutritional, and metabolic	12.3	2.5	4.9
Blood and bone marrow	3.7	1.1	3.4
Mental	8.4	4.8	1.7
Nervous system and eyes and ears	40.6	9.6	4.2
Circulatory system	12.4	13.9	0.9
Respiratory system	123.7	24.0	5.1
Digestive system	17.1	20.2	0.8
Genito-urinary system	18.6	21.2	0.9
Skin and subcutaneous	35.0	5.9	5.9
Musculo-skeletal	6.2	9.9	0.6
Congenital anomalies	61.7	45.8	1.3
Accidents, poisoning, and violence	74.2	26.9	3.7

days for nutritional disorders, and 19 days compared to 5 days for ear infections.

When the Western Australian morbidity statistics for Aborigines are broken down into geographical regions it is striking that the south-west corner of the State has higher morbidity rates for nearly every disorder than other regions. For infective and parasitic diseases and for diseases of the respiratory system, of the skin, and of the digestive system the rates are all very much higher in the south-west, the rates being as much as twice the next highest region. This is true also for diseases of the nervous system as well as for accidents, poisoning, and violence.

Recently the figures for all children under 15 years of age admitted to hospitals in Western Australia in 1976 have been analysed.[8] Although Aborigines in this age-group account for only 4 per cent of the State's population, in this analysis they accounted for 39 per cent of admissions for 'gastroenteritis' and for 58 per cent of the bed-days occupied by children with gastroenteritis. In the Kimberley region the admission rate of Aboriginal infants with gastroenteritis exceeded 100 per cent, a figure which indicates that many infants spent more than one period in hospital during the year.

More detailed analysis of the Kimberley statistics shows that the morbidity patterns for gastroenteritis can vary enormously from community to community. Table 9.4 shows a more than tenfold difference between communities in the incidence of gastroenteritis for infants under one year of age, a difference which reflects the ecological situation of these communities. The two with the very high incidences are close to rural towns, whilst the low-incidence

Table 9.4. Number of episodes of 'gastroenteritis' per 1000 per year in three Kimberley communities

	Age	
	Less than 1 year	1–4 years
Community A (n = 250)	1400	773
Community B (n = 278)	1352	435
Community C (n = 187)	111	158

community is relatively isolated, with good local food and water supplies and where Aboriginal mothers are encouraged to breast-feed their infants. This latter point is of great importance. Many Aborigines, in common with people elsewhere, use bottle-feeding. Under conditions prevailing in most Aboriginal communities the formulae are often inadequately prepared and the bottles are grossly contaminated, resulting in the cross-infection of infants. Moreover, the infants receiving the formula feeds lack the protection of the antibodies against local infections which they would have received from the mother's breast-milk.

Protein-calorie malnutrition

Several studies indicate that infection following protein-calorie malnutrition is the most common cause of death in young children. Those dying or suffering from chronic infection are more severely growth-retarded than the survivors. The apparent improvement in the health status of Aboriginal children from about the age of two years, as measured by their mean growth curves, may therefore be due to the selective mortality of smaller children in the younger age groups.

Another important consequence of growth retardation is its association with a complex of other biological indicators of maladaptation. The growth-retarded children have a significantly higher prevalence of chronic streptococcal infection and higher loads of intestinal parasites. Their serum has increased immunoglobulin levels, with unusually high antibody titres against group A streptococci and also antibodies against a number of tissue antigens similar to the pattern in acute rheumatic fever. Clinical tests of responses to specific antigens show that such children have depressed humoral and cellular responses to some of the antigens. Ford and his colleagues have suggested that these altered humoral and cellular responses are the results of higher loads of infection which, in turn, is a consequence of protein-calorie malnutrition during infancy.[9]

The relationship between malnutrition and intestinal infection is now accepted as a widespread phenomenon, not only among Aborigines but in other disadvantaged populations. The increased level of bacterial contamination in the gut produces damage to the enzyme-secreting cells of the brush border and depresses the activity of the digestive enzymes. This is particularly important for the disaccaridases, the enzymes which break down sugars in the gut. Secondary lactose intolerance, due to deficiency of the disaccharidase, lactase, induced by damage to the mucosal lining of the gut, is one of the main causes for protracted diarrhoea in malnourished children.

Lactase deficiency can also be genetic in origin, and this form of the deficiency is widespread around the world, particularly in Africa and Asia. Elliot and his colleagues[10] believe that lactase deficiency of this type is common in Aborigines, but it is not clear whether this is a primary inherited deficiency or one which is due to secondary effects resulting from damage to the intestinal mucosa caused by parasites.

Whether the lactase deficiency is genetic or secondary in origin, the deficient child is unable to utilize properly a milk diet containing normal amounts of lactose. For example, several investigations have shown marked histological abnormalities of the mucosal lining of the small intestine. In these cases it can be shown that not only is the lactase deficient but the levels of sucrase and maltase are also severely depressed. Mitchell and Grunseit[11] have carried out a controlled milk-feeding trial with two groups of Aboriginal children in

New South Wales. One group received a normal cows' milk diet, while the other group was given a low-lactose milk diet. This was identical with the normal diet except that 85 per cent of the lactose had been hydrolysed into its constituent monosaccharides, glucose, and galactose. The group of infants on the lactose-reduced diet showed a 70 per cent increase in weight gain at the end of the trial compared to the children on the normal milk diet. Mitchell and Grunseit conclude that special diets of this type could be important in helping to overcome the growth-retardation syndrome among Aboriginal children in other parts of Australia.

Some paediatricians have questioned the design and analysis of the trial carried out by Mitchell and Grunseit, and it is important that further studies be undertaken to confirm the significance of their conclusions. However, it is necessary to emphasize that feeding with specially prepared lactose-reduced diets is expensive. A more effective promotion of child growth is likely to result from a general improvement in the environment of the child rather than application of a transient palliative in the form of a modified diet.

Malnutrition causes not only defective digestion as a result of reduced production of digestive enzymes, but also a reduction in absorption across the gut surface. The actual cause of the malabsorption of simple sugars under these conditions is not yet clear. What is clear is the vicious cycle which is established in Aboriginal children when the ecological setting changes. When people are congregated without adequate community planning the environment becomes heavily contaminated. There is, as Michael Gracey[12] puts it, 'a significant breakdown in the normal uneasy truce between the host and the intestinal microflora he harbours when his nutritional status is compromised . . . , it seems very likely that altered immuno-function is closely related to the microbiological abnormalities mentioned above and to the well recognized prevalence of gastrointestinal infections and infestations in malnourished children and the recent demonstration of potentially harmful viruses in the intestinal contents of such individuals'.

Other patterns of disease[13]

The crude death rates provide some guide to the diseases which lead to death. In Table 9.5 the leading causes of death in Aborigines in the Northern Territory are compared with the rates for Australia as a whole and with those prevailing among the Maoris in New Zealand. The overall death rate in Aborigines is nearly 2.5 times that for the total Australian population and 3.4 times that for Maoris. The

Table 9.5. Leading causes of death in Northern Territory Aborigines
1964–5 with comparative figures for Maoris and total
Australian population[13]

Deaths due to:	Death rates per 100 000 population		
	Aborigines	Maoris NZ (1964)	Australia (1963)
All causes	2100	620	870
Pneumonia and influenza	370	55	29
Senility and ill-defined diseases	360	0.5	6
Diseases of infancy	230	50	25
Gastroenteritis and dysentery	220	14	4
Heart disease	130	151	322
Accidents	110	63	49
Malignant neoplasms	80	72	135
Anaemias and malnutrition	70	0.2	4
TB (all forms)	70	15	4
Vascular lesions of CNS	30	37	115

greater part of this increase is due to the diseases of infancy which
were discussed in the last section. By contrast, there are several
categories of disorder which affect non-Aborigines to a greater
extent, e.g. heart disease and cerebral haemorrhages and malignant
neoplasms. Indeed, among the diseases of adults only tuberculosis
is a more common cause of death in Aborigines.

There are, of course, many diseases which are the cause of
considerable morbidity in adult Aborigines and which occur among
them with greater frequency than in whites. Not all these diseases
occur over the entire continent of Australia. Climatic factors, inter-
related in some cases with suitable animal vectors and with density-
dependent variables in the human host population, limit the
distribution of several diseases. A further set of factors, about which
little is known in Aborigines, may also influence the distribution of
some disorders: these are genetic differences which affect susceptibility to some diseases or lead, through disturbance in the normal
processes of development, to congenital abnormalities.

In the first of these categories is a group of diseases which are
found almost exclusively in a tropical environment. These include
leprosy, malaria, filariasis, and hookworm. Some, if not all, of these
may have been introduced into Aboriginal populations across the
northern part of Australia by Malay trepangers during the last few
centuries. Alternatively, introduction of exotic diseases might have
been made more recently by members of pearling fleets or by other

Asian migrants who entered Australia during the gold-rush days in the latter part of the nineteenth century.

Leprosy has been particularly virulent during the last hundred years. In the affected areas in the north of Western Australia, the Northern Territory and Queensland 5–10 per cent of the population at risk have been infected. In some persons the disease is self-limiting but in a large number it results in gross disfigurement, loss of use of hands and feet, and considerable mortality. Only in recent years, with the introduction of treatment by sulphone drugs after early case detection and supplemented with restorative surgery for more advanced cases, has the disease been brought under control.

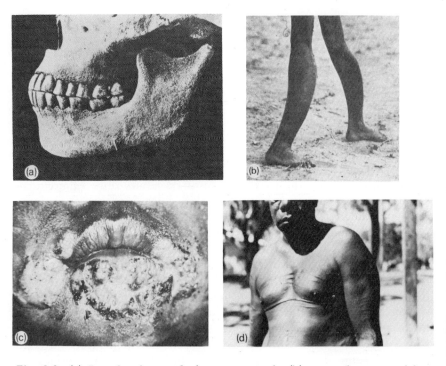

Fig. 9.3. (a) Jaw showing marked wear on teeth; (b) yaws: 'boomerang' leg; (c) yaws: ulceration on lower lip; (d) leprosy: tuberculoid lesion on left breast.

Hookworm is also widespread in settlements across the northern part of the continent. Some surveys have reported 90 per cent of children infected. The hookworm eggs, passing out in the faeces, find a favourable environment in the soils of the wet tropics. As in other parts of the world, too close a settlement pattern, inadequate sanitation, and a preference for walking barefoot, lead to rapid re-infestation. Recently, treatment with drugs such as 'Alcopan' coupled with greater attention to simple hygienic measures has reduced the incidence of hookworm dramatically in closely settled areas. The recent movement of population away from settlements to less densely populated 'out station' camps (cf. Chapter 10) is also important in breaking the man–parasite cycle of dependency.

Infestation with the filarial worm does not seem to have been of great significance in Australia, but filariasis was reported from some localities in the earlier part of this century. Although the mosquito vector which carries the microfilariae from one infected person to another is widespread in the north, the disease has probably never become endemic because the density of human population has been too low to allow the build-up of a sufficient number of infected mosquitoes.

A similar argument explains the absence of malaria as a major health problem, despite its presence in holoendemic form in neigh-bouring New Guinea. The significant difference between otherwise similar ecological situations on both sides of the Torres Strait is the lower density of the human population in Australia. Several malarial epidemics have occurred in northern Australia, but the number of cases affected has always been small and the epidemics have been self-limiting. The complete absence in Aborigines of abnormal haemoglobins or of deficiency for the red-blood-cell enzyme G6PD, one or both of which are found frequently in populations subject to holoendemic malaria, suggests this disease has never been of impor-tance for Aborigines. However, new cases of malaria have been reported during the last few years in the north of Cape York. The disease was probably introduced by contact with Torres Strait Islanders and Papua New Guineans. There is an important warning here, for as the continued development of Australia's northern resources takes place, with consequent increase in population densi-ties, malaria and other tropical diseases could well pose a greater threat to Aborigines than they have done in the past.

Another tropical disease, yaws, or a related treponemal infection, has almost certainly had a long history on the continent, and evidence for infection extends into non-tropical environments. Clinical cases of yaws were commonly noted by early Australian medical workers, and some of the secondary bone deformations similar to those found in cases of yaws in other parts of the world were present in Aborigines.[14] The most striking of these is referred to as 'boomerang tibia' because of the bending of the tibial bone in the leg. Sandison, as noted earlier, found examples of this in the bones he examined from Aboriginal skeletons. One unusual variant of bone deformation was discovered in an isolated group in the Western Desert.[15] Several members of the group had shortened fingers, a secondary development produced by resorption of the mid-phalangeal bones. This expression of treponemal infection has been found only once previously, in Africa.

Although active sores due to yaws are not seen frequently, antibody against treponemal infection is present in nearly one-third of individuals in the Northern Territory and similar high frequencies have been reported from Queensland and Western Australia. An important consequence of this is that in the parts of Australia where infection with the yaws treponemal organisms was very common the immune reaction induced in the population conferred cross-immunity against the closely related organism responsible for syphilis. One of the results of the widespread recent use of anti-biotics in the treatment of yaws has been the removal of this cross-immunity with a consequent increase in the number of cases of both adult and congenital syphilis.

The serious eye disease trachoma is prevalent among Aborigines in many parts of Australia. In parts of Western Australia as many as 80 per cent of the Aboriginal population are infected by the causa-tive virus, and similar high values have been found in many other parts of the continent. Serious impairment of sight frequently develops if the chronic condition is not treated. Trachoma-induced blindness is indeed found, particularly among older people in the more arid areas. In a central Australian survey, carried out by the National Trachoma and Eye Health Program, 28 per cent of Aborigines over 60 years of age had blindness or potentially blinding trachoma lesions.

Middle-ear disease, otitis media, with perforation of one or both drums leading to deafness, is also a widespread disorder. In some communities more than a third of school-age children are affected, and the impairment of hearing is a serious disability for children in a classroom situation.[16]

Infection with hepatitis B virus is also found in many parts of the country, with between 3 and 5 per cent of Aborigines in the Northern Territory and Queensland having persistent virus-like particles in their serum, a rate 30 to 50 times higher than that found in non-Aboriginal Australians. This condition is interesting because the persistent particles were detected for the first time in serum from an Aborigine in Western Australia. Initially, the unknown component was referred to as 'Australia' antigen. Later, when the presence of 'Australia' antigen was being investigated in sera from many other parts of the world it was shown that the viral-like particles detectable in serum by electronmicroscopy were portions of the hepatitis B virus. In some persons infected with the virus the particles persist in the serum, sometimes for many years. Such serum, since it may also contain a small number of infective virions, may give rise to serum hepatitis if transfused into a non-immune recipient.

A disease related closely to living patterns is tuberculosis. Malnutrition is considered to increase susceptibility to the disease, and overcrowded accommodation leads to rapid spread through cross-infection. In Australia both malnutrition and overcrowding were exacerbated after European contact. Aborigines in many parts of the continent were forced to congregate in settlements or in towns and cities, with inadequate food and dilapidated shelters for housing. In the last century tuberculosis was a serious health problem in Aboriginal communities. At Point McLeay during the 35 years before 1900, 13 per cent, and at Point Pearce from 1880 to 1899 28 per cent, of all deaths were due to pulmonary tuberculosis. Early observers noted that the disease appeared to be more acute in Aborigines and a recent study of paired Aboriginal and non-Aboriginal cases in Queensland supports this observation. The Aboriginal cases in this latter study, however, responded rapidly to treatment.

Surveys of the Northern Territory in the mid-1960s show that tuberculosis in Aborigines accounted for 20 per cent of the deaths in people over the age of 20, and the mortality rate above the age of 30 was 360 per 100 000 population at risk. This rate, although comparable with that for Maoris in New Zealand, is 14 times higher than that for the general Australian population. However, the introduction of BCG vaccination from 1951 onwards has reduced the new case rate for tuberculosis to low levels in the younger age-groups.

A number of other diseases are known to occur sporadically in Aborigines and have been discussed by Moodie in his book on Aboriginal health. Typhoid fever has been a persistent disease among Aborigines, with sporadic cases being reported over many years. In 1968 there were outbreaks in at least two Arnhem Land settlements. Cases of bacterial food poisoning have occurred at Palm Island in Queensland, whilst in the same State amoebiasis was present in 80 per cent of children aged 3–5 years at Kowanyama on the west coast of Cape York. Most of these cases are symptomless since *Entamoeba histolytica* is normally a harmless commensal in the gut. Occasionally, however, owing to factors not clearly understood, it becomes pathogenic, causing ulceration of the bowel with spread of the parasite to other organs in the body. Another amoeba, *Acanthamoeba castellani*, may also become a serious threat. Normally free-living, it sometimes invades the central nervous system causing a meningitis. Finally, the highly toxic food-poisoning organism, *Clostridium welchii*, has been found among Aborigines in the Lismore area of New South Wales. Nearly 20 per cent of Aborigines were carriers, and the carrier rate was higher where standards of hygiene in food preservation or storage were lower.

Congenital and genetic defects

The burden of congenital and genetic defect is another factor which affects the standard of general health in any community. Up to the present time there has been no careful documentation of the incidence of these defects in Aborigines. The reasons for this are not hard to find. In the first place, communities of Aborigines are relatively small so that disorders which occur with low frequency will appear in such groups only occasionally. Secondly, medical surveillance until recently has been very inadequate, and even now many Aboriginal communities receive only limited medical attention given during periodic visits. Finally, the diagnosis — or at least its confirmation — in many inherited disorders requires sophisticated pathological or biochemical tests which have not been brought to bear, except in a few instances, on the Aboriginal situation.

Despite these difficulties there have been a number of reports since the end of the 1890s which refer to the occurrence in Aborigines of inherited disorders or congenital anomalies. Thus cases of albinism were reported in Western Australia in 1891, and a further case was reported by an informant in central Australia in the 1920s. But only recently has a reliable report on a young albino child in the Northern Territory appeared in the medical literature. Similar sporadic and frequently poorly documented accounts indicate the rare occurrence of achondroplastic dwarfs, and of polydactyly.

Few studies have been carried out on chromosomes in cases of congenital malformations in Aborigines. For example, some Aboriginal cases of Down's disease (mongolism) have been reported from Darwin, but the type of Down's disease (whether trisomy for chromosome 21 or trans-location) is not known. No other authenticated cases have been reported in Aborigines. Since Down's disease is the most frequent chromosomal aberration in whites its rarity in Aborigines is intriguing. Two factors may explain this rarity. Firstly, trisomy for chromosome 21 increases in frequency rapidly when mothers are above 35 years of age and the lower average age of Aboriginal mothers compared to whites will result in Aborigines having a lower frequency of Down's disease. Secondly, foetuses with chromosome aberrations are more likely to be aborted, and this risk is increased in mothers who are malnourished. This will also lead to a lower frequency of Down's disease babies surviving to full-term in Aborigines compared to the general Australian population.

To date there has been no systematic study of all births to Aboriginal mothers over a number of years which would enable us to give relative incidence figures for specific malformations. It is hoped that with the deployment of more personnel into the Aboriginal health field this situation will soon improve. Amongst paediatricians there appears to be agreement that cystic fibrosis of the pancreas and spina bifida are less common and congenital dislocation of the hip probably less common in Aborigines than in white Australians, but talipes equinovarus (club foot) is more common. For cystic fibrosis the contrast is most marked. So far no authenticated case has been reported among Aboriginal infants, though it is the commonest metabolic disease among white children.

There are some other disorders in Aborigines, also with a clear-cut pattern of inheritance. One of these is a form of pseudohermaphroditism restricted to the Tiwi of Bathurst Island. In a single kinship on the island, there have been 9 cases spread over five generations. Another example is a degenerative neurological disorder, Huntington's Chorea, which is inherited as a dominant trait. Gale and Bennett[17] have collected information on Huntington's Chorea in descendants of families from the Point McLeay Aboriginal Reserve in South Australia. Point McLeay Reserve was established in 1859. A girl born there in 1867 later developed symptoms of chorea and she has had more than 70 descendants who have dispersed into other parts of South Australia, Victoria, and New South Wales, providing approximately 30 fresh foci for its further spread. The Huntington's Chorea gene was probably introduced into this kinship by a European father, possibly of Scottish origin, since this disease is far more common in parts of Scotland than in other places in England or Europe.

In contrast to these examples of specific genetic disorders in, but not peculiar to, Aboriginal populations there are some genetic disorders which so far have not been detected in Aborigines, although a fairly careful search has been made for them. Amongst these are the haemoglobinopathies and red cell enzyme deficiencies which are widespread in many other parts of the world.

Haemoglobinopathies, due either to abnormal haemoglobins or to depression in the production of either the α or β chains of haemoglobin, are found in many parts of the world. Individuals who inherit genes controlling abnormal haemoglobin or the quantity of α or β haemoglobin chains often have breakdown of blood cells. This is more severe when these genes are present in homozygous form. Depression of α or β chain production (thalassaemia) is very common among coastal populations in New Guinea. However, no cases of abnormal haemoglobin or of thalassaemia have been detected among Australian Aborigines.

Deficiency of the red cell enzyme glucose-6-phosphate dehydrogenase (G6PD) is controlled by a gene on the X chromosome. It also produces red cell breakdown under certain conditions. G6PD deficiency is also widespread in coastal areas of New Guinea, sometimes having a frequency of 20 per cent among males, but no case has been detected so far in Aborigines.

Another gene not present in Aborigines of full descent is the Rh-negative gene. This gene has a frequency of approximately 30 per cent in Europeans and a mother homozygous for the Rh-negative gene having an Rh-positive baby can produce antibodies which cause haemolytic disease in the newborn infant. In severe cases the baby may be stillborn or die after birth. Among Aborigines, since they do not possess the Rh-negative gene, haemolytic disease of the newborn due to Rh incompatibility cannot occur. This does not rule out the possibility of neonatal jaundice due to incompatibility between mother and child in the ABO blood group system, but I am not aware of any evidence for this in Aborigines.

Mental health

The incidence of behavioural disorders is difficult to determine in any community. It is even more difficult for communities where the cultural norms are different from those of the culture to which the observer belongs. To try and solve these difficulties several studies have been carried out during the last 20 years, and a new discipline is developing under the title of 'trans-cultural psychiatry'. In Australia, Jones and Kidson have been carrying out such studies in traditionally oriented Aboriginal populations in the desert areas of Western Australia and the Northern Territory, and Cawte has made similar studies in the northern part of the Kimberley and on Mornington Island. These and other investigators have reported also on mental health problems among Aborigines living in cultural transition areas, such as rural townships or large cities.[18]

Despite the difficulty of defining behavioural disorders precisely, there is agreement by the psychiatrists involved in these studies that the framework for recognizing mental disorders in European culture-based groups can be used for categorizing cases in Aboriginal groups.

The analysis of causes, however, reveals important differences between the two.

In the desert areas between 6 and 10 per cent of Aborigines are considered to have a psychiatric disorder, diagnosed according to criteria used in the white community. Table 9.6 shows that about one-tenth of the cases are schizophrenic, one-tenth are depressive, and one-fifth suffering from organic brain disorders. By contrast, classical neuroses, psychosomatic illness, and suicide were not detected. Other reports confirm that suicide is a rarity among traditionally oriented Aborigines.

Table 9.6. Psychiatric disorders in desert Aborigines

Diagnosis	Per cent of cases
Schizophrenia	0.5
Depression	0.5
Affective psychosis	0.3
Organic disorders	1.2
Personality disorders	0.5
Mental subnormality	0.3
Possession syndrome	0.3
Childhood behaviour disorders	0.8
Others	1.6
Total cases out of all in population	6.0

One form of psychosis which occurs in Aboriginal communities is a 'possession syndrome'. The subject believes that he or she has been injured by supernatural means or sorcery. Cases are characterized by withdrawal, inactivity, refusal to eat, and the expectation of death. Sometimes a cure can be effected by persons in the community, such as 'medicine men', who the patient believes have the power to dispel the evil spirits or neutralize the sorcery.

Cawte, in a study of mental illness at Kalumburu, on the far north coast of Western Australia, found some similarity with the pattern of illness in the desert areas. Schizophrenia-like symptoms are present, although Cawte suggests it is difficult to distinguish the schizophrenia in the Kalumburu patients from the behaviour which results from sorcery. He points out also that the converse could be true, and what is diagnosed as sorcery might be schizophrenia. Functional depressive psychosis and suicide are rare, but reactive depression is not uncommon, and personality disorders of both passive–dependent and passive–aggressive type are also present, and paranoid psychoses are common.

A more detailed analysis of mental illness was made by Cawte on

Mornington Island. Here he was able to contrast the patterns in two groups: Lardil, the traditional occupants of the island, and Kaiadilt, originally residents of nearby Bentinck Island who were moved to Mornington Island in 1948. The Kaiadilt, long isolated and few in number, have developed a distinctive genetic constellation of traits, which is reflected in their blood genetic markers, dermatoglyphic patterns, and their physical appearance. As newcomers to Mornington the Kaiadilt live on the periphery of the village and are more poorly integrated.

Depressive states are far more common in the Kaiadilt, 7 out of a total of 60 Kaiadilt adults being classified as having depressive states, either at the time of the survey or immediately before.

This contrasts with the absence of serious depressive states in the other 218 adult Aborigines on the island. Perhaps a more significant fact reported by Cawte is that there had been one suicide, several attempted suicides, and one 'Voodoo'-type death, all among members of the Kaiadilt.

Having noted the genetic distinctiveness of the Kaiadilt, Cawte poses the question whether the Kaiadilt genotype has led to a behaviour phenotype quite different from that of the Lardil. This phenotype would be characterized by temperamental instability, easy arousal, poor emotional control, with a tendency toward quarrelling and depression. Having posed the question, Cawte concludes that the environmental pressures operating on the Kaiadilt are so different from those for the Lardil that it seems likely these are sufficient to account for the behavioural patterns observed. It is related to social disintegration which, Cawte believes, was taking place before their exodus to Mornington Island in 1948. In their Bentinck Island home they were subjected to drastic fluctuations in the abundance of their food resources. Overpopulation led to a struggle for survival, and their behaviour was characterized by acts of violence, robbery, murder, abduction, and revenge. Social disintegration associated with these periodic fluctuations in abundance was already a reality for the Kaiadilt when they were forcibly transplanted to the alien environment of Bentinck Island. Here they were subjected to new stresses which led to further disintegration and development of more behaviour disorders. Cawte suggests that in the development of these disorders disturbance of the ecological balance comes first, followed by interpersonal disturbances, and then intrapsychic disturbances. This sequence spreads out through the community and is passed on in succeeding generations.

10

A PEOPLE IN TRANSITION

At the beginning of this book attention was drawn to the drastic change in the social, economic, and ecological relationships of Aborigines which followed the intrusion of European settlers into Australia just 200 years ago. Population figures for the Aborigines are sufficient testimony in themselves to the impact of this sudden intrusion of an alien culture into a situation where the slow adjustment between man and environment had been proceeding, relatively undisturbed, for many thousands of years. From an estimated total of just over 250 000 at the time of first contact, the Aboriginal population fell to its lowest level of 60 000 in the census of 1921. Since that date the trend has reversed. Broom and Jones[1] estimated a few years ago that if the present demographic pattern continues the Aboriginal population of Australia will reach its former level of 250 000 by about 1990 and may rise to 350 000 to 400 000 by the end of this century. This may be an overestimate, but there is no doubt that the number of Aborigines is increasing rapidly.

This rapid population growth is only one of the many changes now taking place in Aboriginal communities. These communities themselves are diverse in type, and each presents its own biological stresses to which adjustment must be made. Briefly, these varied communities can be categorized as follows:[2]

Those containing predominantly persons of full Aboriginal descent. These are located mainly in the centre and across the north of the continent, including the Kimberley, Arnhem Land, and Cape York, and the majority are Government-sponsored settlements and church-dominated missions or ex-missions. Without exception they are economically dependent, either completely or to a significant extent, on the wealthier white society. Politically these communities are striving increasingly to become independent of the dominant culture, and this is reflected in the strength of the 'Land Rights' movement and in the increasing power exercised by Aborigines as a result of their sharing in the profits derived from the exploitation of minerals, such as uranium, in their territories. It is reflected also in a movement of people away from the settlements to 'out-stations' or 'homelands', accompanied by a resurgence of traditional life-styles. Some of the reasons for and consequences of this latter adaptation will be discussed later.

Camps associated with pastoral properties and containing Abori-gines of full- and part-descent. In the immediate past the pastoral industry provided a major source of employment for Aborigines. Wages were low, provision for physical amenities such as housing and sanitation was of a deplorably low standard, and payment in kind had to be shared between the large numbers of relatives who swelled the population of these camps. Recently, the pattern of employment in the pastoral industry has been changing. Pressure for better working conditions and equality of pay with whites has led to improvement in the standard of housing and other physical ameni-ties but also to a reduction in the number of Aborigines employed. A new development has been the acquisition of pastoral properties for Aboriginal management, the acquisition of the properties being financed by the government.

Communities associated with rural towns. Starting in the last cen-tury and accelerating during the first half of the present century, the remnants of Aboriginal groups in the more densely settled white areas congregated in squattages on the edges of rural towns. Houses were constructed from cast-off materials, sanitation was almost non-existent, and the members of these communities were dependent on sporadic employment in local rural industry. Racial discrimination was intense, and Aborigines were frequently excluded from partici-pating in the community activities enjoyed by the whites of the town. During the last decade some changes have occurred in this pattern. Physical conditions in the squattages have started to improve: more permanent houses are being built either by direct government programmes or indirectly by government-financed Aboriginal housing organizations. In some cases homes for Aborigines have been made available in the main urban area. Integra-tion of this type has presented great difficulty to members of both white and black groups. The stress has been most severe on Aboriginal families moving into the white community, particularly in rural towns. Some of the problems faced by Aborigines in these communities have been studied in the town of Bourke in New South Wales and will be discussed in more detail later.

Communities in large cities. The movement to an urban environment has progressed from the staging-squattages of the rural towns to the centres of the large cities. These cities now have the largest populations of Aborigines. It is difficult to obtain a precise figure, but Sydney has approximately 14 000 Aborigines, nearly all of part-descent. The city-centres have also attracted other ethnic groups who, because of their socio-economic status, align themselves politically with Aborigines. Sydney, for example, has 5000 Torres Strait and other Pacific Islanders.

Physical conditions in the inner-city slums, where the majority of Aborigines and Islanders have congregated, are poor. Government-funded projects, both direct and indirect, have made some improvements, and recently there has been a movement of Aborigines from slum areas into new government housing or flats both in the central and outer suburban areas. Since such movement often involves many families, the stresses are not so acute as they are in attempts to 'integrate' isolated families in the rural towns, and a new urban Aboriginal culture is in process of formation. A small but expanding Aboriginal 'élite' is also taking its place alongside the middle-class white professional urban dweller.

Almost all of the ecological situations in which Aborigines now live have involved abandonment of traditional life-styles and the disintegration of the former Aboriginal culture. Those who require details of the history of this disintegration during the last 100 years will find it fully documented by C. D. Rowley in a series of books: *The remote Aborigines, The destruction of Aboriginal society* and *Outcasts in white Australia*.[3]

Biological effects of social transitions

Demographic factors

Population expansion means large families, and large families, in a poor community mean greater poverty, an increase in overcrowding in houses, and a rise in the incidence of nutritional and communicable disease. All these factors operate in present-day Aboriginal communities, though their magnitude varies from place to place.[4] The size of families is measured by taking the mean number of surviving children for women over the age of 40. For non-Aboriginal Australians in 1970 the mean number of surviving children per woman was 2.5; in the State of Victoria Aboriginal women have an average of 6.5 surviving children; and along the south coast of New South Wales the comparable figure is 5.6. Aboriginal women of full descent in the Northern Territory have only 3.3 surviving children,

Table 10.1. Family size: number of children to women over age 40

	Mean No. of live births per woman
Non-Aboriginal Australians	2.5
Aborigines of part-descent — Victoria	6.5
Aborigines of part-descent — Sydney	4.7
	Mean No. of surviving children per woman
Aborigines of part-descent — NSW South coast	5.6
Aborigines of full-descent — Northern Territory	3.3

Table 10.2. Proportion of women with various number of children

	Aborigines rural NSW (%)	Total population Australia (%)
Women (aged 20–29) with 5 or more children	25.0	4.5
Women (aged 30–39) with 10 or more children	8.3	1.1

but the number is still significantly above that of the non-Aboriginal population.

Where economic conditions are good and social services adequate, large families do not necessarily result in undue biological stress. For Aborigines at present, however, this is not the case. In rural New South Wales the burden of large families falls on young mothers. One quarter of Aboriginal women in the age-group 20–29 have five or more children compared to only one woman in 22 in the same age-group for the total Australian population. Table 10.3 shows that

Table 10.3. Average number of Aborigines per dwelling

Rural NSW	7.0
Walgett, NSW	8.9
Sydney	7.0
(per room)	2.5
Northern Territory	5.2
Australia (total population)	3.6

large families for Aborigines results in overcrowding. In Australia as a whole there is an average of 3.6 persons per dwelling. Aborigines have an average of 5 to 9 persons per dwelling. Norelle Lickiss,[5] in a survey of health problems among Aborigines in Sydney, found a density of 2.5 persons *per room*, whilst at Kowanyama, on the Gulf of Carpentaria coast of Cape York, it is reported that half the Aborigines live in households of 9 or more persons, and in some cases 4 or 5 children share a bed with their parents.

Community health

Overcrowding represents one factor in the syndrome of poverty and social disintegration which characterizes nearly all Aboriginal communities at the present time. In Chapter 9 we have noted that the health of Aborigines, as measured by indices such as infant mortality, is seriously deficient. Studies of morbidity reveal that the burden of ill health is widespread and affects all age-groups.

Similar patterns of morbidity have been revealed through special surveys in several parts of the country. Norelle Lickiss has analysed the ill health of children among a group of Aboriginal households in the inner-city area of Sydney. During the first five years of life one-third of the children had been in hospital at least three times. Almost the same proportion of children had been admitted to hospital at some time with a respiratory infection and one-fifth for gastro-intestinal disorders. Similarly, Fay Gale[6] has recorded the hospital admissions for Aborigines in Adelaide during a 30-month period and found that 22.6 per cent had been admitted at least once. She comments that the long period of hospitalization needed by many of these patients interferes seriously with the opportunities for work among adults and with education for children under the age of fifteen. Both factors contribute to a further deterioration in the standard of life in the community.

More detailed analysis of morbidity patterns has been given by Kamien[7] for Aborigines in Bourke in western New South Wales. Physical and laboratory investigations have revealed that among children 63 per cent have intestinal parasites, 51 per cent have iron deficiency, and 50 per cent some form of eye disease; 17 per cent have respiratory disorders, 16 per cent gastro-intestinal disorders, and a similar number have infectious skin diseases. For adults 31 per cent have eye disorders and the same proportion gastro-intestinal disorders, 21 per cent have respiratory disorders, 19 per cent have urinary-tract infection, 18 per cent intestinal parasites, 15 per cent are hypertensive, 13 per cent are obese, and 5 per cent diabetic.

Mental health

There is much evidence to suggest that stress on individuals in a disintegrating society gives rise to an increased frequency of mental illness. In the previous chapter we noted Cawte's analysis of the manner in which such stresses gave rise to increased mental disorder among the Kaiadilt on Mornington Island. These people are still living close to a traditional parttern of life. The same picture holds for many Aboriginal communities living on settlements in other remote areas and it applies also to those shanty communities on the edge of rural towns and to the congregations of Aborigines in large cities.

Kamien, in his study of community health in Bourke, also included observations on the extent of mental health problems.

The amount of mental illness among Aboriginal adults in Bourke totals 32 per cent. Approximately one half of this is due to sociopathic addictive disorders, nearly all in men. A large proportion of these are chronic alcoholics. About one-sixth of the cases are due to anxiety states and a similar proportion have reactive depression. About 5 per cent of the cases are classified as functional psychoses.

Although these figures for the prevalence of mental illness in Bourke Aborigines seem high, they are not much higher than prevalence figures for two white Australian populations studied in Victoria. For Aboriginal women the prevalence rates in Bourke are similar to those for whites in Victoria. The higher rate for Aboriginal men in Bourke is due to the greater number of alcoholics in the Bourke community. Even higher prevalence rates for mental illness have been reported in other parts of the world, notably in a study of Stirling County, Nova Scotia. Kamien considers that, although many of the life circumstances of Aborigines in Bourke parallel

Table 8.4. Psychiatric disorders among Aborigines in a rural town

Diagnosis	Per cent of cases
Functional psychosis	5.0
Symptomatic psychosis	5.0
Anxiety state	15.7
Reactive depression	17.6
Other psychoneuroses	6.0
Sociopathic addictive personality	47.0
Other personality disorders	3.7
Total cases out of all adults	31.9

those of the depressed areas of Stirling County, the Bourke Aboriginal community does not appear to be as severely disintegrated. Despite the high prevalence of alcoholism among Aboriginal men, alcoholism among Aboriginal women was not so great a problem as in Stirling County, and the chronic hostility in families and broken homes were far less common in Bourke.

Despite these comments that alcoholism, as an indicator of social breakdown, is not so acute in Bourke Aborigines as in some other populations in the world, many observers believe it is one of the more serious problems facing Aboriginal communities at the present time. Alcohol abuse is present in nearly every Aboriginal community, and it has its origin in the contact areas soon after the arrival of Europeans two hundred years ago.

Discussing the disintegration of Aboriginal society, C. D. Rowley points out that the effect of alcohol, even in the early nineteenth century, was obviously catastrophic. There developed a belief that there was a physical difference between Aborigines and whites in their tolerance of alcohol. Rowley points out that it was an error to seek an explanation in a physical rather than a social cause, and as noted in Chapter 8 studies on the rate of metabolism of alcohol confirm that there is no significant difference between Aborigines and whites. As a social scientist Rowley believes that rampant alcohol abuse results from a failure in the social structure to adjust to the disruption of life-styles, and a breakdown in Aboriginal law. Authority in Aboriginal society is very vulnerable, and since fermented or distilled liquors were unknown in Australia before the arrival of Europeans no social controls existed in Aboriginal society to regulate their use. Rowley outlines the steps by which Aboriginal authority was undermined during the early years of contact, and he continues:

probably the first use of alcohol had the effect it has continued to have of reducing the great man to an object of ridicule; and of giving to the doubting and tentatively dissident youth courage to defy him.

Its use by the women must have affected drastically their work of child-raising and socialization. In a group where the habit had changed quickly from a nomadic hunting existence to limited movement, facing the new health hazards arising from comparative immobility, this must have caused high infant death rates. With ineffective shelter and waste disposal, change of diet and new disease as well, alcohol must have formed an important link in the chain of causes which so rapidly obliterated whole groups of people.[8]

The breakdown in social regulation which characterized the contact situation described by Rowley is still taking place in Aboriginal communities, not only in cities and towns, where access to alcohol is easy, but also in more remote areas when alcohol becomes available.

Lee Sackett,[9] for example, has described changes at Wiluna in Western Australia, when restrictions on the drinking of alcohol by Aborigines were removed in 1971. Within two months the number of arrests for drinking and associated offences jumped from 2 to 29, and there was a simultaneous increase in fighting between members of the community and a decrease in the amount spent on food, accompanied by a deterioration both in ritual life and in physical health. Similar accounts of the effects of alcohol on the breakdown of social structure have been given for Aboriginal communities in many other parts of the continent.

A new adaptive response

We have already noted the transition in the population number of Aborigines from decline to rapid increase, which has brought with it associated problems resulting from overcrowding and the higher proportion of people in the infant and child age groups. A further readjustment in social patterns which will have important implications for the biology of Aborigines is now taking place.

Official government attitudes toward the welfare of Aborigines have been characterized during the greater part of this century by indecisiveness and changing philosophies about the responsibilities of the majority culture to members of the minority culture. During the 1960s there was increasing pressure from Aboriginal groups for greater government assistance to help solve some of the problems created by the policies of the Australian Federal government and other agencies. This was coupled with demands for greater self-determination on the part of the Aborigines themselves, a movement which has continued to gain momentum and from which has flowed a number of changes, both official and unofficial.

In 1967 a referendum gave overwhelming support to the proposal that the Australian Federal government take over responsibility for Aborigines in all parts of the continent. This has meant increased expenditure on health services, housing, and education. It has also resulted in increased recognition of Aboriginal Councils and other representative bodies which, in turn, has resulted in a new social awareness of Aboriginal identity and a restoration of pride and confidence in their ability to control social behaviour. During the last decade a large number of social experiments have been initiated, many by Aborigines themselves; and some of these are relevant to our present theme.

Aboriginal health services

The low standard of health in Aboriginal communities is related closely to their socio-economic conditions. These must be improved if the fundamental cause for their ill-health is to be removed. Most effort in the past, however, has been directed to the provision of curative health services — clinics, and hospitals staffed by white doctors and nurses. In remote areas the application of western medicine is palliative at best; and the attitudes of doctors and nurses are frequently irrelevant to the culture of the people they serve. Even in urban areas, Aborigines have found it difficult to avail themselves fully of services designed primarily for the white community.

To overcome some of these problems Aborigines have established their own medical services and in 1980 twenty-one such services were operating, most of them in the larger urban environments. These services are financed mainly by Government funds, but are managed by Aborigines. They employ their own medical and nursing staff and their clinic treatment is supplemented by welfare activities and, in at least one case, by a nutrition programme aimed particularly at pregnant women and young children.[10]

Three of these Aboriginal-controlled health projects have been started in tribal areas, at Papunya and Utopia in the Northern Territory, and at Pipalyatjara in the recently established Bidjandjadjara Traditional Homelands area, embracing Bidjandjadjara territory on the borders of South Australia, Western Australia, and the Northern Territory. This latter project is part of the government support being given to initiatives on the part of Aborigines in remote areas to re-establish a life-style more closely related to that of original populations of the area.

Development of cognitive abilities

One of the effects of low socio-economic conditions is retardation of development of cognitive abilities. This in turn leads to difficulty in integrating into the new patterns demanded by a society in transition and perpetuates the syndrome associated with deprivation.

In the field of education the lessons learned from cross-cultural studies of cognitive abilities is that Aborigines score lower than whites on tests of intelligence and that these tests predict they will do poorly at school or in occupations regarded as useful in white society. Further, since test performance improves in proportion to the degree of contact with white culture it is believed that Aborigines score badly in test situations because they are not exposed during infancy to cultural patterns that emphasize things like predictability, cause-and-effect relationships, and classificatory systems used in white society. A culturally conditioned expectation of failure or a lack of concern for the values implicit in the test may both adversely affect test performance. This cultural disadvantage may be heightened in some cases by the effects of severe malnutrition.

Some anthropologists and psychologists believe that if the above facts and the premises which flow from them are accepted then it should be possible to introduce intervention programmes to alter some of the factors which reduce test scores, and so break the vicious cycle. This does not mean simply giving practice with the test material but involves creating specific educational experiences, the effects of which can be measured by subsequent tests of cognitive ability.

One such trial, supervised by Barry Nurcombe,[11] was carried out over three successive years from 1970 to 1972 among children in a small rural town in western New South Wales. Here, Aborigines, mainly of part-descent, form approximately 25 per cent of the population. Their standards of physical health are poor and many live in substandard houses on the edge of the town.

Receptive verbal IQ was measured at the start of the trial by the Peabody Picture Vocabulary test (PPVT) and linguistic ability by the Illinois Test of Psycholinguistic Abilities (ITPA). Initially Aborigines of pre-school age scored only 68 on the PPVT, but the white pre-school children from the same town scored 77. Similar results were obtained for the ITPA test. The children who scored lowest (about 80 per cent of all those tested) were selected for pre-school education and given predetermined educational programmes. Of these, half in the first year were exposed to a 'traditional' pre-school training, which emphasized a broad range of activities to promote, social, emotional, and motor development, and the other half were given a structured programme emphasizing language development. At the end of the year little or no improvement in test scores was achieved by the children in the 'traditional' programme, but an improvement of 25 points in mean IQ was obtained by those who had received the structured language training. Mid-way through the following year, after all the children had entered the normal primary school, it was found that the white children in the initial trial had retained their gains in IQ. By contrast the Aboriginal children had lost about one-third of their gains.

Variations in the trials were introduced to new groups of pre-school children in succeeding years. In 1972, for example, in addition to the original language programme an Extended Experience

Programme was introduced which emphasized formal language development using situations drawn from the children's own experiences
and involving parents more actively in understanding and supporting
the programme. Retests at the end of the trial period showed
Aboriginal children who had experienced the original structured language programme gained 21 points on the PPVT compared to only
11 points for those on the Extended Experience Programme. For
ITPA the gains were 10.5 and 9 points respectively.

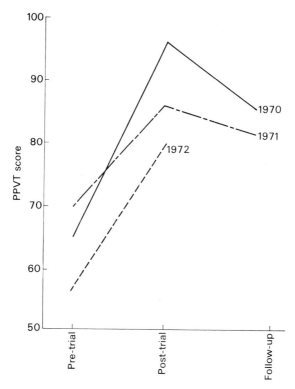

Fig. 10.1. Changes in an intelligence performance score in a pre-school intervention programme for Aboriginal children in a rural town.

Barry Nurcombe and his colleagues conclude from the results of
these trials that the improvements during the pre-school programme
were maintained for at least a year in the case of the white children,
but only partially maintained for Aboriginal children. They believe
there should be a follow-through programme developed in co-
operation with teachers at primary school and that greater home

support be sought for the pre-school programme. It remains to be proved whether conceptual development made possible by competence in the language of instruction underlies the operational thinking necessary for success in primary school. Empirical evidence suggests this is true. Nurcombe and his associates draw attention, however, to one important factor in their trials. It was a programme designed and carried out by whites in an ethnically integrated pre-school. They believe that a long-lasting effect for the Aboriginal children is likely only when the programme has far greater control by Aborigines in the community. This should ensure that the level of interaction between Aboriginal parents and their children is raised and remains at a higher level than at present. 'Without this reinforcement', they conclude, 'the initial gains achieved may become irrelevant to the world of children involved.'

The homelands movement

The development of health programmes under Aboriginal control was referred to earlier, and some of these programmes are associated with traditionally oriented groups of Aborigines who have moved away from the larger government and church mission settlements. H. C. Coombs has recently described the development of these homeland movements and his analysis reveals some of the longer-term implications.[12]

Significant homeland groups have been established at Puta-Puta, about 200 km west of Amata, a government settlement established in Bidjandjadjara territory in South Australia; at Yayayi, some 50 km west of Papunya in the Northern Territory; at One Arm Point, north of Derby in the Kimberley area of Western Australia; and at several localities up to 100 km from the large government settlement of Maningrida, in Arnhem Land. Many other homeland groups, some only transient, have been established in other parts of the country.

These homeland groups are small, usually from a single clan or the same language group. For the most part they are comprised of a few families who, for one reason or another, have sought to escape from the internal conflicts and alien supervision which are associated with the large aggregations of people in government and other settlements.

Coombs believes it is possible to categorize the reasons for setting up the homelands in three ways. The first is the desire by Aborigines to establish a 'presence' on land which, by tradition, they regard as theirs. Often the homelands are close to 'sacred' sites so that it is possible to hold ceremonies associated with these sites. Secondly in the smaller, culturally more homogeneous, homeland group the traditional group leaders are able to reassert their social control. The

larger settlements bring together people of different tribes and varying loyalties. Committee structures based on those in white communities exercise social authority and so bypass traditional methods
of control. The social disintegration in the larger government
communities has been extreme in many instances and the recognition
of the problems associated with these artificial aggregations of people
has led to the desire by some to move away and establish smaller
groups. Thirdly, it is recognized that the exercise of authority in the
context of Aboriginal law is easier when it takes place at some
distance from the administration of justice in the context of white
law. This is true, particularly for the control of alcohol abuse, a constant source of conflict with white authority in the larger settlements.

The homeland groups have benefited in several ways. Some health
hazards due to overcrowding and social disintegration have been
reduced, social tensions have been ameliorated, and there appears to
be greater contentment. Traditional skills in craft have been revived,
and hunting and food-gathering have re-emerged as a base for
economic activity. But none of the homeland groups has reverted
to a completely traditional manner of living. All require some goods
and services from outside.

Store foods supplement those gathered locally. Rifles are used in
hunting and other modern tools for gathering or in developing small
vegetable gardens. Motor vehicles are needed for transport, radios for
communication and entertainment, and some form of schooling must
be provided for the children. All these compromises indicate the
dilemmas facing groups which wish to remove themselves from direct
contact with white society yet who have already incorporated into
their own structure some of the material goods and values of that
society.

There are other implications of the 'homeland' movement which
Coombs examines in detail for the Bidjandjadjara in central Australia.
At the end of 1976 there were at least 14 homeland groups in South
Australia, Western Australia, and the Northern Territory. They all
speak closely related languages and share a common cultural tradition. There is a preponderance of children in these homeland groups,
and on present indications their population will double in less than
25 years.

The central Australian environment in which these groups live is
very arid, with effective rainfall giving a growing period for vegetation as low as four weeks about one year in four. In consequence
water is a principal determinant for plant and animal life. Permanent
streams are non-existent, but run-off after rain from rocky slopes
provides water to water-courses and to temporary or permanent

water-holes at the bases of hills. Water in rock holes can be supple-meted by surface-water which is available after rain, but its quality deteriorates the further removed it is from the hills. Ground-water can also be collected by seepage into wells. These sources of water make it possible to establish small settlements in the foothills and alluvial fans. Most of these settlements have started vegetable gardens, but Coombs states that few of these have contributed substantially to the settlements' needs of fruit and vegetables and many do not continue to produce at all. The main cause of their failure seems to be that white advisers do not stay long at the settle-ments and constant changes of personnel make it difficult for the Aborigines' interests and skills to become firmly established.

White settlement in the centre of the continent and more seden-tary patterns of life for Aborigines have led to important changes in plant and animal associations. Rabbits, together with feral forms of once domesticated animals, such as cattle, donkeys, and camels, have seriously damaged plant life. Wild foxes and feral cats have reduced the numbers of small marsupials and probably many of the reptiles. By contrast, many of the larger marsupials, the kangaroos and euros, have increased in number despite the use of guns for hunting. However, the number of emus seems to have decreased. Because of damage to the plant associations on which they depend certain insects and larvae such as witchety grubs and sugar-ants, which were important items in the diet of Aborigines, appear to be less numerous.

These ecological changes mean that significant changes have occurred in the diet of present-day Bidjandjadjara groups compared to that of similar groups before white settlement. Kangaroo is still an important source of animal protein, but is supplemented now by rabbits and cats, with emus as a rare luxury. However, store foods, flour, bread, and biscuits have largely replaced natural grains and seeds, with a consequent fall in protein and some vitamins.

Coombs recognizes the important role which the movement to homelands is playing in re-establishing a cultural identity for tradi-tionally oriented people. But he draws attention to the threat of damage to the environment which their present life-style poses. Around the camps is an increasing area of devastation. Trees are being cut down for firewood and to provide wood for the manufac-ture of artefacts, one of the few means of earning money for the pur-chase of items from outside. In addition, smaller vegetation is being eaten or trampled out of existence by the grazing of stock animals.

As the number of homeland groups increases and as the people living in them continue to become more sedentary and to introduce into the area new species of plants and animals and develop productive processes aimed at increasing their cash income, the effect on the whole ecosystem could be serious. Only further study of the effects on the environment, and consequently on the health and physique of the people themselves, will reveal if this movement represents an adaptation capable of leading traditionally oriented Aborigines out of the transition period into one of new balance and relative stability.

REFERENCES

This list is not exhaustive but is intended as a guide to the more important books and articles dealing with the human biology of Australian Aborigines. Under each chapter references are given to general works as well as to specific articles by persons mentioned in the text. However, details of citations to nineteenth-century sources of historical interest have not been included.

Chapter 1

1. General background information on the geography and climate of Australia will be found in: Leeper, G. W. (ed.) (1970). *The Australian environment* (4th edn, revised). CSIRO and the University of Melbourne Press, Melbourne.

   Spate, O. H. K. (1959). *Australia — a study of warm environments and their effect on British settlement* (7th edn). Methuen, London.

   Walker, D. (ed.) (1972). *Bridge and barrier: the natural and cultural history of Torres Strait*. Australian National University: Department of Biogeography and Morphology. Publication BG/3, Canberra.

2. Fitzpatrick, E. A. and Nix, H. A. (1970). The climatic factor in Australian grassland ecology. In *Australian grasslands* (ed. R. M. Moore). Australian National University Press, Canberra.

3. Peterson, N. (1976). The natural and cultural areas of Aboriginal Australia. In *Tribes and boundaries in Australia* (ed. N. Peterson) pp. 50–71. Australian Institute of Aboriginal Studies, Canberra.

4. *Atlas of Australian resources* (1967). *Surface water resources*. Department of National Development, Canberra.

5. Carnahan, J. A. (1976). *Atlas of Australian resources: natural vegetation*. Division of National Mapping, Canberra.

   Ride, W. D. L. (1970). *A guide to the native mammals of Australia*. Oxford University Press, London.

   Moore, R. M. (ed.) (1970). *Australian grasslands*. Australian National University Press, Canberra.

   Macintosh, N. W. G. (1974). Early man and the dog in Australia. In *Grafton Elliot Smith: the man and his work* (ed. A. P. Elkin and N. W. G. Macintosh). University of Sydney Press, Sydney.

6. Chappell, J. (1976). Aspects of late Quaternary palaeography of the Australian–East Indonesian region. In *The origin of the Australians* (ed. R. L.

Kirk and A. G. Thorne) pp. 11-22. Australian Institute of Aboriginal Studies, Canberra.

7. Nix, H. A. and Kalma, J. P. (1972). Climate as a dominant control in the biogeography of Northern Australia and New Guinea. In *Bridge and barrier: the natural and cultural history of Torres Strait* (ed. D. Walker) pp. 61-91. Australian National University, Publication BG/3, Canberra.

8. Jones, Rhys (1980). Hunters in the Australian coastal savannah. In *Human ecology in savannah environments* (ed. David R. Harris) pp. 107-45. Academic Press, London.

9. Calaby, J. H. (1971). Man, fauna and climate in Aboriginal Australia. In *Aboriginal man and environment in Australia* (ed. D. J. Mulvaney and J. Golson) pp. 80-93. Australian National University Press, Canberra.

10. Gillespie, R., Horton, D. R., Ladd, P., Macumber, P. G., Rich, T. G., Thorne, A. R., and Wright, R. V. S. (1978). Lancefield Swamp and the extinction of the Australian megafauna. *Science, N.Y.* 200, 1044-8.

Chapter 2

1. Birdsell, J. B. (1977). The recalibration of a paradigm for the first peopling of a greater Australia. In *Sunda and Sahul* (ed. J. Allen, J. Golson, and R. Jones) pp. 113-67. Academic Press, London.
   Chappell, J. (1976). Aspects of late Quaternary palaeography of the Australian–East Indonesian region. In *The origin of the Australians* (ed. R. L. Kirk and A. G. Thorne) pp. 11-22. Australian Institute of Aboriginal Studies, Canberra.

2. Bowler, J. M., Thorne, A. G., and Polack, H. A. (1972). Pleistocene man in Australia: age and significance of the Mungo skeleton. *Nature, Lond.* 240, 46-50.
   Bowler, J. M. and Thorne, A. G. (1976). Human remains from Lake Mungo: discovery and excavation of Lake Mungo III. In *The origin of the Australians* (ed. R. L. Kirk and A. G. Thorne) pp. 127-140. Australian Institute of Aboriginal Studies, Canberra.

3. Thorne, A. G. (1971). Mungo and Kow Swamp: Morphological variation in Pleistocene Australians. *Mankind* 8, 85-9.

4. Thorne, A. G. (1977). Separation or reconciliation? biological clues to the development of Australian society. In *Sunda and Sahul* (ed. J. Allen, J. Golson, and R. Jones) pp. 187-204. Academic Press, London.
   Brace, C. L. (1980). Australian tooth size clines and the death of a stereotype. *Curr. Anthrop.* 21, 141-64.

5. Freedman, L. and Lofgren, M. (1979). Human skeletal remains from Cossack, Western Australia. *J. hum. Evol.* 8, 283-99.

6. Jones, R. (1977). Australia felix — the discovery of a Pleistocene prehistory. *J. hum. Evol.* 6, 353-62.

7. Mulvaney, D. J. (1975). *The prehistory of Australia* (revised edn). Penguin, Harmondsworth.

8. White, Carmel (1967). Early stone axes in Arnhem Land. *Antiquity* 41, 149-52.

9. Dortch, C. E. and Merrilees, D. (1973). Human occupation of Devil's Lair, Western Australia during the Pleistocene. *Archaeol. Phys. Anthropol. Oceania* 8, 89-115.

10. Luebbers, R. (1975). Ancient boomerangs discovered in South Australia. *Nature, Lond.* 253, 39.

11. Flood, J. (1974). Pleistocene man at Clogg's Cave: his tool kit and environment. *Mankind* 9, 175–88.
12. Bowdler, S. (1977). The coastal colonization of Australia. In *Sunda and Sahul* (ed. J. Allen, J. Golson, and R. Jones) pp. 205–46. Academic Press, London.
13. Jones, R. (1977). Man as an element of a continental fauna: the case of sundering of the Bassian bridge. In *Sunda and Sahul* (ed. J. Allen, J. Golson, and R. Jones) pp. 317–86. Academic Press, London.
    Davidson, D. S. (1937). Relationship of Tasmanian and Australian cultures. In *Twenty-fifth anniversary studies* (ed. D. S. Davidson) pp. 47–62. Philadelphia Anthropological Society, Philadelphia.
14. Edwards, R. and Ucko, P. J. (1973). Rock art in Australia. *Nature, Lond.* 246, 274–7.
    See also:
    Ucko, P. J. (ed.) (1977). *Form in indigenous art.* Australian Institute of Aboriginal Studies, Canberra.
15. Macintosh, N. W. G., Smith, K. N., and Bailey, A. B. (1970). Lake Nitchie burial — unique Aboriginal burial. *Archaeol. Phys. Anthropol. Oceania.* 5, 85–101.

Chapter 3

1. Krzywicki, L. (1934). *Primitive society and its vital statistics.* (English edn). Macmillan, London.
2. The original estimates were given by:
   Radcliffe-Brown, A. R. (1930). The Aboriginal population: former numbers and distribution of the Australian Aborigines. *Official Yearbook of the Commonwealth of Australia.* No. 23. Government Printer, Melbourne.
   A review of estimates by other authors is in Lawrence, R. (1968) *Aboriginal habitat and economy.* Department of Geography Occasional Papers No. 6. Australian National University, Canberra.
   See also:
   Bellshaw, J. (1978). Population distribution and pattern of seasonal movement in northern New South Wales. In *Records of times past* (ed. Isobel McBride) pp. 65–81. Australian Institute of Aboriginal Studies, Canberra.
   Recent studies of the demography of Aborigines are:
   Jones, F. L. (1970). *The structure and growth of Australia's Aboriginal population.* Australian National University Press, Canberra.
   Smith, L. R. (1975). The Aboriginal population of Australia. Ph.D. Thesis, University of New South Wales, Sydney.
3. Meggitt, M. J. (1972). *Desert people.* Angus and Robertson, Sydney.
4. Jones, R. (1974). Tasmanian tribes. In N. B. Tindale's *Aboriginal tribes of Australia.* Australian National University Press, Canberra.
5. Good reviews of Aboriginal social structure will be found in:
   Berndt, R. M. and Berndt, C. H. (1977). *The world of the first Australians* (2nd edn). Ure Smith, Sydney.
   Elkin, A. P. (1974). *The Australian Aborigines: how to understand them.* (revised edn). Angus and Robertson, Sydney.
   Maddock, K. (1972). *The Australian Aborigines: a portrait of their society.* Penguin, Harmondsworth.
   Stanner, W. E. H. (1965). Aboriginal territorial organization: estate, range, domain and regime. *Oceania* 36, 1–26.

Hiatt, L. R. (1965). *Kinship and conflict. A study of an Aboriginal community in northern Arnhem Land.* Australian National University Press, Canberra. For a discussion of the concept of local group, or 'horde' see:

Birdsell, J. B. (1970). Local group composition among the Australian Aborigines: a critique of the evidence from fieldwork conducted since 1930. *Curr. Anthrop.* 11, 115–42.

6. Long, J. P. M. (1971). Arid region Aborigines: the Pintubi. In *Aboriginal man and environment in Australia* (ed. J. Mulvaney and J. Golson), pp. 262–70. Australian National University Press, Canberra.

7. Berndt, C. H. and Berndt, R. M. (1975). *Pioneers and settlers: the Aboriginal Australians.* Pitman Australia, Melbourne.

8. Piddington, R. (1970). Irregular marriages in Australia. *Oceania* 40, 329–43.

9. Kaberry, P. M. (1939). *Aboriginal women, sacred and profane.* Routledge, London.

10. Rose, F. G. G. (1960). *Classification of kin, age structure and marriage amongst the Groote eylandt Aborigines.* Akedemic-Verlag, Berlin.

11. White, N. G. (1976). A preliminary account of the correspondence among genetic, linguistic, social and topographic divisions in Arnhem Land, Australia. *Mankind* 10, 240–7.

12. Yengoyan, A. A. (1968). Demographic and ecological influences on Aboriginal Australian marriage sections. In *Man the hunter* (ed. R. B. Lee and I. de Vore) pp. 185–99. Aldine Publishing Co., Chicago.

Yengoyan, A. A. (1976). Structure, event and ecology in Aboriginal Australia. In *Tribes and boundaries in Australia* (ed. N. Peterson) pp. 121–32. Australian Institute of Aboriginal Studies, Canberra.

13. Tindale, N. B. (1974). *Aboriginal tribes of Australia.* Australian National University Press, Canberra.

14. Denham, W. W. (1975). Population properties of physical groups among the Alyawara tribe of central Australia. *Archaeol. Phys. Anthropol. Oceania.* 10, 114–51.

15. Sharp, R. L. (1940). An Australian Aboriginal population. *Hum. Biol.* 12, 481–507.

16. Hart, C. W. M. and Pilling, A. R. (1963). *The Tiwi of North Australia.* Holt, Rinehart, and Winston, New York.

17. Birdsell, J. B. (1953). Some environmental and cultural factors influencing the structuring of Australian Aboriginal populations. *Am. Nat.* 87, 171–207.

18. Tindale, N. B. (1940). Results of the Harvard-Adelaide Universities anthropological expedition 1938–9. Distribution of Australian Aboriginal tribes: a field survey. *Trans. R. Soc. S. Aust.* 64 (1).

19. Birdsell, J. B. (1973). A basic demographic unit. *Curr. Anthrop.* 14, 337–56.

20. Berndt, R. M. (1959). Concept of the 'tribe' in the Western Desert of Australia. *Oceania* 30, 82–107.

21. Dixon, R. M. W. (1976). Tribes, languages and other boundaries in northeast Queensland. In *Tribes and boundaries in Australia* (ed. N. Peterson) pp. 207–38. Australian Institute of Aboriginal Studies, Canberra.

Chapter 4

1. Hallam, Sylvia (1975). *Fire and hearth.* Australian Institute of Aboriginal Studies, Canberra.

2. Jones, R. (1980). Hunters in the Australian coastal savannah. In *Human*

ecology in savannah environments (ed. D. R. Harris) pp. 107–45. Academic Press, London.

3. Meehan, B. (1977). Hunters by the seashore. *J. hum. Evol.* 6, 363–70.

   Meehan, B. (1977). Man does not live by calories alone: the role of shell-fish in a coastal cuisine. In *Sunda and Sahul* (ed. J. Allen, J. Golson, and R. Jones) pp. 493–532. Academic Press, London.

4. Golson, J. (1971). Australian Aboriginal food plants: some ecological and culture-historical implications. In *Aboriginal man and environment in Australia* (ed. D. J. Mulvaney and J. Golson) pp. 196–238. Australian National University Press, Canberra.

5. McArthur, M. (1960). Food consumption and dietary levels of groups of Aborigines living on naturally occurring foods. In *Records of the American-Australian scientific Expedition to Arnhem Land. 2. Anthropology and nutrition* (ed. C. P. Mountford) pp. 90–134. Melbourne University Press, Melbourne.

6. Scarlett, N. H. (1976). Riitja and Gathul: the role of monsoon and mangrove forests in Yualngu traditional economy. Australian Institute of Aboriginal Studies Ethnobotany Workshop, Canberra. Mimeographed.

7. Peterson, N. (1977). The traditional pattern of subsistence to 1975. In *The nutrition of Aborigines in relation to the ecosystem of central Australia* (ed. B. S. Hetzel and H. J. Frith). CSIRO, Canberra.

8. Sahlins, M. D. (1968). Notes on the original affluent society. In *Man the hunter* (ed. R. B. Lee and R. Devore) pp. 85–9. Aldine, Chicago.

9. Hiatt, B. (Meehan) (1968). The food quest and the economy of the Tasmanian Aborigines, *Oceania* 38, 99 133, 190–219.

10. Lawrence, R. (1968). *Aboriginal habitat and economy.* Department of Geography Occasional Papers No. 6. Australian National University, Canberra.

11. Allen, H. (1974). The Bagundji of the Darling basin: cereal gatherers in an uncertain environment. *World Archaeol.* 5, 309–22.

12. Tindale, N. B. (1974). *Aboriginal tribes of Australia.* Australian National University Press, Canberra.

13. Gould, R. (1973). *Yiwara: foragers of the Australian desert.* Charles Scribner, New York.

14. Gould, R. (1969). Subsistence behaviour among the Western Desert Aborigines of Australia. *Oceania* 39, 253–74.

15. Thomson, D. (1975). *Bindubi country.* Thomas Nelson, Melbourne.

16. Sweeney, G. (1947). Food supplies of a desert tribe. *Oceania* 17, 289–99.

17. Flood, J. (1976). Man and ecology in the highlands of southeastern Australia. In *Tribes and boundaries in Australia* (ed. N. Peterson) pp. 30–49. Australian Institute of Aboriginal Studies, Canberra.

   Flood, J. (1980). *The moth hunters.* Australian Institute of Aboriginal Studies, Canberra.

18. Meggitt, M. J. (1962). *Desert people: a study of the Walbiri Aborigines of Central Australia.* Angus and Robertson, Sydney.

19. Lawrence, R. (1971). Habitat and economy: a historical perspective. In *Aboriginal man and environment in Australia* (ed. D. J. Mulvaney and J. Golson) pp. 249–61. Australian National University Press, Canberra.

Chapter 5

1. Birdsell, J. B. (1950). Some implications of the genetical concept of race in terms of spatial analysis. In *Origin and evolution of Man. Cold Spring*

Harb. Symp. quant. Biol. **15**, 259–314.
2. See, for example:
  Abbie, A. A. (1966). Physical characteristics. In *Aboriginal man in south and central Australia* pp. 9–45. Government Printer, Adelaide.
  Abbie, A. A. (1969). *The original Australians.* A. H. and A. W. Reed, Sydney.
3. Basedow, H. (1925). *The Australian Aboriginal.* Preece, Adelaide.
  Walker, A. C. (1969). Albinism in a full-blood Aboriginal child. *Med. J. Aust.* **2**, 300–2.
4. Prokopec, M. (1977). An anthropometric study of the Rembarranga: comparison with other populations. *J. hum. Evol.* **6**, 371–91.
5. Fenner, F. J. (1939). The Australian Aboriginal skull: its nonmetrical morphological characters. *Trans. R. Soc. S. Aust.* **63**, 248–306.
6. Hrdlicka, A. (1928). Catalogue of human crania in the United States National Museum collections. Australians, Tasmanians, South African Bushmen, Hottentots and Negro. *Proc. U.S. Nat. Mus.* **71**, Art. 24, 1–140.
  Morant, G. M. (1927). A study of the Australian and Tasmanian skulls, based on previously published measurements. *Biometrika* **19**, 417–40.
  Wagner, K. (1937). *The craniology of the Oceanic races.* Skrifter Utgitt av det Norske Videnskaps-Akademi 1 Oslo 1. Matematisk Naturvidenskapelig Klasse **2**, 1–193.
  Turner, W. (1908). The craniology, racial affinities and descent of the Aborigines of Tasmania. *Trans. R. Soc. Edin.* **46**, 365–403.
7. Macintosh, N. W. G. and Larnach, S. L. (1973). A cranial study of the Aborigines of Queensland with a contrast between Australian and New Guinea crania. In *The human biology of Aborigines of Cape York* (ed. R. L. Kirk) pp. 1–12. Australian Institute of Aboriginal Studies, Canberra.
8. Kellock, W. L. and Parsons, P. A. (1970). A comparison of the incidence of minor non-metrical cranial variants in Australian Aborigines with those of Melanesia and Polynesia. *Am. J. Phys. Anthrop.* **33**, 235–40.
  Richards, L. C. and Telfer, P. J. (1979). The use of dental characters in the assessment of genetic distance in Australia. *Archaeol. Phys. Anthrop. Oceania* **14**, 184–94.
9. Parsons, P. A. and White, N. G. (1973). Genetic differentiation among Australian Aborigines with special reference to dermatoglyphics and other anthropometric traits. In *The human biology of Aborigines in Cape York* (ed. R. L. Kirk) pp. 81–94. Australian Institute of Aboriginal Studies, Canberra.
  Parsons, P. A. and White, N. G. (1976). Variability in anthropometric traits in Australian Aborigines and adjacent populations. In *The origin of the Australians* (ed. R. L. Kirk and A. G. Thorne) pp. 227–43. Australian Institute of Aboriginal Studies, Canberra.
  White, N. G. and Parsons, P. A. (1976). Population genetic, social, linguistic and topographical relationships in north-eastern Arnhem Land, Australia. *Nature, Lond.* **261**, 223–5.
  White, N. G. (1978). A human ecology research project in the Arnhem Land region: an outline. *Newsletter* **9**, 39–52. Australian Institute of Aboriginal Studies, Canberra.
10. Margetts, B. H. and Freedman, L. (1977). Morphometrics of Western Australian Aboriginal skulls. *Rec. West. Aust. Mus.* **6**, 63–105.

11. Pietrusewsky, M. (1979). Craniometric variation in Pleistocene Australian and more recent Australian and New Guinea populations studied by multivariate procedures. *Occasional papers in human biology* 2, Australian Institute of Aboriginal Studies, Canberra.

12. Yamaguchi, Bin (1967). *A comparative osteological study of the Ainu and the Australian Aborigines*. Australian Institute of Aboriginal Studies, Canberra.

13. Giles, E. (1976). Cranial variation in Australia and neighbouring areas. In *The origin of the Australians* (ed. R. L. Kirk and A. G. Thorne) pp. 161–72. Australian Institute of Aboriginal Studies, Canberra.

14. Howells, W. W. (1973). *The Pacific Islanders*. Weidenfeld and Nicolson, London.
    Howells, W. W. (1973). *Cranial variation in man*. Papers of the Peabody Museum of Archaeol. and Ethnol. 67. Harvard University, Cambridge.

Chapter 6

1. White, N. G. and Parsons, P. A. (1976). Population, genetic, social, linguistic and topographical relationships in north-eastern Arnhem Land, Australia. *Nature, Lond.* **261**, 223–5.

2. Tindale, N. B. (1953). Tribal and intertribal marriage among Australian Aborigines. *Hum. Biol.* **25**, 169–90.
   For a discussion of trade-routes in Australia see:
   McCarthy, F. D. (1939–40). 'Trade' in Aboriginal Australia and 'trade' relationships with Torres Straits, New Guinea and Malaya. *Oceania* **9**, 105–38; **10**, 80–104, 171–95.
   Mulvaney, D. J. (1976). The chain of connection: the material evidence. In *Tribes and boundaries in Australia* (ed. N. Peterson) pp. 72–94. Australian Institute of Aboriginal Studies, Canberra.

3. General reviews of the distribution of blood groups among Aborigines are:
   Kirk, R. L. (1965). *The distribution of genetic markers in Australian Aborigines*. Australian Institute of Aboriginal Studies, Canberra.
   Simmons, R. T. (1976). The biological origin of Australian Aborigines. In *The origin of the Australians* (ed. R. L. Kirk and A. G. Thorne) pp. 307–28. Australian Institute of Aboriginal Studies, Canberra.

4. Forbes, J. F., Bashir, H., Cross, R., Alpers, M., Ting, A., and Morris, P. J. (1973). Leucocyte antigen studies in Australia and New Guinea. In *The human biology of Aborigines in Cape York* (ed. R. L. Kirk) pp. 95–102. Australian Institute of Aboriginal Studies, Canberra.

5. For a detailed review of the distribution of serum protein and red cell enzyme markers see:
   Kirk, R. L. (1976). Serum protein and enzyme markers as indicators of population affinities in Australia and the Western Pacific. In *The origin of the Australians* (ed. R. L. Kirk and A. G. Thorne) pp. 329–46. Australian Institute of Aboriginal Studies, Canberra.
   Kirk, R. L. (1966). Population genetic studies in Australia and New Guinea. In *The biology of human adaptability* (ed. P. T. Baker and J. S. Weiner) pp. 395–430. Clarendon Press, Oxford.
   Blake, N. M. (1979). Genetic variation of red cell-enzyme systems in Australian Aboriginal populations. *Occasional papers in human biology* 2, 39–82. Australian Institute of Aboriginal Studies, Canberra.

6. McDermid, E. M. and Cleve, H. (1972). A comparison of the fast-migrating

Gc variant of Australian Aborigines, New Guinea indigenes, South African Bantu and Black Americans. *Hum. Hered.* 22, 249-53.

7. Curtain, C. C., van Loghem, E., and Schanfield, M. S. (1976). Immunoglobulin markers as indicators of population affinities in Australasia and the Western Pacific. In *The origin of the Australians* (ed. R. L. Kirk and A. G. Thorne) pp. 347-64. Australian Institute of Aboriginal Studies, Canberra.

8. Blake, N. M. and Kirk, R. L. (1978). Widespread distribution of variant forms of carbonic anhydrase in Australian Aborigines. *Med. J. Aust.* 1, 183-5.

9. Birdsell, J. B. (1976). Realities and transformations: the tribes of the Western Desert of Australia. In *Tribes and boundaries in Australia* (ed. N. Peterson). Australian Institute of Aboriginal Studies, Canberra.
   See also:
   Birdsell, J. B., Simmons, R. T., and Graydon, J. J. (1979). Microdifferentiation in blood group frequencies among twenty-eight adjacent Aboriginal tribal isolates in Western Australia. *Occasional papers in human biology* 2, 1-38. Australian Institute of Aboriginal Studies, Canberra.

10. Balakrishnan, V., Sanghvi, L. D., and Kirk, R. L. (1975). *Genetic diversity among Australian Aborigines.* Australian Institute of Aboriginal Studies, Canberra.

11. Swadesh, M. (1971). *The origin and diversification of language* (ed. J. Sherzer). Aldine Atherton, Chicago.

12. Wurm, S. A. (1972). *Languages of Australia and Tasmania.* Mouton, The Hague.

13. Capell, A. (1962). *A new approach to Australian linguistics* (2nd edn). Oceania Linguistics Monographs No. 1, University of Sydney.

14. Osborne, C. R. (1974). *The Tiwi language.* Australian Institute of Aboriginal Studies, Canberra.

15. Dixon, R. M. W. (1980). *The languages of Australia.* Cambridge University Press, Cambridge.

16. Hale, K. (1964). Classification of northern Paman languages, Cape York Peninsula: a research report. *Oceanic Linguist* 3, 248-66.

17. Steinberg, A. G. and Kirk, R. L. (1970). Gm and Inv types of Aborigines in the Northern Territory of Australia. *Archaeol. Phys. Anthropol. Oceania* 5, 163-72.

18. Keats, Bronya (1977). Genetic structure of the indigenous populations in Australia and New Guinea. *J. hum. Evol.* 6, 319-39.

19. Kirk, R. L. (1979). Genetic differentiation in Australia and the Western Pacific and its bearing on the origin of the first Americans. In *The first Americans: origins, affinities and adaptations* (ed. W. S. Laughlin and A. B. Harper). Gustav Fischer, New York.

20. Nei, M. (1975). *Molecular population genetics and evolution.* North Holland, Amsterdam.

21. Nei, M. and Roychoudhury, A. K. (1972). Gene differences between Caucasian, Negro and Japanese populations. *Science N.Y.* 177, 434-6.

22. Booth, P. B. and Taylor, H. W. (1976). Genetic distance analysis of some New Guinea populations. In *The origin of the Australians* (ed. R. L. Kirk and A. G. Thorne) pp. 415-30. Australian Institute of Aboriginal Studies, Canberra.

Chapter 7

1. Keats, B. (1976). Population genetic studies in Australia and New Guinea. Ph.D. thesis, Australian National University, Canberra.
2. Kettle, E. S. (1966). Weight and height curves for Australian Aboriginal children. *Med. J. Aust.* 1, 972-7.
   See also:
   Propert, D. N., Edmonds, R., and Parsons, P. A. (1968). Birth weights and growth rates up to one year for full-blood and mixed blood Australian Aboriginal children. *Aust. paediat. J.* 4, 134-43.
3. Brown, T. and Barrett, M. J. (1971). Growth in central Australian Aborigines: stature. *Med. J. Aust.* 2, 29-33.
4. Brown, T. and Barrett, M. J. (1973). Dental and craniofacial growth studies of Australian Aborigines. In *The human biology of Aborigines in Cape York* (ed. R. L. Kirk) pp. 69-80. Australian Institute of Aboriginal Studies, Canberra.
5. Cheek, D. B., Graystone, J. E., Holt, A. B., Sutherland, G. C., Chopra, S. A., and Spargo, R. M. (1978). Assessment of protein reserves (cellular mass) in Aboriginal children. *Am. J. Clin. Nutr.* 31, 1328-33.
6. Barrett, M. J. (1953). Dental observations on Australian Aborigines: Yuendumu, central Australia, 1951-52. *Aust. J. Dent.* 57, 127-38.
7. Spencer, B. and Gillen, F. J. (1927). *The Arunta: a study of stone age people* Vol. 1, p. 176. Macmillan, London.
8. Brace, C. L. (1980). Australian tooth size clines and the death of a stereotype. *Curr. Anthropol.* 21, 141-64.
   See also the discussion by:
   Wright, R. V. S. (1976). Evolutionary process and semantics: Australian prehistoric tooth size as a local adjustment. In *The origin of the Australians* (ed. R. L. Kirk and A. G. Thorne). Australian Institute of Aboriginal Studies, Canberra.
9. Barrett, M. J. and Brown, T. (1971). Increase in average height of Australian Aborigines. *Med. J. Aust.* 2, 1169-72.
10. Porteus, S. D. (1917). Mental tests with delinquents and Australian Aboriginal children. *Psych. Rev.* 24, 32-42.
11. Comprehensive reviews of studies on cognition in Aborigines are given in:
    Kearney, G. E. and McElwain, D. W. (eds.) (1976). *Aboriginal cognition: retrospect and prospect.* Australian Institute of Aboriginal Studies, Canberra.
    Kearney, G. E., de Lacy, P. R., and Davidson, G. R. (eds.) (1973). *The psychology of Aboriginal Australians.* John Wiley, Sydney.
12. de Lemos, M. M. (1973). The development of conservation. In *The psychology of Aboriginal Australians* pp. 71-88. John Wiley, Sydney.
13. de Lacey, P. R. (1973). Classificatory ability. In *The psychology of Aboriginal Australians* pp. 59-70. John Wiley, Sydney.
14. Dasen, P. R., de Lacey, P. R., and Seagrim, G. N. (1973). Reasoning ability in adopted and fostered Aboriginal children. In *The psychology of Aboriginal Australians* pp. 97-104. John Wiley, Sydney.
15. Kearins, J. (1976). Skills of desert Aboriginal children. In *Aboriginal cognition: retrospect and prospect* (ed. G. E. Kearney and D. W. McElwain) pp. 199-212. Australian Institute of Aboriginal Studies, Canberra.

Chapter 8

1. Birdsell, J. B. (1967). Preliminary data on the trihybrid origin of the Australian Aborigines. *Archaeol. phys. Anthropol. Oceania* 2, 100-55.
2. A review of earlier work is given in:
   Hicks, C. S. and O'Connor, W. J. (1938). Skin temperature of Australian Aborigines under varying atmospheric conditions. *Aust. J. exp. Biol. med. Sci.* 16, 1-18.
   A good review of early physiological studies of Aborigines is given by:
   Macpherson, R. K. (1966). Physiological adaptation, fitness and nutrition in the peoples of the Australian and New Guinea regions. In *The biology of human adaptability* (ed. P. Baker and J. S. Weiner) pp. 431-68. Clarendon Press, Oxford.
3. Scholander, P. F., Hammel, H. T., Hart, J. S., LeMessurier, D. G., and Steen, J. (1958). Cold adaptation in Australian Aborigines. *J. appl. Physiol.* 13, 211-18.
   Hammel, H. T., Elsner, R. W., LeMessurier, D. G., Andersen, H. T., and Milan, F. A. (1959). Thermal and metabolic responses of the Australian Aborigine exposed to moderate cold in summer. *J. appl. Physiol.* 14, 605-15.
4. Morrison, P. (1965). Body temperature in some Australian mammals. V. Aboriginals. *J. appl. Physiol.* 20, 1278-82.
5. Wardlaw, H. S. H., Davies, H. W., and Joseph, M. R. (1934). Energy metabolism and insensible perspiration of Australian Aborigines. *Aust. J. exp. Biol. med. Sci.* 12, 63-74.
6. Roberts, D. F. (1952). Basal metabolism, race and climate. *J.R. anthrop. Inst.* 82, 169-83.
7. Macfarlane, W. V. (1973). Functions of Aboriginal nomads during summer. In *The human biology of Aborigines in Cape York* (ed. R. L. Kirk) pp. 49-68. Australian Institute of Aboriginal Studies, Canberra.
   Macfarlane, W. V. (1976). Palaeophysiology. In *The origin of the Australians* (ed. R. L. Kirk and A. G. Thorne) pp. 183-94. Australian Institute of Aboriginal Studies, Canberra.
   Macfarlane, W. V. (1977). Aboriginal desert hunter/gatherers in transition. In *The nutrition of Aborigines in relation to the ecosystem in Central Australia* (ed. B. S. Hetzel and H. J. Frith). Commonwealth Scientific Industrial Organization, Melbourne.
8. Wyndham, G. H., Macpherson, R. K., and Munro, A. (1964). Reactions to heat of Aborigines and Caucasians. *J. appl. Physiol.* 19, 1055-8.
9. Kuno, Y. (1934). *The physiology of human perspiration*. Churchill, London.
10. See for example:
    Van Dongen, R., Davigongs, V., and Abbie, A. A. Aboriginal blood pressure at Beswick, South-Western Arnhem Land and correlation with physical dimensions. *Med. J. Aust.* 2, 286-9.
11. Nye, L. J. J. (1937). Blood pressure in the Australian Aboriginal, with a consideration of possible aetiological factors in hyperpiesia and its relation to civilization. *Med. J. Aust.* 2, 1000-1.
12. Edwards, F. M., Wise, P. H., Thomas, D. W., Murchland, J. B., and Craig, R. J. (1976). Blood pressures and electrocardiographic findings in the South Australian Aborigines. *Aust. N.Z.J. Med.* 6, 197-205.
13. Fenna, D., Mix, L., Schaffer, O., and Gilbert, A. L. (1971). *Canad. Med.*

Assoc. J. **105**, 472–6.

14. Goedde, H. W., Harada, S., and Agarwal, D. P. (1979). Racial differences in alcohol sensitivity: a new hypothesis. *Hum. Genet.* **51**, 331–4.

15. Reed, T. E. (1978). Significant racial differences in rate of alcohol metabolism. *14th International Congress of Genetics – Moscow.* Abstracts (2), 412.

16. Marnovich, N., Larsson, O. and Barber, K. (1976). Comparative metabolism rates of ethanol in adults of Aboriginal and European descent. *Med. J. Aust.* **1**, 44–6.

Chapter 9

1. Sandison, A. T. (1980). Notes on some skeletal changes in pre-European contact Australian Aborigines. *J. hum. Evol.* **9**, 45–8.
   Prokopec, M. (1979). Demographical and morphological aspects of the Roonka population. *Archaeol. phys. Anthropol. Oceania* **14**, 11–26.

2. Basedow, H. (1932). Diseases of the Australian Aborigines. *J. trop. Med. Hyg.* **35**, 177–85.

3. Jones, R. (1971). The demography of hunters and farmers in Tasmania. In *Aboriginal man and environment in Australia* (ed. D. J. Mulvaney and J. Golson) pp. 271–87. Australian National University Press, Canberra.

4. Barwick, D. (1971). Changes in the Aboriginal population of Victoria 1863–1966. In *Aboriginal man and environment in Australia* (ed. D. J. Mulvaney and J. Golson) pp. 288–315. Australian National University Press, Canberra.

5. Doherty, R. L. (1973). The health status of Aboriginal communities in Cape York. In *The human biology of Aborigines in Cape York* (ed. R. L. Kirk) pp. 37–48. Australian Institute of Aboriginal Studies, Canberra.
   Jose, D. G., Self, M. H. R., and Stallman, N. D. (1968). A survey of children and adolescents on Queensland Aboriginal settlements, 1967. *Aust. paed. J.* **5**, 71–88.

6. Jose, D. G. and Welch, J. S. (1970). Growth retardation, anaemia and infection, with malabsorption and infestation of the bowel. *Med. J. Aust.* **1**, 349–56.

7. Director General of Health (1979). *Annual Report 1977–78.* Commonwealth Department of Health, Canberra.

8. House of Representatives Standing Committee on Aboriginal Affairs (1976). *Aboriginal Health and related matters in the south-west of Western Australia.* Australian Government Publishing Service, Canberra.

9. Ford, G. W., Belbin, R., Jose, D. G., Vorbach, E. A., and Kirke, D. K. (1976). Growth and immune function in Aboriginal children during recovery from malnutrition and infection. *Aust. N.Z.J. Med.* **6**, 321–8.

10. Elliott, R. B., Maxwell, G. M., and Vawser, N. (1967). Lactose maldigestion in Australian Aboriginal children. *Med. J. Aust.* **1**, 46–9.

11. Mitchell, J. D. and Grunseit, F. (1978). Aboriginal infants: lactose malabosrption and small bowel mucosal abnormalities. *New Doctor* **8**, 20–3.

12. Gracey, M. (1977). Nutritional problems of Australian Aborigines. *Proc. Nutr. Soc. Aust.* **2**, 11–16.

13. An excellent review of health problems in Aborigines is given in:
    Moodie, P. M. (1973). *Aboriginal health.* Australian National University

Press, Canberra.

14. There is a detailed discussion of treponemal disease in:
    Hackett, C. J. (1936). Boomerang leg and yaws in Australian Aborigines. *Trans. R. Soc. Trop. Med. Hyg.* 30, 137-50.

15. Riseborough, A. W., Joske, R. A., and Vaughan, B. F. (1961). Hand deformities due to yaws in Western Australian Aborigines. *Clin. Radiol.* 12, 109-13.

16. For a discussion of child morbidity in a central Australian community see:
    Middleton, M. and Francis, S. (1976). *Yuendumu and its children — life and health on an Aboriginal settlement.* Department of Aboriginal Affairs, Canberra.

17. Gale, F. and Bennett, J. H. (1969). Huntington's chorea in a South Australian community of Aboriginal descent. *Med. J. Aust.* 2, 482-4.

18. Cawte, J. (1972). *Cruel, poor and brutal nations.* University Press of Hawaii, Honolulu.
    Jones, I. H. (1972). Diagnosis of psychiatric illness among tribal Aborigines. *Med. J. Aust.* 1, 345-9.
    Kidson, M. A. (1968). Psychiatric disorders among Aborigines of the Australian Western desert. *Arch. gen. Psychiat.* 19, 413-17.
    Kamien, M. (1976). Psychiatric disorders in Bourke Aboriginal adults. *Med. J. Aust.* 2, Suppl. Nov. 27 11-16.

Chapter 10

1. Broom, L. and Jones, F. L. (1973). *A blanket a year.* Australian National University Press, Canberra.

2. Discussion of the characteristics of the various types of communities will be found in:
    Long, J. P. M. (1970). *Aboriginal settlements — a survey of institutional communities in eastern Australia.* Australian National University Press, Canberra.
    Schapper, H. P. (1970). *Aboriginal advancement to integration — conditions and plans for Western Australia.* Australian National University Press, Canberra.
    Stevens, F. (1974). *Aborigines in the Northern Territory cattle industry.* Australian National University Press, Canberra.

3. Rowley, C. D. (1972). *The Remote Aborigines.* Penguin, Sydney.
    Rowley, C. D. (1972). *Outcasts in White Australia.* Penguin, Sydney.
    Rowley, C. D. (1972). *The destruction of Aboriginal Society.* Penguin, Sydney.

4. Frith, N., Hausfeld, R. G., and Moodie, P. M. (1974). *The coast-town project — action research in Aboriginal community health.* Australian Government Publishing Service, Canberra.

5. Lickiss, N. (1970). Health problems of Sydney Aboriginal children. *Med. J. Aust.* 2, 995-1000.

6. Gale, F. (1972). *Urban Aborigines.* Australian National University Press, Canberra.

7. Kamien, M. (1978). *The dark people of Bourke — a study of planned social change.* Australian Institute of Aboriginal Studies, Canberra.

8. Rowley, C. D. (1972). *The destruction of Aboriginal Society* p. 31. Penguin, Sydney.

9. Sackett, L. (1977). Liquor and the law: Wiluna, Western Australia. In *Aborigines and change* (ed. R. M. Berndt) pp. 90-9. Australian Institute of Aboriginal Studies, Canberra.

10. Descriptions of some of the changes in attitudes to the delivery of health care are given in:

    Nathan, P. (1980). *A home away from home: a study of the Victorian Aboriginal health service in Fitzroy.* Preston Institute of Technology, Melbourne.

    Reid, J. (1978). Change in the indigenous medical system of an Aboriginal Community. *Newsletter* 9, 61-71. Australian Institute of Aboriginal Studies, Canberra.

    Reid, D. (1978). Aboriginal medical service, Perth, Western Australia. *Med. J. Aust.* 1, 53-5.

11. Nurcombe, B., de Lacey, P., Moffitt, P., and Taylor, L. (1973). The question of Aboriginal intelligence: the first three years of the Bourke pre-school experiments. *Med. J. Aust.* 2, 625-30.

12. Coombs, H. C. (1978). *Kulinma: listening to Aboriginal Australians.* Australian National University Press, Canberra.

AUTHOR INDEX

SUBJECT INDEX

marriage 46
  intertribal 111
marsupials 12, 13, 73, 83, 84
  extinct 19, 29
  giant 16
  mice 13, 72
  moles 13
  phalangers 13
  possums 13, 72, 73
  rats 72
matrilineal descent 44
maxillary arch 144
'maze' tests 148
medicine men 189
Melanesia and Melanesians 95, 99, 103, 114,
    127, 128
menstrual pattern 165
mental disorders 188, 189, 196
metabolism 154, 156–8
mice 13, 72
Micronesians 99
middens 34, 37, 68
migration
  coastal 32
  waves of 24
Milingimbi 135, 136
millet 75
Miriwun 24, 25, 28
moieties 44
moisture index 7
moles 13
molluscs 13, 75
mongoloids 95, 107
monsoon 5, 68
monsoonal climate 28
morbidity 177, 195
Mornington Island 112, 136, 188, 190, 196
morphological adaptation 154
morphological distance 106
mosquitoes 183
moth feasts 83
Motu 128, 134
Mount Cameron West 37
mulbo 81
mulga 11
mullet 66
Mungo I 32, 37
Mungo III 19, 32, 37
Murrayians 89, 95
Murray River 3, 9, 19, 24, 32, 40, 54, 55,
    89, 102, 105, 145, 170
Murrumbidgee River 3
mussels 32, 72
mutton fish 72
Myoporum 74

negritos 89

New Britain 103–5
New Caledonia 95, 103, 105
New Guinea and New Guineans 1, 2, 11, 12,
    14, 16, 18, 25, 28, 96, 102, 104,
    106, 116, 127, 130, 133, 183,
    188
New South Wales 94, 95, 101, 105, 146,
    171, 173, 179, 185, 187, 192,
    193, 199, 202
New Zealand 103, 181, 185
ngaru 79
Northern Territory 37, 40, 41, 95, 119,
    136, 139, 181, 182, 184, 186,
    193, 199, 202
Norwegians 157
Nullarbor Plain 37, 77

obesity 195
ochre 36, 37
Oenpelli 26
One-arm Point 202
Ooldea 94
orange 74
origins, trihybrid theory 88
ossification, timing of 142
overcrowding 203
oxygen consumption 156
oysters 72

Pacific populations 129
Pacific slope 9
Palm Island 147, 185
palms 69
Pandanus 69
Panicum 75, 83
Papunya 199, 202
Parsis 116
pastoral properties 192
Patagonia 158
patrilineal descent 44
Pattern Intensity Index 99
Peabody picture vocabulary test 200
Perth 151
phalangers 13
phenyl thiocarbamide tasting 167
Philippines 108
physiological adaptation 154
pigface 72, 74
pigweed 74
Pipalyatjara 199
plant growth determinants 7
Pleistocene period 1, 3, 13, 15–17, 19, 22,
    24–6, 28, 29, 33, 35, 54
plums 69
Point McLeay 148, 185, 187
Point Pearce 173
polygyny 51

Map of Australia showing states and main localities mentioned in text